The Jordan Automobile

The Jordan Automobile

A History

James H. Lackey

McFarland & Company, Inc., Publishers
Jefferson, North Carolina

The present work is a reprint of the illustrated case bound edition of The Jordan Automobile: A History, *first published in 2005 by McFarland.*

LIBRARY OF CONGRESS CATALOGUING-IN-PUBLICATION DATA

Lackey, James H., 1936–
The Jordan automobile : a history / James H. Lackey.
p. cm.
Includes bibliographical references and index.

ISBN 978-1-4766-6277-0 (softcover : acid free paper) ♾
ISBN 978-1-4766-0921-8 (ebook)

1. Jordan automobile—History. 2. Jordan, Ned, 1881–1958.
3. Jordan Motor Car Company—History.
4. Advertising—Automobiles—United States—Biography.
5. Automobile engineers—United States—Biography. I. Title.
TL215.J58L35 2015 629.222'2—dc22 2005022633

BRITISH LIBRARY CATALOGUING DATA ARE AVAILABLE

Cover art: From the second version of the "Somewhere West of Laramie" ad, August 1923

Printed in the United States of America

McFarland & Company, Inc., Publishers
Box 611, Jefferson, North Carolina 28640
www.mcfarlandpub.com

This book is dedicated to:

The memory of Shelva Lackey, Father—
He taught me to work hard and be honest.

Lola Lackey, Mother—
She taught me to love God and keep His Commandments.

The memory of Scott C. Watts, with whom I made my home while in high school. He taught me to be proud of myself and stand up straight.

The memory of Nancy Watts, Scott's wife. She taught me to strive for the highest goals and that you are never defeated unless you quit.

Ann Jordan and the memory of Don Jordan—They gave their collection of Jordan literature, books, Jordan arrow lapel pin, ads and everything they had concerning Jordan, to this effort. Don was my biggest booster.

Rachel Lackey, my wife. She has endured this nonsense for 38 years and has been my faithful companion for 46. She did all the typing and computer work.

Acknowledgments

A Special Thank You

To the memory of Ralph Dunwoodie, Sun Valley, Nevada, the best friend an automotive historian ever had.

To Mark and Lisa Bias, Barboursville, West Virginia: without their help this book would not have been completed.

Thank You

Mark Patrick, Detroit, Michigan (Detroit Public Library, National Automotive History Collection); Stuart McDougall, Philadelphia, Pennsylvania (Free Library of Philadelphia, Automotive History Collection); Ann Sindilar, Cleveland, Ohio (Western Reserve Historical Society Library); the late Arthur Michnevitz, Spring Grove Illinois; Katy Matthews, Topeka, Kansas; James and Myrtle Emmitt, Haines City, Florida; Barry and Diane Fohrman, Hinkley, Illinois; John and Marge Fye, Dundas, Illinois; Bob and Wilda Boyd, Stoneboro, Pennsylvania; the late Don Jordan and Ann Jordan, Sinclairville, New York; Anson "Skip" and Jackie Loose, Manheim, Pennsylvania; the late Allan and Shirley MacNicol, New London, New Hampshire; Dan and Tracy Jordan, Chino Hills, California; Jess and Peggy Jordan, Atlantic Highlands, New Jersey; Ken and Schreall Baumgardt, Glenville, Pennsylvania; John and Peggy Willi, Cleveland, Ohio; Jim and Connie Stecker, Cleveland, Ohio; Donald and Betty Weir, Friendship, New York; Arthur and Mamie Grove, Carlisle, Pennsylvania; Art and Dee Worledge, Yuma City, California; Kate W. Jordan Wallace, Dominican Republic; William Bailey, Royal Oak, Michigan; John Conde, Keego Harbor, Michigan; Duey and Alice Anderson, Minneapolis, Minnesota; Joel and Sunnie Andress, Newport, Vermont; Julius and Theresa Baron, Little Silver, New Jersey; Olan and Janie Jordan Bentley, Washington Court House, Ohio; Charles and Marlene Boles, Fresno, California; Greg Loftness, Blaine, Minnesota; Floyd and Donna Jordan, Granite City, Illinois; George and Lana Kline, Stockton, California; Irvin C. and Wilma Leach, Decatur, Illinois; Les and Tracy Lunceford, Gresham, Oregon; Dale and Jill Robinson, Guilford, Connecticut; Skip Weeks, Collinsville, Connecticut; Stan Hurd, Rio, Wisconsin; Dan Kirchner, Dearborn, Michigan; Howard Applegate, Mt. Gretna, Pennsylvania; Brooks Brierley, Baltimore, Maryland; Laurie Thompson, New York, New York; Charles P. Bradley, Sun City, California; Ray Unsworth, South Burlington, Vermont; Sharon Thatcher, Merrill, Wisconsin; Beverley King, Merrill, Wisconsin; Kim Miller, Hershey, Pennsylvania (AACA Library & Research Center); Rudolph H. Garfield, Cleveland, Ohio; Mrs. Joseph Fewsmith, Jr., Florida; Mary Ross, Louisiana; Patterson Barnes, Gates Mills, Ohio; Dorothy Paviol, Office of Selectmen, Canaan, Connecticut; Cathy Jacob, University of Wisconsin Archives; Helene Gross, Greybull, Wyoming; Roger Anderson, Seattle, Washington; the late Michey Mishne, Medina, Ohio; Patrick Jordan; Gary and Dorothy Hein, Prescott, Arizona; Robert and Dotty Blake, Gastonia, North Carolina; Macdonald H. Leach, Edgewater, Maryland; Richard Barrie, American Nurses Association, Washington, D.C.; Diane Gallagher, Nursing Archives Association, Boston University, Boston Massachusetts; Fred and Jan Hansen, Irving, New York; Jeff and Pam Willis, South Point, Ohio; John and Cuza Chandler, Huntington, West Virginia; Paul Hamilton, Huntington, West Virginia; Bennie Ashworth, Milton, West Virginia; Sandy McCaw, Wakefield, Rhode Island; and *The Jordan Register* (Art Worledge, President), 2099 Pheasant Drive, Yuba City, California 95993

Table of Contents

Acknowledgments vii

Preface 1

ONE
Ned Jordan
3

TWO
The Founding of the Jordan Motor Car Company, 1916
10

THREE
Early Growth, 1917
22

FOUR
"A Million Dollar Idea," 1918–1919
31

FIVE
Surviving the First Pinch, 1920–1922
40

SIX
"Somewhere West of Laramie," 1923–1924
51

SEVEN
New Models and All Steel Bodies, 1925–1926
63

EIGHT
Little Car, Big Blunder, 1927–1928
76

NINE
Dashed Hopes of Recovery, 1929
90

TEN
Last Gasps, 1930–1932
103

Between pages 116 and 117 are
16 color plates containing 43 photographs

ELEVEN
Aftermath
117

Twelve
Advertising
123

THIRTEEN
Dealers and Distributors
133

Chapter Notes 141
Appendix I. Partial List of Distributors and Dealers 147
Appendix II. Chassis Specifications 149
Appendix III. Engine Specifications 154
Appendix IV. Serial Numbers 155
Appendix V. Wiring Diagrams 157
Bibliography 173
Index 177

Preface

Having loved everything with an engine since my earliest memories, it must have been predetermined that I would someday get into the antique car hobby. My first was a 1931 Model A Ford Tudor which I purchased in 1963. I have owned many different makes and models since then, but Jordan has always been my favorite.

I found a copy of *Antique Automobile* on the newsstand in 1963 and was hooked forever. An article about Jordans appeared in that publication in 1966 and I immediately wanted to own one. I was struck by the "Somewhere West of Laramie" ad and decided that a Playboy would be the one. A 1923 Playboy would be the one in particular.

After looking for several years I finally found it in Friendship, New York, and a few years later was able to purchase my dream. It was such a mess that some people, including my wife, doubted my sanity when I brought it home. One of my grandsons looked at it and said, "PaPa, what happened to your car, did it rust?" However, a few years later that derelict turned into an AACA Grand National Senior Winner.

Long ago I started collecting anything Jordan I could find (and afford) until today I have, in all probability, the largest collection of Jordan memorabilia in the world. I am a charter member of the Jordan Register and have been the club historian for many years.

A book was the last thing I thought about, but after reading everything I could find about Jordan, much of which is replete with errors, and after considerable urging by my Jordan friends I now find myself consumed with the subject.

What you will find herein is 36 years of research and hard work. I have strived to make this work as accurate as humanly possible and to restrict it to well verified fact. There is very little personal opinion here. During my research, I have found that if I could not obtain information by one method, I could not just give up. Persistence and repeated attempts are necessary. Every known repository of Jordan material has been visited or contacted. I obtained Ned Jordan's personal scrapbook in the late 1990s and drew some valuable historical material from it. In addition, many enthusiasts of the Jordan car and friends of the author have contributed liberally to this cause.

One

Ned Jordan

Edward Stanlaw "Ned" Jordan was born November 21, 1881, in Merrill, Lincoln County, Wisconsin.[1] He was the youngest of a family of six children and the only son of John and Katie Griffin Jordan. His older sister, Katie, had died at the age of eight before Ned was born.

Ned's father, John, was born May 10, 1841, at Erie, Pennsylvania, the son of Irish immigrants. In his childhood the family moved to Ravenna, Portage County, Ohio, where John spent his youth on the family farm.[2] (There is some evidence that he was in fact born at Ravenna.) One of the skills he acquired was that of carpentry, but like most young men, he craved adventure and excitement. His opportunity would arrive before he reached the age of 21. The Civil War had been brewing for some time and finally erupted on April 12, 1861.

Ohio was solidly for preservation of the Union, and these being John's sentiments, he enlisted as a private in Company C, 34th Regiment, Ohio Volunteer Infantry at Camp Dennison, Ohio, on September 10, 1861.[3] He served with distinction and was promoted to corporal on March 18, 1862. He was discharged early for the purpose of re-enlisting and did so on February 29, 1864, at Camp Russell, Charleston, West Virginia.[4]

John was a good soldier and was promoted to sergeant on April 24, 1864. Just a few days later on May 10, 1864, he was wounded in action at the fierce battle of Cloyd's Mountain, Virginia, where Confederate General Albert Galatin Jenkins was fatally wounded while leading his troops. Sergeant Jordan had been hit in the left elbow by a gunshot, dislocating the joint. After a comrade re-set the joint, Jordan continued to fight. He carried his arm in a sling for six weeks but never sought hospitalization as his unit was in constant conflict. Later in life this would be a source of contention between Jordan and the U.S. government as he sought to obtain a pension.

Still assigned to Company C, he was promoted to first sergeant on July 11, 1864. Sergeant Jordan was again promoted on December 9, 1864, to 2nd lieutenant, assigned to Company D, 34th Regiment.[5]

At Beverly, West Virginia, on January 11, 1865, Jordan along with 579 others was captured by the Confederate Army and marched through the bitter cold and deep snow to Staunton, Virginia. Later he was transported to prison at Richmond where he was held until February 21, 1865, when he was paroled at Varina, Virginia. He was transported to the U.S. Army Officers Hospital at Annapolis, Maryland, on February 23, 1865, where he was granted a 30 day leave.[6] The 34th Regiment, badly depleted by this time, was merged with the 36th Regiment, Ohio Volunteer Infantry.

Jordan was discharged and mustered out on April 17, 1865, at Cumberland, Maryland, under the provisions of Paragraph 10, Special Orders 41 concerning consolidation of units.[7] The war was over and his services were no longer needed.

John Jordan would try unsuccessfully for many years to get a pension from the U.S. government. He never succeeded until May 20, 1912, when he was granted six dollars per month. By that time he was a resident of the National Home for Disabled Volunteer Veterans in Milwaukee, Wisconsin. His pension was raised to $30 per month on May 20, 1916, less than a year before his death on April 23, 1917.[8]

His obituary stated that he had been a close friend to the martyred President William McKinley. In truth it is doubtful that he was a close friend. He did know McKinley as a superior officer during the Civil War, when the future president was a major with the 23rd

Regiment, Ohio Volunteer Infantry. Had he been a close friend, McKinley most likely would have intervened on his behalf. McKinley was elected president in 1896 and took office in 1897. Surely the president of the United States had enough clout to see an old friend treated fairly.

Ned's mother, Kate M. Griffin, the daughter of John and Nancy Kinney Griffin, was born September 27, 1842. According to Ned, she was born at Union Corners (near Buffalo), New York.[9] While she was still a young girl her parents left Union Corners and sailed the Great Lakes to Milwaukee and then traveled by wagon train to the lead works near Shullsburg, Wisconsin. Another source has her being born at Shullsburg. She was educated in the schools of Sinsinewa Mound.[10]

After the Civil War, westward expansion was accelerating at a rapid pace. The Union Pacific Railroad was pushing westward from Omaha, Nebraska, and hordes of the eastern population were following. Kate, her two sisters and three brothers decided to join in the westward movement and left Wisconsin by wagon train seeking their fortune. While ferrying the wagons across the Mississippi River, Kate's brother Ned was drowned. Kate and the others pushed on across Iowa to Council Bluffs where they crossed the Missouri River into Nebraska at Omaha.[11]

Kate's sister, Mary, established a small general store at Fremont. She later married A.B. Moore, one of Omaha's wealthiest citizens. Kate's other sister, Jenny, later opened a store at Laramie, Wyoming. The ever adventurous Kate pushed on to Green River, Wyoming, to establish her own general store.[12]

After his discharge from the U.S. Army, John Jordan still craved excitement and decided to head west. He traveled to St. Louis, then to Fremont, Nebraska, where he found carpentry work on the Union Pacific Railroad as a bridge builder foreman.[13]

Somewhere along the Union Pacific tracks between Fremont and Green River, John and Kate met. On May 10, 1869, when the golden spike was driven at Promontory, Utah, John and Kate were there. She had taken a work train down from Green River to the ceremony.

With the railroad completed, John was out of a job. A few days later he and Kate were married at Corrine, Utah.[14] There is some speculation that they may have been married at Fremont during 1868. No record of the marriage exists in Nebraska or Utah. There is some evidence that Kate may have been married previously as John listed her name as Bryant on one of his pension applications, but on other papers he listed her as not having been married previously.

The new couple headed back east to Omaha and then down to Maryville, Missouri, where Kate's brother Frank had established a newspaper. Finding few work opportunities there, they moved on to Fort Scott, Kansas. John's occupation was still carpentry, but before long he was employed as a policeman and later, supposedly, police chief.[15]

The couple's first daughter, Minnie Estelle, was born at Fort Scott on March 18, 1870. Daughter Katie Eveline came along on February 22, 1872, and daughter Ella May on September 2, 1874.[16]

The family lived at Fort Scott until about 1876 when they moved to Fond du Lac, Wisconsin, where John found work as a carpenter. In Fond du Lac daughter Blanche Edith was born April 5, 1877. Daughter Katie passed away on June 6, 1880, from complications of diphtheria.[17] Daughter Anne was born on May 8, 1881. The family moved to Merrill, Wisconsin, shortly after Anne's birth, where John found work at one of the many lumber mills then operating in that area.

Edward Stanlaw came along on November 21, 1882.[18] He was named for his uncle, Ned Griffin, who drowned while heading West with Kate and the rest of his sisters and brothers.

It is not known whether John and Kate Jordan were educated, but they insisted on their children getting as much of an education as possible. The girls all taught school or worked at professions which required a good formal education.

Ned's oldest sister, Minnie, married Herbert Charles Miller, a bookkeeper at one of the local lumber mills on November 11, 1890.[19] The third Jordan daughter, Ella May, died December 11, 1902, from complications of an earlier accident.[20] She had fallen down the steps of a cellar while visiting with friends and suffered for two years before succumbing.

Ned's early life was not unlike that of many boys growing up in a small town with a good economy. He loved to fish, hunt, and canoe and did so as much as possible. The Merrill area was a paradise for these activities. Ned was very industrious and worked at everything he could manage during his youth. His endeavors included driving a livery (horse taxi), swamping, pumping the church organ, setting bowling pins, working as a plumber's helper, and being a newspaper boy.

He also found time for mischief and practiced that art as often as possible. One of his favorite tricks was to stuff rags in someone's stove pipe, then hide and watch them come running out of the house. Another sport was hopping trains for a ride, but this pursuit proved dangerous. Once he came close to meeting his demise when he fell and the wheels of the caboose ran over the brim of his cap.[21]

Ned apparently was a good student, especially in the subjects he liked, and graduated from Merrill High School on June 9, 1899, at age 17. Ned gave an oration entitled "The White Man's Burden" at his graduation ceremony. By the time he graduated, he had been working at the local newspaper (*The Merrill Advocate*) for two or three years.[22]

He had apparently left home after his sophomore year of school and had a room at one of the local boarding houses. He was making his own way at 15 years of age and his coming and going at all hours necessitated that he be independent. That he was, and it was a trait that would characterize him for the rest of his life.

After graduation, he continued to work at the *Advocate* and there is some evidence that he also worked at a newspaper in Wausau for a short while.

Working at a small newspaper as a printer and reporter for two years after high school taught Ned that if you wanted to succeed, you needed an advanced education. He left Merrill with $50 in his pocket and what few possessions he had and headed to the University of Wisconsin at Madison for the fall 1901 semester. Ned later liked to say that he decided to go to college on the spur of the moment, but that is highly unlikely. Then, as now, one made considerable preparation before entering college. It is true, though, that his admission papers were dated well past the usual time for entering college. Ned probably had been planning to enroll for some time but lacked the financial resources.

Arriving in Madison, Ned immediately looked up Amos P. Wilder, editor of the *Wisconsin State Journal*. A

Merrill High School 1899 graduating class; Ned Jordan at center indicated by arrow (Merrill Historical Society) (courtesy Sharon Thatcher).

determined young man, Ned left armed with a part time job and set out to make his mark in the academic field.[23]

It wasn't long before he was a big man on campus. By the time he graduated in 1905, he was part of most things that happened except sports, and he wrote about those. Some of his accomplishments and memberships while at the University of Wisconsin were as follows:

Yellow Helmet (Junior and Senior Honorary Society)
Iron Cross (Senior Honorary Society)
Daily Cardinal (student newspaper): Associate Editor, junior year; Editor, senior year
Wisconsin Literary Magazine: Associate Editor, junior year; Editor, senior year
Badger Board (yearbook): Chairman Literary Committee, junior year
Sphinx (student political publication): Editorial Board, senior year
Class President, first semester, junior year; Sergeant at Arms, second semester
Student Conference Committee: Secretary, senior year
Social Settlement Benefit Committee: Chairman, senior year
Faculty Alumni—Student Athletic Conference: Secretary, senior year
Cap and Gown Committee, senior year
Quiller's (honorary writers society): President, senior year

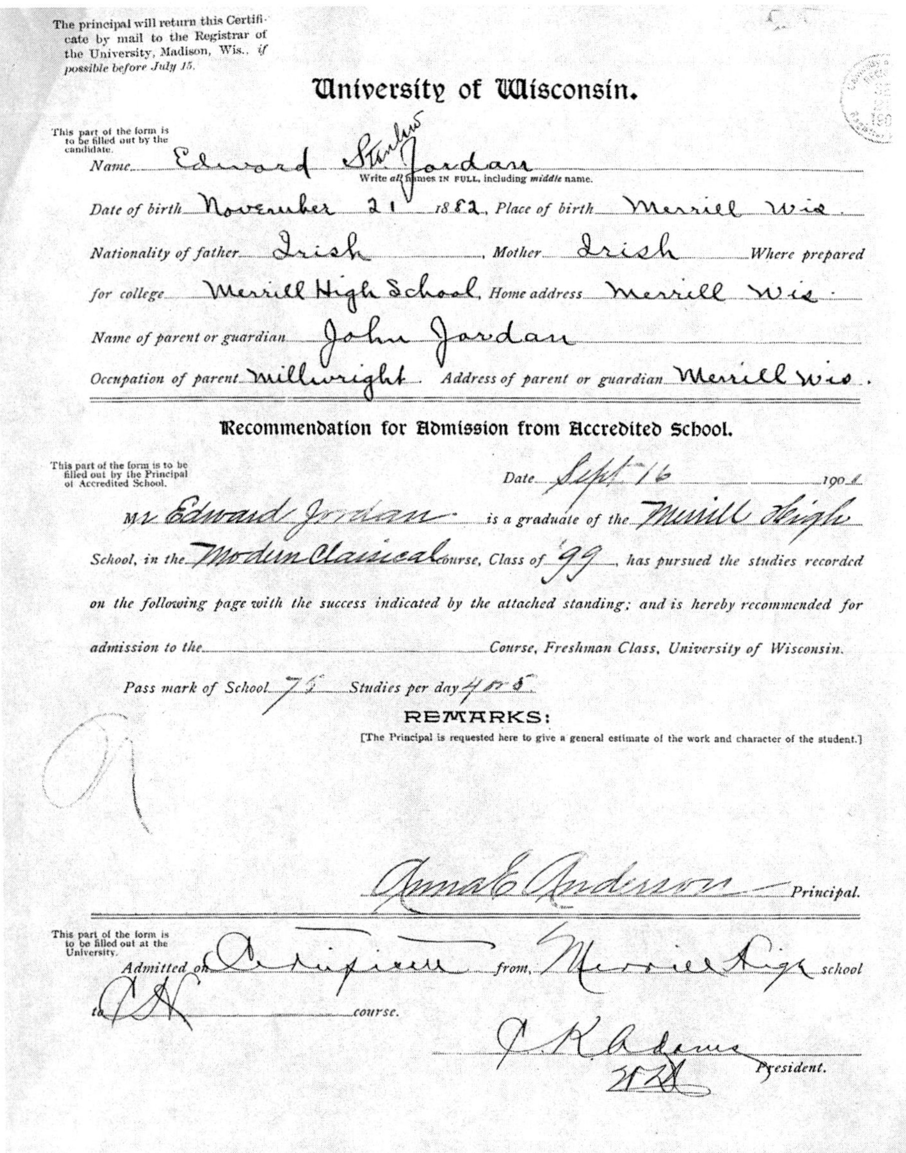
The principal will return this Certificate by mail to the Registrar of the University, Madison, Wis., *if possible before July 15.*

University of Wisconsin.

This part of the form is to be filled out by the candidate.

Name Edward Stanley Jordan
Write *all* names IN FULL, including *middle* name.

Date of birth November 21 1882, *Place of birth* Merrill Wis.

Nationality of father Irish, *Mother* Irish *Where prepared for college* Merrill High School, *Home address* Merrill Wis.

Name of parent or guardian John Jordan

Occupation of parent millwright *Address of parent or guardian* Merrill Wis.

Recommendation for Admission from Accredited School.

This part of the form is to be filled out by the Principal of Accredited School.

Date Sept 16 1901

Mr Edward Jordan *is a graduate of the* Merrill High *School, in the* Modern Classical *course, Class of* 99, *has pursued the studies recorded on the following page with the success indicated by the attached standing; and is hereby recommended for admission to the* ______ *Course, Freshman Class, University of Wisconsin.*

Pass mark of School 75 *Studies per day* 4 & 5

REMARKS:

[The Principal is requested here to give a general estimate of the work and character of the student.]

Anna E Anderson *Principal.*

This part of the form is to be filled out at the University.

Admitted on Certificate *from* Merrill High *school*
to C H *course.*

C. K. Adams *President.*

Ned Jordan's admission papers at the University of Wisconsin, 1901.

He was also a member of Phi Gamma Delta fraternity; his nickname was "Senator."

Ned Jordan met his wife while at the university. Charlotte Eva (Lottie) Hannahs was born January 11, 1883, at Kenosha, Wisconsin.[24] Her parents were Fred C. and Amelia (Millie) Harrington Hannahs. She was the oldest of three children and the only daughter.[25] Her parents were prominent citizens of Kenosha and owned the Crib Furniture Manufacturing Company (later Hannahs Manufacturing Company), makers of household furniture.[26] Charlotte graduated from Kenosha High School, Class of 1901, and entered the University of Wisconsin for the fall term.

An average student in high school, Charlotte did well at the university. During her sophomore year she was a member of the Woman's Athletic Board. By her junior year she, too, was fairly prominent on campus, being the first vice-president of the Junior Class (first semester) while her future husband was president. She was a member of the Alpha Phi Sorority, and her nickname was "Hop."

Charlotte and Ned graduated together in 1905.[27] She returned to Kenosha and Ned stayed on as city editor of the *State Journal* for a while.

Ned was a pretty fair journalist.

To achieve the city editorship of a major newspaper while going to college full-time is no mean feat. One of his greatest triumphs was sneaking aboard a train and interviewing President Theodore Roosevelt, who ascended to the presidency when President William McKinley was assassinated at the Pan American Exposition at Buffalo, New York, in September 1901. This interview brought him considerable fame and some money. He sold copies to newspapers throughout the United States for $25 each. He needed money at the time because paying one's way while working part time is not an easy task. Rumor has it that he graduated with $5,000 in the bank.[28] That is probably untrue as Ned stated he was flat broke when he got married.

Ned's parents moved from Merrill to Milwaukee shortly before Ned graduated from college. Ned followed them after graduation and worked a short while as a reporter for the *Milwaukee Journal*. He didn't stay long but soon took a position with the *Cleveland Press* in Cleveland, Ohio. Before Ned went to work in Cleveland he wrote a series of articles for *Collier's*, on professionalism in college athletics, which the magazine was trying to expose.[29]

The romance which had blossomed at the University of Wisconsin culminated in the marriage of Ned and Lottie on February 1, 1906.[30] She moved to Cleveland and their life together began. Their only son, John Stanlaw ("Jack"), was born in Cleveland on August 9, 1906.[31]

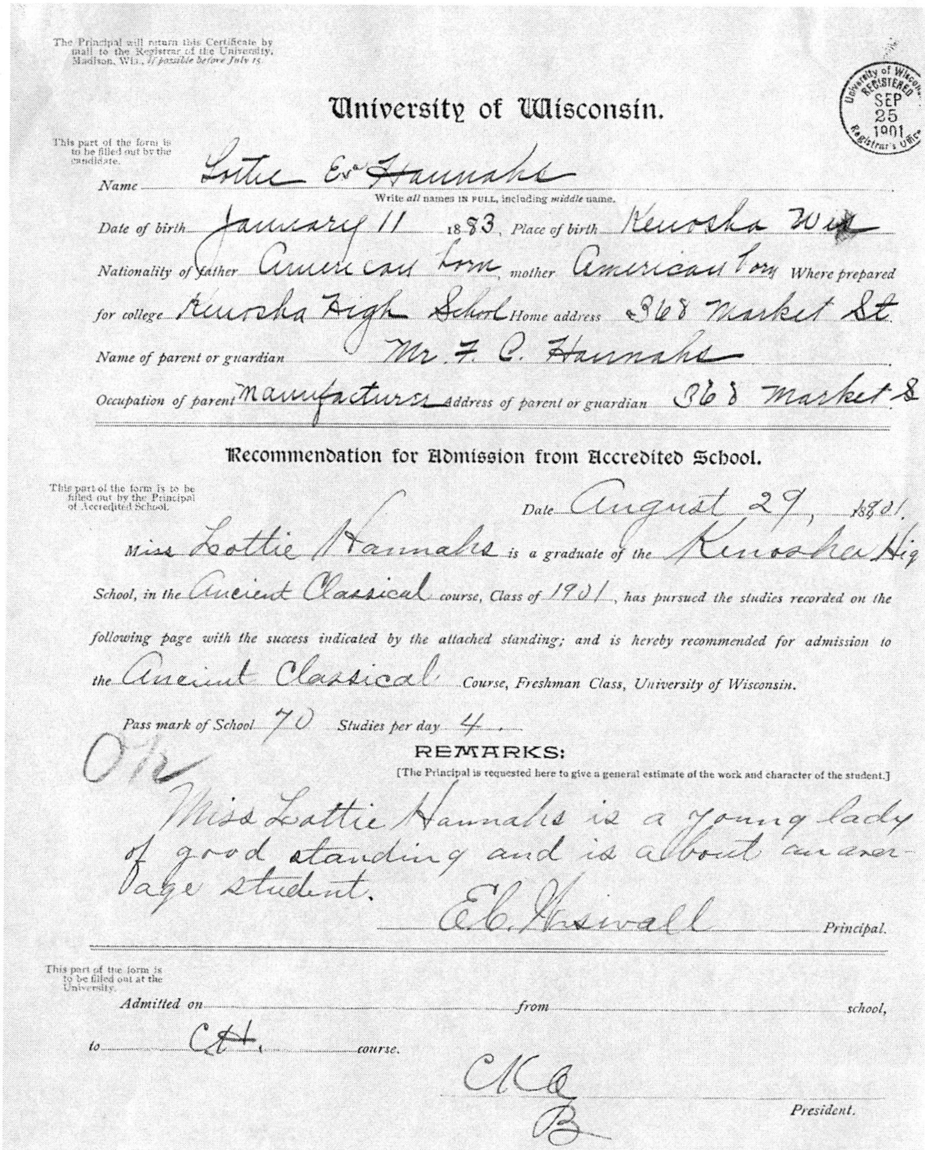

The Principal will return this Certificate by mail to the Registrar of the University, Madison, Wis., if possible before July 15.

University of Wisconsin. REGISTERED SEP 25 1901 Registrar's Office

University of Wisconsin.

This part of the form is to be filled out by the candidate.

Name Lottie Ev Hannahs

Write all names IN FULL, including middle name.

Date of birth January 11 1883, Place of birth Kenosha Wis

Nationality of father American born mother American born Where prepared for college Kenosha High School Home address 368 Market St.

Name of parent or guardian Mr F C Hannahs

Occupation of parent manufacturer Address of parent or guardian 368 Market S

Recommendation for Admission from Accredited School.

This part of the form is to be filled out by the Principal of Accredited School.

Date August 29, 1901.

Miss Lottie Hannahs is a graduate of the Kenosha Hig School, in the Ancient Classical course, Class of 1901, has pursued the studies recorded on the following page with the success indicated by the attached standing; and is hereby recommended for admission to the Ancient Classical Course, Freshman Class, University of Wisconsin.

Pass mark of School 70 Studies per day 4.

OK

REMARKS:

[The Principal is requested here to give a general estimate of the work and character of the student.]

Miss Lottie Hannahs is a young lady of good standing and is about an average student.

E C Hiswall Principal.

This part of the form is to be filled out at the University.

Admitted on ... from ... school, to CA course.

President.

Charlotte Eva (Lottie) Hannah's admission papers at the University of Wisconsin, 1901.

Ned's stay at the *Press* was enjoyable, and he later claimed that the biggest thrill of his life was when he scooped the San Francisco earthquake and the *Cleveland Press* beat all the newspapers that depended on the Associated Press to the streets.[32] An article he wrote about the corruption of city officials caught the eye of John Patterson of Dayton, Ohio. The owner of the National Cash Register Company, Patterson was always looking for bright young people to work for N.C.R. His offer to double Ned's salary was inducement enough, so Ned and his family headed for Dayton.

John Patterson was a very opinionated and temperamental man who was always feuding with the local newspapers. He demanded perfection in everything and when he didn't get his way, he didn't like it one bit. He once sued one of the local papers, the *Dayton News*, for $373,000, charging libel. Not getting the coverage he desired (which was to dominate the news), he established the Ohio Press Bureau and hired Ned to run it the way he wanted. It is unclear what Ned's job was. He was supposed to be the press agent for National Cash Register. Apparently, he wrote NCR's press releases and news items and supplied them to the *Dayton Journal*.[33]

Ned stayed at NCR for about a year. After the *Journal* carried an article, edited by Ned, about Patterson's rantings he got his walking papers along with 93 others in August 1907.[34]

Ned's wife and son were in Kenosha visiting her parents at the time. He stayed in Dayton just long enough to get his affairs settled and then headed for Kenosha. It is not clear how he landed a job with Thomas B. Jeffery & Company, makers of the Rambler automobile. Ned's in-laws were prominent citizens of Kenosha and may have intervened on his behalf, or he may have gotten in on his own initiative. Charles T. Jeffery, Thomas B.'s eldest son, met him at the railroad station (whether by accident or design) and a meeting was arranged. Ned convinced Charles that he had the training necessary to work for Jeffery and walked away with the job of advertising manager.[35]

The Jeffery Company had been started by Thomas Buckland Jeffery, who was born in England in 1845 and immigrated to the U.S. in 1863. He had a good education and was very mechanically skilled. He settled in Chicago and found work as an instrument maker. He soon started his own shop making telescopes and microscopes. He later became enamored with the bicycle and eventually started his own business manufacturing them. In 1881, he took on a partner, Philip Gormully, an old schoolmate who had immigrated to the United States, and they expanded the business. The company grew to be very successful, especially after Jeffery and Gormully fended off a lawsuit by Colonel Albert Pope, the giant of the bicycle industry. The biggest break came when G & J invented the clincher pneumatic tire in 1891. Soon, Gormully & Jeffery were the second largest bicycle manufacturer in the United States, trailing only Colonel Pope. By the time the Chicago World's Fair came to town in 1893, the G&J Cycles were known as the Rambler.

College yearbook photographs of Edward S. Jordan, 1905, and Charlotte Eva Hannahs, 1906 (University of Wisconsin Archives). Yearbooks were not printed until the following year.

In 1895, Jeffery and his son, Charles, saw an exhibition of automobiles in Chicago and the idea for manufacturing them was planted. Gormully passed away and Jeffery, stuck with handling the business affairs of a large company, was not happy. And the company's prospects were not bright, for when Colonel Pope merged his bicycle empire with the sporting goods business of Albert G. Spalding, they gobbled up just about all of the bicycle trade. Tom Jeffery knew it was time to get out and sold to the Pope conglomerate.

The plans for making automobiles were now becoming a reality as Charles had been experimenting with cars for a few years. From the sale of G&J, enough money was raised to afford a good retirement, but Tom Jeffery, ever the inventor, bought a former bicycle factory in Kenosha, Wisconsin, for the purpose of pursuing his dreams. Charles had been the branch manager for his new boss, Colonel Pope, but he resigned to help his father in the new endeavor. Charles became the chief designer for the company, but he also had to learn the business of building automobiles. The younger of Jeffery's two sons, Harold, was also trained in the production end of the venture. Thomas B. Jeffery & Company was now in the business of making automobiles.

The first car appeared in February 1902, and by the end of the year, Jeffery was second only to Olds in the production of gasoline engine powered automobiles. The new car was named Rambler, after the bicycle which had been so successful for the owners.[36]

On that day in August 1907 when Edward S. Jordan stepped off the train and into the job he would hold for the next eight and one-half years, he was joining a growing, prosperous company. Ned and Lottie moved in with her parents at 368 Market Street, Kenosha, and Ned settled into his new job. They would make their home with Lottie's parents until 1912.[37] Although he had no previous experience with the automobile, Ned was capable of doing his job. Soon, ads began appearing in magazines which formerly had no auto advertising. Farmers and doctors began seeing ads in the publications they read. Ned Jordan had ideas and Tom Jeffery liked what he was seeing.[38]

The Jordan family settled into Kenosha society with Lottie becoming very active in the Woman's Club.

She took up painting and became a fairly good artist, but her greatest achievement would come later in the field of sculpture. Ned petitioned Kenosha Lodge #47, Free & Accepted Masons, and was accepted. He became a member of several other Masonic Organizations and served as High Priest of Kenosha Chapter #3 Royal Arch Masons and was a Knight Templar and Shriner.[39]

The Jordan family increased on September 7, 1908, when daughter Jane was born. Another daughter, Joan, came along on December 8, 1909.[40]

On April 2, 1910, shock and sadness settled over the Jeffery family and employees as news came that Thomas B. Jeffery had died suddenly while vacationing in Italy. The whole city of Kenosha was saddened as the elder Jeffery was one of the most respected citizens of that city and had touched the lives of nearly everyone who resided there. Charles would now be in charge, but he and Ned were good friends and not much would change.[41]

The Jordan family suffered a loss on May 25, 1912, when Ned's mother, Kate, passed away. Ned and Lottie journeyed to Milwaukee where they, along with Ned's father, three sisters, and brother-in-law, Herbert Miller, accompanied the body by train to Merrill where she was buried in the local cemetery. A brief graveside service was performed by Reverend J.S. Wilson.[42] Ned and his mother were very close. He attributed his drive and ambition to her, and her death affected him deeply.

Ned and his father apparently were never close and may indeed have been estranged. Ned wrote often and glowingly of his mother but said very little of his father except when he wanted to brag about his exploits in the Civil War, which Ned tended to exaggerate.

Ned was doing well at Jeffery. Advertising for the Rambler was excellent and paying dividends in more sales and steady employment for the workers. After Thomas B. passed away and Charles ascended to the leadership, the company was reorganized and incorporated under the name of the Thomas B. Jeffery Company with ownership remaining in the hands of the Jeffery family. Charles, less conservative than his father, slowly began to increase production. In 1913 he made another bold move. Though the Rambler was a respected name in the automobile trade, Charles decided to change the name to Jeffery in honor of his father. It was a risky venture but was completed without harm to the company, thanks in part to the good advertising Jordan wrote for the new car to smooth the transition from Rambler to Jeffery. Somewhere about this time Ned was promoted to secretary and general sales manager.

The company had also gone into the truck business and was manufacturing the Quad, a four wheel drive vehicle, which had enormous appeal to the military.

The Jeffery dynasty nearly came to an end on May 2, 1915, when Charles, on a trip to Europe aboard the *Lusitania*, ended up in the sea after the ship was torpedoed by a German submarine. His wife had bought him an excellent life preserver before the trip and insisted he wear it at all times. He didn't, but was able to retrieve it from his cabin and that probably saved his life.[43] After this incident, Charles was a changed man and his interest in manufacturing automobiles began to fade.[44]

Ned's future at Jeffery was secure, but he was an ambitious young man and wanted more than Jeffery could offer. It was time to move on.

Two

The Founding of the Jordan Motor Car Company, 1916

On Thursday, January 13, 1916, Edward S. Jordan resigned his position as secretary and general sales manager of the Thomas B. Jeffery Company.[1] Two days later, he called a press conference and announced that he would soon form a company for the manufacture of automobiles.

This was only a formality as friends and insiders at Jeffery knew this had been coming for some time. Jordan left with the blessing of Charles T. Jeffery, who had inherited the leadership of the Jeffery Company after the death of his father, Thomas, in April 1910. Ned had been a very close friend of the elder Jeffery and his wife, Kate. Thomas had told his son to keep Ned with the Jeffery firm under any circumstance.[2] Ned and Charles were also good friends, and Charles stated that when Ned told him he was leaving, he felt as if his wife had asked for a divorce.[3]

When Charles's enthusiasm for making automobiles waned, Jordan recognized the need to make a move. Knowing he could never raise enough money to purchase the Jeffery Company, he started to make plans for his own automobile empire. His instincts proved him to be a prophet, as the Jeffery company was sold to Charles Nash within six months and the Jeffery name disappeared from the list of great automobile manufacturers.[4] However, Charles Nash would lead the company to bigger and better things under the new name.

Ned had started at Jeffery as advertising manager without previous experience in the automobile industry, but he had learned the business quickly, and turned out some great advertising for the Rambler.[5] Under Tom Jeffery, a cautious and conservative businessman, Ned was never allowed to go as far as he wished in advertising the company product. Though he enjoyed more freedom after Charles ascended to the leadership of the company, he still could never go as far as he really wanted. He would now be able to do his own thing, and automobile advertising would never be the same.

Ned had learned well in the past eight and one-half years, and his education would pay dividends. He was a good judge of people and took with him some of the brightest young men Jeffery had. He needed them because he knew very little about designing and manufacturing an automobile. He would leave that to those who knew their trade. Advertising and merchandising was his game and he could play with the best. Two of the Jeffery Company employees who left with Ned were Paul Zens and Russell Begg.[6]

Paul Zens would be a partner in the new company. He was a native of Kenosha and had been with Jeffery for thirteen years, starting as an office boy and working his way up to chief purchasing agent.[7] He had gained favor with the Jefferys as a young lad while delivering ice cream to their home. Kate Jeffery saw potential in the young man and persuaded her husband Thomas to give him a job. They were not disappointed as he was a good worker and a faithful employee until the day he left. He had been a purchasing agent at Jeffery for six years and had many contacts in the industry. These would prove invaluable in his new role as automobile manufacturer.

Russell Begg was a brilliant engineer, a graduate of the University of Michigan who had previously been employed at Hudson, Packard and Thomas and was the

***Top, left:* Paul Zens, co-founder and major stockholder in the Jordan Motor Car Company (*Motor Age*, December 10, 1920). *Top, right:* Ned Jordan circa 1916 (courtesy Art Michnevitz). *Bottom:* Russell Begg, Jordan chief engineer (Detroit Public Library, National Automotive History Collection).**

chief experimental engineer at Jeffery when he left the company.[8]

W.B. Riley, Jeffery assistant sales manager would soon follow the others in their move to Cleveland.

On January 25, Ned went to Chicago and called a meeting of college buddies, friends, and potential stockholders.[9] The next day, he raised $200,000 in a matter of hours.

Ned had made a lot of friends while at Jeffery. He traveled extensively and visited as many dealers as possible. These people would be the ones who would make substantial investments in the new company.

The prospectus called for a total capitalization of $800,000 including $500,000 preferred and $300,000 common stock. Of the preferred, $200,000 was to be held in the treasury while the common was to be given as a bonus with the preferred on the basis of one-half share to every share of preferred.[10] The preferred was to pay 7 percent cumulative and could be redeemed, at the company option, at 110 percent in two years. Of the preferred, $100,000 was reserved for friends and associates of the first stockholders. The Jordan Motor Car Company would be a co-operative effort with suppliers and dealers, who agreed to sell Jordans, owning as many shares of stock as they could afford.

Ned was a small man with a large ego, but he had the spunk to make a go of it. Without question, the new company would be called the Jordan Motor Car Company and the new car would be named Jordan.

Back in Kenosha, on February 8, it was announced that the company had taken an engineering office in the Goldberg Building in Detroit, Michigan. Here, Russell Begg would begin designing the new car.[11] Designing a chassis and selecting the proper engine, transmission, axles, and all the necessary components would be a mighty task, but he was a very capable engineer and that was what he had been trained to do. Detroit was the hub of automobile manufacturing at that time, and since the new company did not have a home it was a good place to start. Russell Begg knew the town well and having worked there previously, had many connections in the industry.

The Jordan would be what was known in the trade at the time as an assembled car. Jordan would not manufacture any of the components but would have some made to its specifications by reputable firms and purchase everything else from firms who furnished parts for much of the automobile industry. It would have been impossible to start a company which manufactured all of its components in house with only $800,000. Assembled automobiles were the only alternative. Moon, Crawford, Stephens, Biddle and Crow-Elkhart were just a few of the other manufacturers in the assembled car field, which composed approximately 25 percent of the industry at the time.

Jordan envisioned a high quality automobile that would sell in the upper middle price range. Jordan never wanted to challenge Ford, General Motors, Packard or any of the well established companies. They were too large and fiscally sound to be challenged by an upstart. The trick was to find a niche where the Jordan would fit in: just above the Buick and below the Cadillac, Packard, Pierce Arrow and Peerless.[12] Competing in the low priced field was out of the question. Ford with its Model T had that market covered, and Chevrolet was producing the Model 490 about this time. Studebaker, Dodge Brothers, Willys-Overland, and several others filled virtually every other position. These companies produced nearly everything they needed in-house, and no small new company was going to muscle in.

Ned and Paul Zens soon began looking for a factory site and more financing. They had been invited to Jackson, Michigan, by Captain William Sparks, who was co-owner of the Sparks-Withington Company (maker of "Sparton" automobile horns, among other things), and for a time it looked as if Jackson would get the new factory. Captain Sparks was born on May 9, 1873, in Burrington, Devonshire, England. His family migrated to America when he was six years old. As a young man he worked long hours and studied business at night. After a stint as owner of a grocery store, working in a department store and as a laborer in a manufacturing plant, he was hired by Colonel (later General) Winthrop Withington and Major Philip Withington (presumably of the Michigan National Guard) to work for a new company they were starting. It is not known when he became a partner, but the "Sparton" horn was perfected in 1912. The company grew and so did the stature of William Sparks. He was later a captain in the Michigan National Guard and was the leader of an American Legion Marching Group. He distinguished himself as a community leader and philanthropist and served three terms as mayor of Jackson.[13]

Sparks-Withington employee badge.

An automobile assembly plant would have been a great boost to the Jackson area, and the fact that Jordan would be buying all of its components meant that Sparks-Withington would be in a position to supply many of them. However, Phil Withington, Sparks's partner, invited Jordan and Zens to come to Cleveland (where Sparks-Withington also had a factory managed by Phil Withington) to look over some prospective plant sites and meet with financiers.

When Jordan and Zens arrived in Cleveland on March 30, Withington took them to meet George Coulton, president of the Union National Bank. They were taken to the Union Club for lunch where they met Charles and Alva Bradley, Mr. Little (president of the Chamber of Commerce), Benedict Crowell and Mr. Lundoff. The Bradleys were associated with George Coulton in the banking business and Mr. Lundoff was a partner with some of the aforementioned in the contracting business.[14]

Phil Withington had done his work well, and by four o'clock that afternoon, Jordan and Zens had found a plant site, secured financing and signed a contract to have the new factory constructed.

Sparks and Withington were not at odds. Regardless of whether the factory was in Jackson or Cleveland they benefited. They had factories in both cities and would sell Jordan many parts for the new car, especially "Sparton" horns and radiators.

Paul Zens and Ned Jordan had known both William Sparks and Phil Withington while employed at Jeffery, and this friendship would now pay dividends for the new company. The Union National Bank was now the financier for Jordan, and Ned plunked down the money he had previously raised. The Jordan Motor Car Company was now in business.

Phil Withington would become one of the officers of the new company and one of its major stockholders. Withington stood to gain in several ways, in fact. He was also the president of the Burchard-Roberts-Wales Company, Consulting Engineers, who would draw the plans for the new Jordan factory. He may also have had some connection with the realty company that owned the land and the construction company who erected the building. If not, he at least had done his work well and Ned Jordan and Paul Zens were able to leave Cleveland with the assurance that the Jordan Motor Car Company now had a home.

Cleveland was a good choice, as it had steel mills, water and rail transportation, good highways and streets. Several of the companies who would supply parts for the Jordan had factories located there. Ned was at home in the city, having worked for the *Cleveland Press* a decade earlier. His father had been raised a short distance from there, too.

The new plant was located on five acres at East 152 Street, adjacent to the Nickel Plate railroad tracks.[15] This would be important as most cars were shipped by rail. A rail siding next to the plant saved much time and money, thereby putting Jordan in a more competitive position. Highways were almost nonexistent in many parts of the country, and truck transportation was in its infancy. If a dealer did not drive his purchase away, it usually had to go by rail. A few were shipped by boats which sailed the Great Lakes.

Ground was broken and construction of the new factory began on April 5, 1916, with completion scheduled by June 1. It would cost $50,000 and would contain 30,000 square feet of space. Construction was finished on May 25, and the new building was turned over to the owners who were eager to get started.[16]

The new building now had to be equipped with the machinery necessary for the assembly of automobiles. An assembly line was installed; overhead conveyors, hoists, and cranes were added. A boiler room for steam to drive the air compressors and heat the building was constructed and equipped. A water tower to supply the boiler and necessary fire protection was an absolute must.

The factory boasted an engine test section with several dynamometers. Although Continental would make all Jordan engines, they would be tested by Jordan's own employees.[17]

A large body paint area with the latest equipment was a necessity. Jordan bodies were received at the factory in primer only. All those beautiful colors were applied by a highly skilled crew of craftsmen. Add a final test and inspection area and you have an automobile assembly plant.

Jordan employees were treated well with spacious offices for the management staff, nice rest rooms, a cafeteria for everyone and pleasant working conditions. This assured the new company of successful labor relations, and many former employees later remarked that working for Jordan was the best job they ever had. Hiring and training a staff had been going on while the factory was under con-

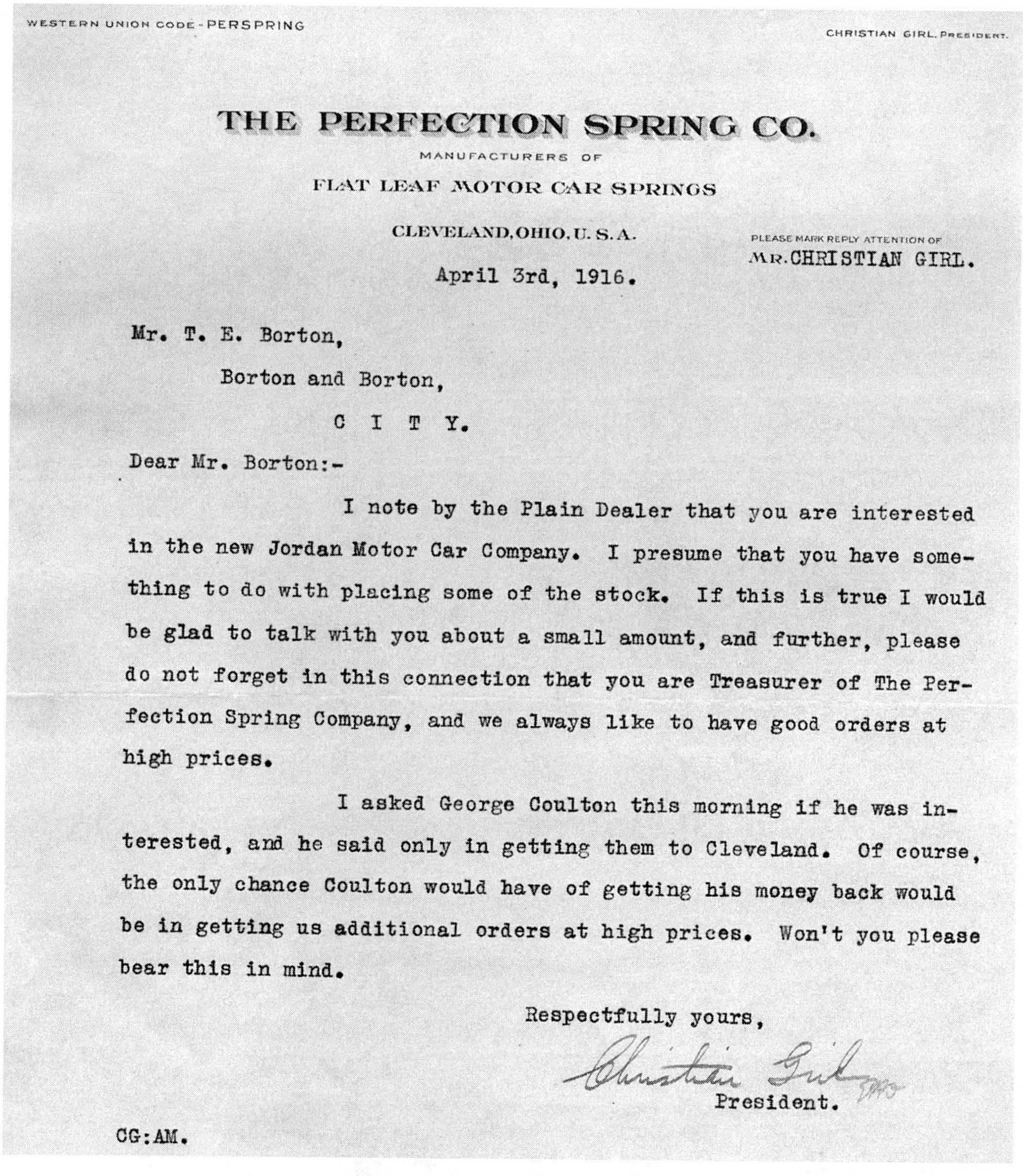

WESTERN UNION CODE-PERSPRING

CHRISTIAN GIRL, PRESIDENT.

THE PERFECTION SPRING CO.

MANUFACTURERS OF

FLAT LEAF MOTOR CAR SPRINGS

CLEVELAND, OHIO, U. S. A.

PLEASE MARK REPLY ATTENTION OF MR. CHRISTIAN GIRL.

April 3rd, 1916.

Mr. T. E. Borton,

Borton and Borton,

C I T Y.

Dear Mr. Borton:-

I note by the Plain Dealer that you are interested in the new Jordan Motor Car Company. I presume that you have something to do with placing some of the stock. If this is true I would be glad to talk with you about a small amount, and further, please do not forget in this connection that you are Treasurer of The Perfection Spring Company, and we always like to have good orders at high prices.

I asked George Coulton this morning if he was interested, and he said only in getting them to Cleveland. Of course, the only chance Coulton would have of getting his money back would be in getting us additional orders at high prices. Won't you please bear this in mind.

Respectfully yours,

Christian Girl

President.

CG:AM.

Letter from Perfection Spring Co., found in Ned Jordan's scrapbook.

Top: The Jordan factory, first phase (*Motor World*, August 16, 1916). *Bottom*: Jordan engine testing area (courtesy Art Michnevitz).

struction. Many of the employees had held similar jobs in other industries and others left jobs at automobile factories then operating in Cleveland. Getting qualified workers was not much of a problem. A minimal staff was hired at first and increased as the need arose. A profit sharing plan contributed greatly to the successful employment of workers.

New models were usually announced in August or September, and Jordan had to be up and running by that time. A prototype model had been under construction even before the factory was built, and was finished in April. It had actually been driven by officers and stockholders of the company on May 4.[18]

On May 6, Sparks-Withington signed a contract to be the sole supplier of horns for the new car. Being a large stockholder was paying dividends.[19]

On June 9, officers of the company were announced:

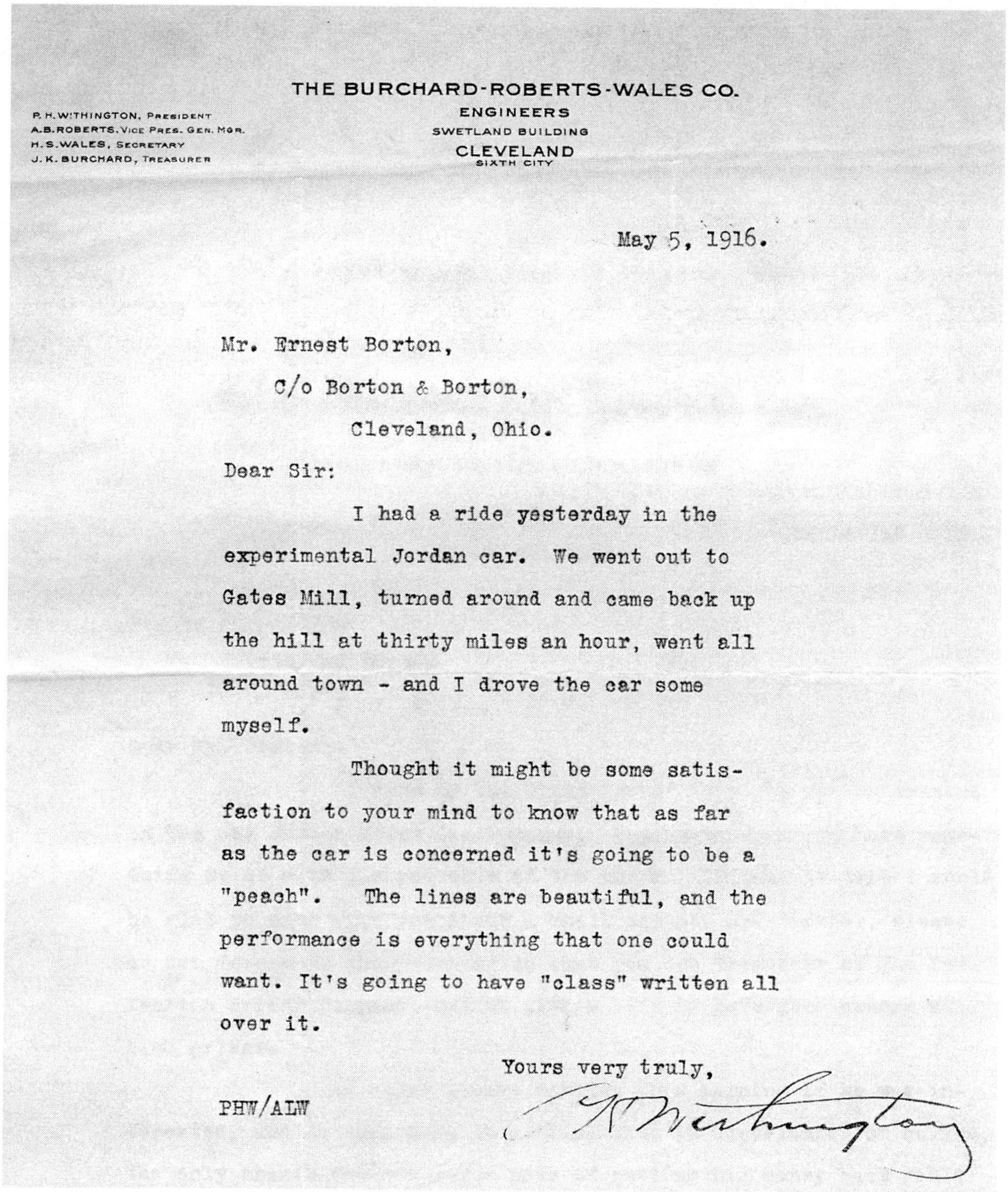

THE BURCHARD-ROBERTS-WALES CO.
ENGINEERS
SWETLAND BUILDING
CLEVELAND
SIXTH CITY

P. H. WITHINGTON, PRESIDENT
A. B. ROBERTS, VICE PRES. GEN. MGR.
H. S. WALES, SECRETARY
J. K. BURCHARD, TREASURER

May 5, 1916.

Mr. Ernest Borton,
C/o Borton & Borton,
Cleveland, Ohio.

Dear Sir:

I had a ride yesterday in the experimental Jordan car. We went out to Gates Mill, turned around and came back up the hill at thirty miles an hour, went all around town - and I drove the car some myself.

Thought it might be some satisfaction to your mind to know that as far as the car is concerned it's going to be a "peach". The lines are beautiful, and the performance is everything that one could want. It's going to have "class" written all over it.

Yours very truly,

PHW/ALW

Letter from Phil Withington to Ernest Borton reporting a test ride in a Jordan prototype, May 5, 1916; Ned Jordan saved this letter in his scrapbook.

Edward S. Jordan, President and General Manager.

P.H. Withington, Vice President, Partner in Sparks-Withington Company (Manufacturer of Sparton horns, also associated with American Fork and Hoe Co.). Also President of the Burchard-Roberts-Wales Company, Engineers.

Paul Zens, Secretary, Assistant General Manager, Purchasing Agent, formerly with Jeffery and co-owner of the new company.

T.E. Borton, Member of Board of Directors. A Cleveland financier and also a stockholder in Perfection Spring Company. He would handle much of Jordan's stock.

Russell Begg, Designer and Chief Engineer, Board of Directors. Formerly with Jeffery, Hudson, Thomas, and Packard.

J.L. Davidson, Works Manager, Board of Directors (formerly with Studebaker Corp.).

W.B. Riley, Sales Manager. Formerly with Thomas B. Jeffery Company; joined the new company shortly after its founding.

F.G. Tyler, Cost Accountant and Systems Manager (20 years' experience).[20]

Ned Jordan, Paul Zens, Russell Begg and the others who came from Jeffery would not have an easy time of it. They invested every dime of their saving sin the new company. They all lived in Cleveland Heights in duplex houses and owned one automobile between them.

Everyone left for work at the same time and if one was late, he had to take a streetcar. Ned said that when they were able to purchase a Ford Model T truck they thought they were "going to town."[21] All were on very small salaries and they had to make a go of the new company to see their investment pay off.

Manufacturing began in early June, shortly after the plant was completed, and ads for the new car began appearing in the trade magazines on July 6.[22]

Businessmen of Cleveland (of which many were stockholders) were invited to tour the factory and have a look at the new car on the same date. They were treated to a luncheon and a pep talk by Ned Jordan in which he outlined the plans of the company, gave them the specifications of the new car, and announced who would supply the components.[23]

The prototypes had been seen in all the right places around Cleveland for a couple of months. Ned Jordan wanted to whet the people's appetite for the new car and did a masterful job of doing so.

The first ads carried the Jordan Arrowhead but no name.[24] Insiders knew but the public would be teased for a few weeks. The Jordan logo would later become as recognizable as the Chevrolet bowtie.

Photos and prices of all body styles were released to the trade magazines on July 20.[25] On this date, Jordan released an eight-page article in *The Automobile*, a trade magazine, entitled "The Realization of a Great Ideal." It gave a glowing account of the new company with photos of the three body styles they would soon start delivering to dealers.

Jordan released photos and prices to the trade magazines early because most dealers nationwide were subscribers and potential Jordan distributors. Jordan needed as many as possible as soon as possible. It must have worked as they had 2,600 applications by August 21.

The *Saturday Evening Post* carried the first public ad on September 2, featuring only the Seven Passenger Touring car. The new company had been building the touring as rapidly as possible in order that dealers might have at least one car to show the public when the news broke. The first shipment to leave the factory arrived in New York City on August 15 and was consigned to the John G. Dale Agency.[26]

The model design would be Model 60,[27] though the car was sometimes referred to as 6–60 (6 cylinder, 60 horsepower) and later as the Model B. All would be sold as 1917 models. The Model B designation was never used officially by Jordan at the time of manufacture. Trade magazines and others began using it after Jordan came out with a Model 60 Series C version, and the company began using it later when releasing serial numbers to insurance companies.

The Seven Passenger Touring (Luxury) was the only car the early public ad showed, but they stated you could also have the Four Passenger Sport Touring and the Roadster. The other models would be supplied to dealers as quickly as they could be manufactured.[28]

Businessmen inspect the new Jordan (*Motor Age*, July 13, 1916).

Once Reporter on Press, Now Heads Auto Firm

TEN YEARS AGO JORDAN WAS "DOING" POLICE FOR THE CLEVELAND PRESS

NOW HE IS THE HEAD OF THE JORDAN MOTOR CAR CO.

Edward S. Jordan

Ten years ago Edward S. Jordan was "doing police" for the Cleveland Press.

Now he is head of the Jordan Motor Car Co., a new concern.

The plant opened Tuesday.

Jordan came to Cleveland fresh from college in 1905 at the suggestion of Newton Baker and Frederic C. Howe, fraternity brothers.

He was a reporter on The Press two years. Then he joined the National Cash Register Co. Later he became secretary and general manager of the Jeffery Motor Car Co., at Kenosha, Wis.

He left the Jeffery company Jan. 15, and since has organized an $800,000 company, originated a [illegible], and built a plant on E. 152d-. Production will begin this week.

The plant site covers five acres. The building includes 30,000 feet of floor space.

Cleveland Press article lauding Ned Jordan, June 28, 1916.

All three models would have five hood louvers. A later version of the Seven Passenger Touring car would be shown in ads with six, probably the result of an artist taking liberties. The Roadster would have the spare tire mounted perfectly vertically, but it would soon be placed at an angle.

All models were powered by a Continental 7 N six cylinder engine with bore and stroke of 3½ × 5¼ inches. The wheelbase was 127 inches with 35 × 4½ inch wheels. The cars used a Brown Lipe clutch and transmission and Timken axles and bearings. Bijur supplied the starter and lighting and Bosch the ignition. Fedders supplied the radiators which were topped off with a Boyce Motometer, and Stromberg carburetors were used. The bodies were aluminum and the chassis rode on Mather semi-elliptic springs. Willard batteries and Gemmer steering came as standard equipment, and Marshall coil springs in the seats assured a comfortable ride. The Jordans would ride on Firestone tires, and Stewart Warner would furnish the vacuum fuel feed.[29] Parish & Bingham would supply the frames.

The Seven Passenger luxury car and the Roadster were priced at $1,650; wire wheels were $100 extra. The Sport Four was $1,750 with wire wheels standard.

Leather upholstery was standard and paint could be had in either maroon or light green. Weight was 3,050 lbs. for the luxury car. The interior appointments were elegant with mahogany wood and nickel used liberally.

Who supplied the early bodies has always been a mystery, but it is almost certain that the Walker-Wells Company of Amesbury, Massachusetts, supplied most, if not all, of the early closed bodies (introduced in the late fall) and probably those of the open cars as well.[30] Walker-Wells was licensed to produce the Springfield bodies which Jordan used on the Sedan and Coupe and, of all the companies doing such work, was the most likely builder of the open bodies. It is certain that they did supply at least part of what Jordan required.[31]

Ned Jordan himself had a great influence on the design of all Jordan bodies. Some slick promotion was used when it came to that subject. They were never advertised as "custom" but rather as "custom style," riding on a chassis of finished mechanical excellence.

Jordan was quick to point out the quality components which made up the car but strangely silent when it came to the subject of bodies. They apparently wanted the public to believe they were building their own, and it is rumored that they did do at least some, but no reliable evidence has been found to substantiate this. Jordan craftsmen designed and built the prototypes, but it is highly unlikely that they did anything else.

Jordan had announced that only 100 dealers would sell the new car nationwide, but "dealers" were actually distributors that furnished cars to many small dealerships, some of which carried several brands.

This distinctively American emblem will mark a new luxury car. The name will soon be nationally known

A New Luxury Car

For 1917—with a choice of Custom Style Bodies.

PEOPLE who know, realize that in the motor car of the future, the determining factor is to be the body.

A standard chassis of finished mechanical excellence, fitted to suit the buyer, with a choice of distinctive and comfortable custom style bodies, is both practical and fashionable.

Those in whom good taste is inherent, value a motor car for its distinctive appearance, quality of detail, body comfort, and performance.

In this advanced style class, a new luxury car will shortly assume a positive leadership.

It is the first American car in which body lines, finish, and body arrangement in their relation to the mental and body comfort of the passengers is given first consideration.

It is a light, perfectly balanced automobile with wonderful acceleration, and with unusual flexibility of applied power.

The chassis includes all of the finest universally approved mechanical units chosen after the joint endorsement of the greatest American automobile engineers.

The touring bodies are straight as an arrow from motometer tip to top cover, fashionably long and low.

The racy roadster and four passenger sporting models are low and rakish, yet the seats are cleverly arranged for real comfort.

The enclosed types include Sedan, Limousine, and Coupe, and are fitted with bodies of the permanent top style—exclusively 1917 vogue.

To inspire the owner's pride and save depreciation, twenty painting operations, a detailed finish, hand-buffed leather, and custom style mahogany cabinet work are provided, encouraging the owner to keep his car year after year.

There is more room for the driver; more room in the rear seat and a distinct innovation in seat cushions is introduced for the first time. The effect is almost pneumatic.

The passenger will feel that he is sitting down in the car instead of on top of it. The rear seat is actually wide enough for three people.

It is a body in which there is not a cramp or a squeeze for driver or passengers; a body of real riding comfort.

A single chassis designed and built with extreme accuracy, to be produced in limited numbers under the most rigid inspection system, maintaining the highest standard of quality and efficiency by using the one best unit available for each purpose.

On special order, the standard chassis may be fitted with custom made bodies by the world's leading makers.

Only 100 well established dealers will be authorized to sell this car.

Delivery schedules will be provided for these in accordance with daily production.

Further interesting details next week.

Dealers and individuals desiring advance information may address

The New All American Car
Care of Motor Age. Chicago.

The first Jordan ad, which appeared in *Motor Age* on July 6, 1916.

Above, left: Model 60 7 Passenger Touring. *Above, right:* Model 60 4 Passenger Touring. *Left:* Model 60 Roadster.

Interior of Model 60 Seven Passenger Luxury Car.

Parish & Bingham furnished frames for early and late Jordans (*The Automobile*, December 1916).

Jordan found itself cramped for space almost immediately and erected a large tent (6,000 square feet) on the opposite side of the Nickel Plate railroad tracks where final inspection would take place. The Jordan Building Company had taken formal title to the new factory about this time. The Citizens National Bank had financed the project and the final cost would be $75,000—approximately one-half more than originally anticipated.[32]

On October 16 it was announced that a new building would be erected on the spot where the tent was used temporarily. It would be of the same size and construction as the original building, which had a capacity of 30,000 square feet.[33]

The railroad track which ran along the west side of the plant would be enclosed at the front but would have large doors in order to facilitate the loading of automobiles. The track would remain uncovered between the two plants. Cars without bodies could now be transported through the enclosed portion to the final assembly point and never be subjected to the elements.

Bodies were shipped to the factory with only a primer coat of paint. The body supplier would furnish two painters who would see them finished to specifications. These two men would be employed until Jordan's own painters could be trained to do the job. Customers who wanted to commission a special body to their specifications could buy a Jordan chassis.[34]

Production, which had started at three cars per day, was now up to five and shooting for ten. The work force was quickly gaining skill and would soon meet the higher goal.

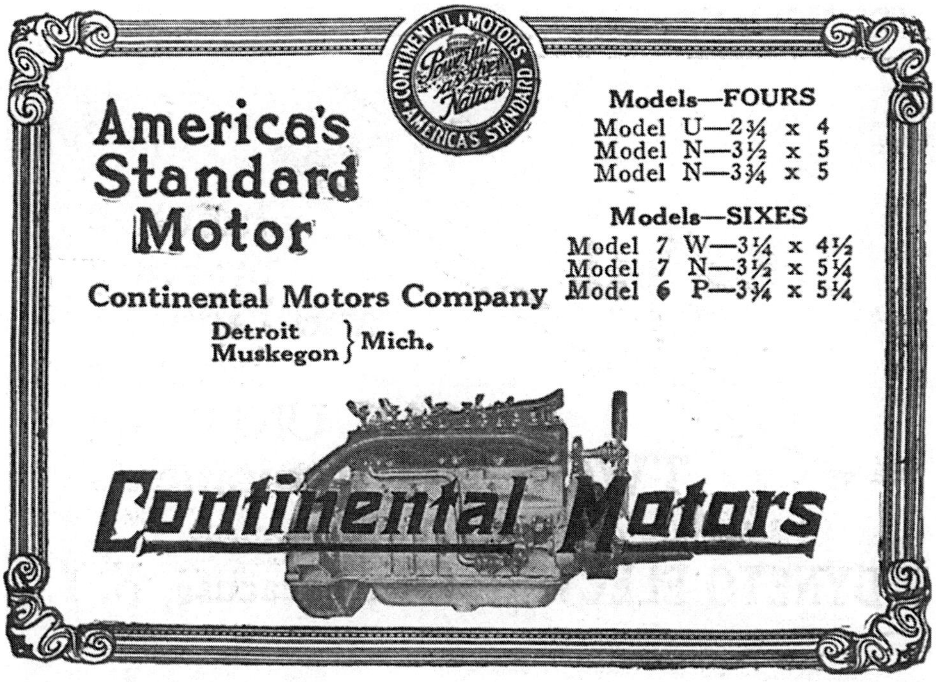

Continental Motors ad. The Model 7N was Jordan's first engine (*The Automobile*, October 12, 1916).

The trade magazines announced that Jordan added three new enclosed models on November 30, but the *Saturday Evening Post* carried the first ad for these new automobiles on November 18.[35] All closed models would have five hood louvers but they would soon be increased to ten. The Sedan, Coupe, and Limousine had the same mechanical specifications as the previous models. The Sedan and Coupe bodies were of the Spring-

Rendering of the Jordan factory showing (at left) the addition that would double its capacity (*Jordan Success* brochure, November 30, 1916).

Above, left: **Model 60 Coupe.** ***Above, right:*** **Model 60 Sedan.** ***Left:*** **Model 60 Limousine (Free Library of Philadelphia).**

field type; the pillars could be lowered thereby creating what we know today as the hard top.

The Coupe sold for $2,300, the Sedan for $2,350 and the Limousine for $3,000. Wire wheels were $100 extra on any model. A Dictograph speaking system—basically a speaking tube between front and rear compartments—was employed on the Limousine, along with a heater for winter driving comfort. Wooden wheels were standard on most body styles but 75 percent of the cars were shipped with wire spokes.[36]

Jordan placed an eight page ad entitled "Jordan Success" in the November 30 issue of *Motor Age* magazine. It contained glowing stories of Jordan performance, durability, reliability, gas mileage and the joys of owning a Jordan. Drawing on his knack for journalism and advertising, Ned Jordan never missed an opportunity to take advantage of anything favorable to his cause.

Jordan entered 1917 with orders for more cars than it could build, a new plant, an addition in the planning stage and 3,000 prospective dealers who wanted to sell the new offering.

From a dream to reality in less than a year was more than they could have hoped for, but they had worked extremely hard and long working hours were common. They were now set to reap the benefits of their labor.

THREE

Early Growth, 1917

As 1917 dawned, Jordan was doing well. Production was increasing as the employees became more efficient, the company had orders for more cars than it could build, finances were in good shape and there were no foreseeable problems. The war which had been raging in Europe was beginning to involve the United States, however, as diplomatic relations with Germany were severed on February 3. The U.S. Congress declared war on Germany on April 6, but Jordan's production would not be affected.

The six body styles were carried into the new year unchanged. All cars which had been made previously were designated as 1917 models because they were released at the beginning of that model year. This would be the way Jordan would continue, as most other makers were also doing, but they would introduce a new model or body style anytime they chose.

Jordan went to the National Automobile Chamber of Commerce National Automobile Show in New York City early in January. The show was held at the Grand

Top, left: 1917 Model 60 Sedan, second version with ten hood louvers. Top, right: 1917 Model 60 Coupe, second version. Bottom, left: 1917 Model 60 Roadster, second version. Bottom, right: 1917 Model 60 Limousine, second version (all photographs: Free Library of Philadelphia).

Central Palace, which was bedecked with floral arrangements. This was Jordan's first show, and being one of the new kids on the block, they were relegated to the fourth floor among the accessory and motorcycle manufacturers. Their fate was not much better at the Chicago show as they ended up in the basement with a lot of other smaller manufacturers. Jordan was not yet a member of the N.A.C.C. but would be before the 1918 shows were held.

Some ambitious plans for production were announced on February 9. Jordan released a projection of producing 5,000 cars during the 1917 calendar year. This was a very optimistic statement, and the company would actually produce less than half that amount.

At a stockholders meeting held on the same date, all officers of the company were re-elected. Plans for the new addition, which would double the size of the factory and had been in the works for some time, were shown to the attendees and it was announced that construction would start as soon as practical.[1]

By early 1917, it became evident that the price of some cars needed a little tweaking and on March 15, Jordan announced that prices on four models would be increased to become effective April 1.[2]

The Seven Passenger Luxury Touring and the Roadster would sell for $1,795, while the Four Passenger Sport Touring would sell for $1,895 with wire wheels as standard equipment. The Sedan would now go for $2,495. Prices of the Four Passenger Coupe and Limousine would remain unchanged at $2,300 and $3,000 respectively.

Construction of the new addition began about the middle of March, and barring any unforeseen problems, the building was expected to be occupied by late June.[3]

An array of new spring colors was announced on April 10. This would be Jordan's first opportunity to give customers a choice of colors as the first cars had to be rushed into production as quickly as possible.[4] Jordan never did believe in the Ford theory of "any color you wish as long as it's black." The new colors would make a rainbow blush, but customers, then as now, wanted something to suit their individual tastes and Jordan did not disappoint them. Nine new colors were offered, each restricted to a certain model. There would be but 25 cars made in each color.

1. Apache Red—Four Passenger Sport with khaki top and white wire wheels.

2. Ocean Sand Gray—Seven Passenger Luxury car with semi-bright leather top and black wire wheels.

3. Italian Tan—Four Passenger Sport Model with mustard color top with fenders and splash aprons to match the body.

4. Egyptian Bronze—Seven Passenger Luxury Touring with patent leather top with fenders and splash aprons to match the body.

5. Apple Blossom Green—Four Passenger Sport Model with white leather top with fender and splash aprons to match the body and white wire wheels. To add distinction the hood louvers were painted brilliant Chinese blue.

6. Chinese Blue—Seven Passenger Luxury Touring with top in a harmonizing shade with fenders and splash aprons to match the body color. Red wire wheels complemented the treatment.

7. Venetian Green—Seven Passenger Luxury Touring with semi-bright hand buffed leather upholstery and white wire wheels with fenders and splash aprons in body color. The Four Passenger Sport model was available with the same features.

8. Savage Red—Four Passenger Sport Model with Italian tan top and white wire wheels.

Plant addition under construction, June 15, 1917 (*Jordan Arrow*, courtesy Arthur Grove).

9. Submarine Gray—Four Passenger Sport Model with egg-shell finish, khaki top and orange wheels.

All the special paint jobs were on open cars. With spring in the air, owners wanted cars that reflected their personalities. Ned Jordan was only too willing to oblige and it would be a safe bet that he made more than 25 of each color if the demand was there. Strangely, no special colors were offered for the Roadster.

On April 23, the Welden W. Shaw Company of Chicago, one of the largest taxicab companies in the United States, added ten new Jordan Seven Passenger Touring cars to its fleet. The Chicago Motor Company, Jordan Distributors, made the sale.[5]

On April 27, Jordan announced that it had spent only $387.50 on repairs of the 1,000 Jordan cars sold to that date, on a sales volume of $1,700,000.[6]

On May 10, a four page insert in *Motor Age* entitled "This is the inside story of how Jordan made good" extolled the virtues of the new company, its automobiles and the people who made it go in a lot of high class prose by Ned Jordan.[7]

The new addition to the factory was occupied on May 11, about six weeks ahead of schedule. Jordan had been in dire need of more space and was actually using about two-thirds of the building before completion.[8]

Jordan shipped 287 cars during May, the majority to the southwestern and northeastern parts of the United States. Those areas had seen a 50 percent increase in the past two months.[9] Jordan was constantly adding distributors and dealers wherever they could be found. Production would increase as demand grew. By doubling the size of the factory, they were in a position to meet that demand.

Ned Jordan in a casual pose with W.E. Wheeler, president of the Northwestern Automobile Company of Minneapolis (*Jordan Arrow*, courtesy Arthur Grove).

James L. Davidson, factory manager (*Jordan Arrow*, courtesy Arthur Grove).

Paul Zens talking to L.E. Barger of the Barger-Mitchell Company, Jordan distributors in Toledo (*Jordan Arrow*, courtesy Arthur Grove).

Jordan testers Lester Vought, foreman; H.F. Rolf; E. Frost; and Gus Rye (*Jordan Arrow*, courtesy Arthur Grove).

On June 18, a new Sport Roadster was unveiled. It had basically the same appearance as the earlier version but would have ten hood louvers. It was 200 pounds lighter than the previous model, mainly because it lacked a rumble seat, and was equipped with high speed gearing. It was available in three colors, Mercedes Red, Liberty Blue, or Briarcliff Green.[10]

The steering column was adjustable and the chassis was equipped with special vanadium steel springs which allowed it to sit lower to the ground. The trunk lid had locks at both corners. All other mechanical specifications would be the same as previous Model 60s.

The July color options were announced on the 5th, and several new colors were introduced:

1. Liberty Blue—Seven Passenger Touring, Sport Model Touring, and Sport Roadster.
2. Pershing Gray—Seven Passenger Touring and Four Passenger Sport Touring.
3. Italian Tan—Sport Model Touring.
4. Jordan Maroon—Seven Passenger Touring and Sport Touring.
5. Mercedes Red—Sport Roadsters.
6. Venetian Green—Optional on all three open models.[11]

These colors were in addition to all the others offered.

On July 12, Jordan announced the sale of 1,545 cars as of June 25 at a value of $2,626,500. Output was now ten cars per day but they were working hard to increase that number.[12]

On July 9, the Jordan Motor Car Company was elected to the National Automobile Chamber of Commerce. Membership in the NACC was based entirely on the standing of the manufacturer as to the permanency of the business and of its importance in relation to the trade as a whole. Election was a prestigious achievement to be proud of.[13]

Top: Ned Jordan at the wheel of a 1917-1918 model 60 Roadster (Applegate & Applegate collection). **Bottom:** Another view of a 1917-1918 Model 60 Sport Roadster (Detroit Public Library, National Automotive History Collection).

Ned Jordan pins the emblem of the Loyal Order of the Red Arrow on E.J. Schroeter (*Jordan Arrow*, courtesy Arthur Grove).

The Loyal Order of the Red Arrow emblem (*Jordan Arrow*).

About June or July, Jordan formed an owners organization called the Loyal Order of the Red Arrow. Any owner of a Jordan for at least one year was eligible for membership and could receive a gold pin bearing the red arrow insignia.

On August 22, a leading trade magazine reported that Jordan would soon begin to manufacture trucks.[14] Details of the program would be discussed at a dealers' conference which was to begin on August 24. Apparently the dealers did not respond enthusiastically and the subject of truck production was dropped and never brought up again. Although an article in *Motor* in November 1917 stated that Jordan would soon begin production of trucks, this probably was just some late reporting of the earlier announcement as nothing ever came of the idea. Later there would be a few small trucks, but these were built on passenger car chassis to be used as service vehicles. No trucks were ever offered for public consumption.

The dealer conference, at which ideas for selling Jordans were discussed, coincided with the unveiling of the new line for the 1918 model year.[15] Four new enclosed models made their appearance, representing a radical departure from the previous line. On these Custom Style Enclosed Carriages[16] fenders were now double crowned compared to the previous models which were flat. The windshield was radically slanted and all but the new town car had triangular side windows ahead of the front door posts.

1918-1919 Model 60 C Sport Limousine (Free Library of Philadelphia).

There were no hood louvers and the engine would be of a new design. The instruction manual shows all cars except roadsters, and it must be assumed that they all had the new engines. A Continental 10 N was now the power plant, and most of the previous models would also be similarly equipped. The new engine would have the same bore and stroke of the previous 7 N engine (3½ × 5¼ inches) but would be balanced for much smoother performance. The 10 N engine must have been made exclusively for Jordan as it had an arrowhead cast into the crankcase where the engine data plate was affixed. The new models, as well as the old ones which were retained, would be designated as Model 60 C. Most of the other specifications would remain the same.

The former Sedan and Coupe would be dropped, but the popular sport roadster would continue on as the Model 60 and would still be powered by the Continental 7 N engine.

The four new models were the Sport Limousine, Brougham, Town Car, and Sedan. All were fitted with aluminum bodies. The Sport Limousine had a capacity of seven passengers and was fitted with many fancy interior appointments. The two auxiliary seats folded under the front seat when not in use. A toilet case for both men and women, equipped with virtually anything one might need, came as standard equipment. The car also boasted a host of other refinements, including special dome lights front and rear with door switches which could be disabled for daytime use, Dictograph and reading lamps with individual switches, all standard. A hat rack, silk roller curtains on each rear compartment window, including the window dividing the front from the rear compartment, and two coat hooks were also standard.

The interior could be finished in a variety of worsted and patterns. In addition to the window curtains, it was equipped with drapery curtains for the rear compartment and a Waltham clock and Yale door locks. Colors were Italian Tan, Pershing Gray, Egyptian Bronze, Chrome Yellow and Permanent Maroon. Fancy indeed. The price was $3,300 and wire wheels were $100 extra.

The Brougham was equipped with most of the appointments of the Sport Limousine but seated only four passengers. The passenger side front seat folded forward for entry and could be revolved so the front passenger could face rearward. The driver's seat was adjustable. The body was finished in Liberty Blue, Brewster Green, or Italian Tan. A small compartment at the rear held tools and two pieces of luggage. The price was $2,900 plus $100 for wire wheels.

The Town Car had the same appointments as the Sport Limousine except that the auxiliary seats faced the rear. The front compartment was open but was fitted with a weatherproof cover and curtains for driving in inclement weather. The front compartment seats were finished in hand buffed leather and carriage lights added a touch of elegance. The Town Car was available in Ocean Sand Gray, Permanent Maroon, Venetian Green, Liberty Blue, or Italian Tan with the upper portion finished in Stygian Black. A very elegant car, it was also very expensive, at $3,200 including wire wheels.

The sedan was not so finely finished as the previous models. It seated seven passengers with auxiliary

Interior of Model 60 C Limousine.

seats facing forward when in use. The body was aluminum and was the Springfield type as was the previous Model 60 Sedan. Silk roller curtains graced the windows and the upholstery was the same as the Limousine and Town Car. Colors were Permanent Maroon, Venetian Green, or Liberty Blue with the upper body finished in Stygian Black. The price was $2,650 with wire wheels at an extra cost.[17]

After a Friday morning session devoted to pep talks and tips for having successful sales, the dealers were treated to a session with Ned himself and then given a preview of the new models. Some of the new cars were used to transport the dealers to Shore Acres on the banks of Lake Erie where a luncheon was served.[18]

At two o'clock in the afternoon there was a short business session back at the factory with Ned Jordan speaking, followed by a sales talk from W.B. Riley, Jordan sales manager. The meeting adjourned for a 25 mile ride to Broadlawn Villa in Mentor, Ohio, where dinner would be served on the veranda.

While chatter abounded and liquid refreshment

Top: 1918-1919 Model 60 C Brougham. *Bottom:* Interior of Model 60 C Brougham. (Both photographs: Free Library of Philadelphia.)

flowed, Ned played his ace. A brand new model, never seen by anyone other than the factory insiders, slowly cruised by. It was driven by the beautiful Mrs. Paul Zens, who was accompanied by an announcer with a bullhorn, repeating "I Am the Sport Marine." Dealers for-

1918-1919 Model 60 C Town Car (Free Library of Philadelphia).

Top: 1918-1919 Model 60 C Sedan. *Bottom:* Interior of 1918-1919 Model 60 C Sedan. (Both photographs: Free Library of Philadelphia.)

Left: 1918-1919 Model 60C Sport Marine (Applegate & Applegate collection). Right: Model 60 C Sport Marine with top lowered (John Conde).

Left: Model 60 C Sport Marine rear interior. Right: Model 60 C Sport Marine front interior. (Both photographs: Free Library of Philadelphia.)

got about dinner and besieged sales manager Riley with requests to purchase the new model.[19]

Sporty it was! Finished in Copenhagen Blue, its aluminum body had straight lines and smaller wheels, slung two inches lower than the previous models. Unlike the closed cars it retained the flat fenders of the early Model 60. This really enhanced its appearance rather than detracted, and a front bumper (a Jordan first) gave it the appearance of speed. And speedy it was with a 75 mph speedometer and special gears. Tires were 32 × 4 Silvertown Cords. Paint was velvet finish and would later be offered in Italian Tan, Briarcliff Green, and Ascot Maroon. A Waltham clock was standard, Macbeth lenses graced the headlights and the upholstery was genuine leather. The price was $2,375.

Only one car per dealer would be furnished at first. A drawing was held to see who would get the very first one, and Charles E. Baker, the Detroit dealer, held the ace of hearts and took home the prize.[20] It would be December before the factory could furnish a sufficient number of the Sport Marine for sale to the public. In fact, *The Literary Digest* carried the first public ad for the Sport Marine on December 29. Jordan would advertise the new model very heavily during the next year. After dinner the dealers returned to town and attended a cabaret performance. Saturday, the meeting concluded with a full day of meetings and more pep talks with Ned. A banquet that night officially brought the first dealer conference to a close.

On September 1, a press release stated that 1,788 cars were manufactured during the first year of business (Sept. 1, 1916–Sept. 1, 1917), on a volume of $3,189,600.

Detroit dealer Charles Baker of Baker-Fisk-Hugill Co. got the first Sport Marine (*Jordan Arrow*).

On October 1, new prices were announced effective as of that date.[21] The Seven Passenger, Touring, Sport Roadster and Four Passenger Sport Touring would sell for $1,995, the Sport Limousine for $3,300, the Town Car for $3,000, the Brougham for $2,900 and the Sedan for $2,650. By now the Roadster had given way to the Sport Roadster. If not, both would still be carried on as Model 60s. All the new models could have wire wheels for $100 extra and wheel and tire sizes were optional on the Sport touring. By late December, Disteel pressed steel wheels were optional on most models.[22]

Jordan would conduct an extensive advertising campaign for the Sport Marine. In fact, the first known Jordan color ad was for this car. Where else would it be depicted than the seashore?

Jordan was now doing well with the factory producing at full capacity. They could not build enough cars to satisfy demand and were adding more dealers every day. On December 6, Jordan announced that it had a net profit of $30,699 for the previous year.[23]

A shortage of railroad cars, due to the war effort, began to affect delivery of cars during 1917. Ned would organize a group of college students, form a caravan and make deliveries to dealers within a radius of a hundred or so miles.

By the end of the year, the Sport Marine was being supplied to dealers. Optional colors of Briarcliff Green and Ascot Maroon were now being offered in addition to the original color of Copenhagen Blue. A modest profit was realized, production was increasing, a new addition to the plant was completed and a line of cars to fit any customer demand was available to the consuming public as the year ended.[24]

JORDAN PRICE SCHEDULE

EFFECTIVE DECEMBER 1st, 1917

ENCLOSED MODELS

Touring Sedan	$2750.00
Brougham	$3000.00
Town Car	$3300.00
Limousine	$3500.00

FIVE WIRE WHEELS (EXTRA) $125.00

PRICES F. O. B. CLEVELAND, OHIO

JORDAN MOTOR CAR COMPANY

CLEVELAND, OHIO

Price schedule as of December 1, 1917.

FOUR

"A Million Dollar Idea," 1918–1919

In 1918 the United states was fully involved in World War I, but most civilian production had not been curtailed. Thousands of American soldiers were fighting "over there" and their families were anxiously awaiting their safe return. Sadly, the war had cost the lives of over 8 million servicemen from all countries involved. Meanwhile in the fall a great flu epidemic engulfed the United States, killing some 675,000 in a matter of months.

Good news came on November 11, as the Armistice to end the war was signed. The boys would be coming home to wives and sweethearts, to begin their life anew. Jordan wanted to be part of that experience.

As the new year began, Jordan also had something new. A seven passenger touring model, the Suburban Seven, made its appearance at the January Chicago Auto Show.[1] Ned had picked a familiar name, reverting to his Jeffery days, when in 1912 he was instrumental in naming a car Suburban. The new car went into production February 1, but it would be April before dealers would have them in stock. The car was nothing more than a stretched version of the Sport Marine, having the same mechanical specifications.[2] Weight was increased to 3,100 pounds. The wheelbase was still 127 inches but the body was stretched to accommodate two jump seats. The spare tire, which had been mounted at an angle on the Sport Marine, would now become vertical on the Suburban Seven. Price was $2,375.

On February 11, a press release stated that Jordan had manufactured 1,727 cars during the 1917 calendar year. Their goal of 2,000 cars a year was yet to be met, and the prediction of 5,000 was just a dream.[3] On February 19, the U.S. Patent Office granted Jordan's trademark for the arrowhead (#120,583) which had been used on the radiator emblem since August 6, 1916. Jordan had applied for the trademark on June 26, 1917.

On August 1, another new automobile made its appearance.[4] Without fanfare a new Brougham eased into the picture. The body was a copy of the Model 60 C but it had flat fenders. The rear seat was devoid of

Left: **Model 60 C Suburban Seven (Applegate & Applegate collection).** ***Right:*** **Model 60 C Suburban Seven (Free Library of Philadelphia).**

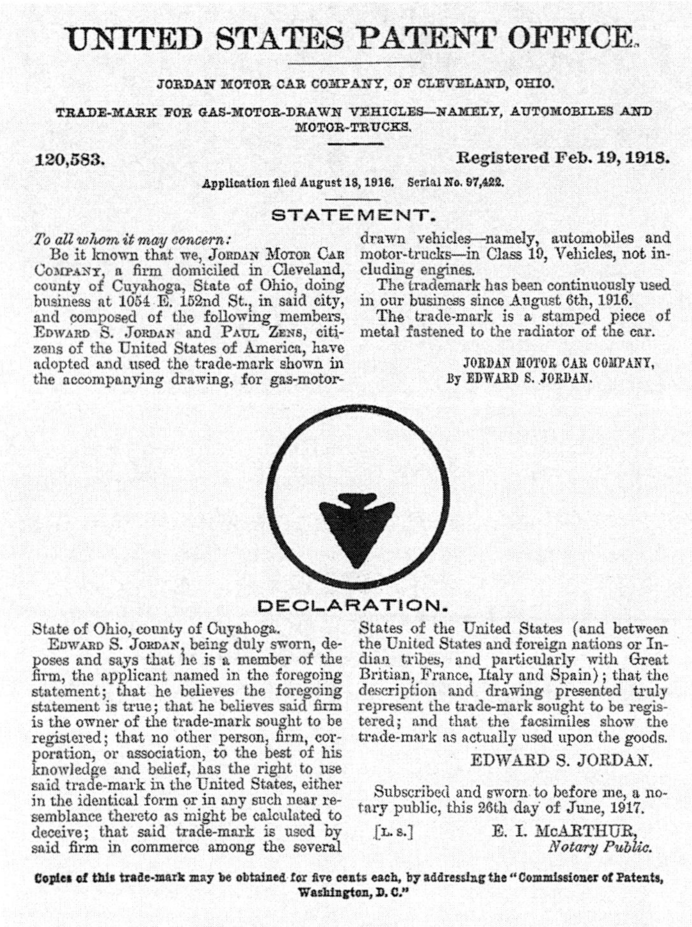

UNITED STATES PATENT OFFICE.

JORDAN MOTOR CAR COMPANY, OF CLEVELAND, OHIO.

TRADE-MARK FOR GAS-MOTOR-DRAWN VEHICLES—NAMELY, AUTOMOBILES AND MOTOR-TRUCKS.

120,583. Registered Feb. 19, 1918.

Application filed August 18, 1916. Serial No. 97,422.

STATEMENT.

To all whom it may concern:

Be it known that we, JORDAN MOTOR CAR COMPANY, a firm domiciled in Cleveland, county of Cuyahoga, State of Ohio, doing business at 1054 E. 152nd St., in said city, and composed of the following members, EDWARD S. JORDAN and PAUL ZENS, citizens of the United States of America, have adopted and used the trade-mark shown in the accompanying drawing, for gas-motor-drawn vehicles—namely, automobiles and motor-trucks—in Class 19, Vehicles, not including engines.

The trademark has been continuously used in our business since August 6th, 1916.

The trade-mark is a stamped piece of metal fastened to the radiator of the car.

JORDAN MOTOR CAR COMPANY,
By EDWARD S. JORDAN.

DECLARATION.

State of Ohio, county of Cuyahoga.

EDWARD S. JORDAN, being duly sworn, deposes and says that he is a member of the firm, the applicant named in the foregoing statement; that he believes the foregoing statement is true; that he believes said firm is the owner of the trade-mark sought to be registered; that no other person, firm, corporation, or association, to the best of his knowledge and belief, has the right to use said trade-mark in the United States, either in the identical form or in any such near resemblance thereto as might be calculated to deceive; that said trade-mark is used by said firm in commerce among the several States of the United States (and between the United States and foreign nations or Indian tribes, and particularly with Great Britian, France, Italy and Spain); that the description and drawing presented truly represent the trade-mark sought to be registered; and that the facsimiles show the trade-mark as actually used upon the goods.

EDWARD S. JORDAN.

Subscribed and sworn to before me, a notary public, this 26th day of June, 1917.

[L. S.] E. I. McARTHUR,
Notary Public.

Copies of this trade-mark may be obtained for five cents each, by addressing the "Commissioner of Patents, Washington, D. C."

Arrowhead trademark certificate.

1919 60 C Brougham. "Drive Your Own Car" was the theme for women.

any frills, making it wider, thus accommodating three passengers. With two riding in the front, the Brougham was a five passenger vehicle. The body was aluminum and the hood sported ten louvers. Jordan was now touting the "drive your own car" theory. Other than the rear seat, the interior was identical to the previous Brougham.

The new Brougham sported a front bumper, and wood wheels were standard. It is unknown what engine powered the new creation, but it probably was the Continental 10 N. It is unlikely that it would be the old 7 N, but Jordan was still using it in the Sport Roadster and could have done the same with the latest addition. Very little advertising was done for the new model and it never showed up in ads designed for public consumption.

On August 29, Jordan pulled another surprise. A new Sedan made its appearance, billed as the "Aluminum Sedan," the body being a reasonable copy of the previous sedan.[5] The car had one door on the driver's side and one center door on the right. The Sedan followed the Brougham with flat fenders, ten hood louvers, front bumper and Macbeth headlight lens. It seated seven passengers and was 200 pounds lighter than the average sedan owing to its aluminum body. Colors were Liberty Blue or Venetian Green with upper body in Stygian Black. It is assumed that it was powered by a Continental 10 N, but the possibility of the 7 N exists. Price was $3,200. Like the new Brougham, advertising was almost nonexistent for the new Sedan.

1919 Aluminum Sedan, a Model 60 C.

The Four Passenger Brougham and Seven Passenger Sedan were the only new models for the 1919 model year. However, the Suburban Seven had made its appearance in January as a late 1918 arrival. Little was said when Jordan dropped anything from the line; it just didn't appear in the lineup anymore.

As 1919 dawned things were going well. The Sport Marine and Suburban Seven were not selling as well as expected, despite heavy advertising, but the rest of the line was doing well. The new year would be one not soon forgotten. The flu epidemic which had started the previous year devastated the United States and some 675,000 Americans died as a result. (The worldwide toll is estimated between 20 million and 70 million.) Congress passed the Volstead National Prohibition Act, and those who drank alcoholic spirits would find it harder to imbibe. Bathtub gin would soon become very popular. Captain John Alcock and Lieutenant Arthur Brown of Britain made the first non-stop flight across the Atlantic. Jack Dempsey knocked out Jess Willard on July 4 to become the heavyweight champion, and the Chicago White Sox threw the World Series to the Cincinnati Reds in a scandal that would forever change baseball. With the war over, thousands of young men were returning home.

The Chicago auto show saw the introduction of a new Jordan model. The Town Sedan was a four door version of the Sedan retaining flat fenders and the 10 hood louvers but the windshield was straight and had no visor.[6] The cowl was ventilated, a first at Jordan. Wood wheels were standard but there was no front bumper. Little else is known about this model; there is no information about engine, body color, or price.

There is some mystery about this model as another Town Sedan made its appearance in February.[7] This version had exactly the same body style as the previous model except that the fenders were now double crowned and it sported wire wheels. The body was aluminum. As on the previous model, the roof was lower, giving the appearance of greater length.

It is possible that soon after the new car was introduced with the flat fenders, it was decided to update it to the new style as Jordan would never again make anything with flat fenders. This is only speculation but seems the only plausible answer.

The second Town Sedan was offered in Liberty Blue and Brewster Green, and it, too, had the cowl ventilator. The inside metal fittings were in platinum (very fancy) and it seated seven passengers. Windows were framed in Circassian walnut.

While all this was going on a price reduction for the older models was announced. The Seven Passenger Luxury Touring and Four passenger Sport Touring were reduced from $2,750 to $2,475, and the Sedan, Four Passenger Brougham, and Town Car from $3,700 to $3,500.[8]

April brought big news at Jordan as a new line of cars was introduced.[9] The Jordan Silhouette would

Top and bottom: **1919 Model 60 C Town Sedan (Applegate & Applegate collection).**

1919 Model F Town Sedan.

1919 Model F Silhouette 7 Passenger Touring. The four passenger version was identical except for two jump seats (Detroit Public Library, National Automotive History Collection).

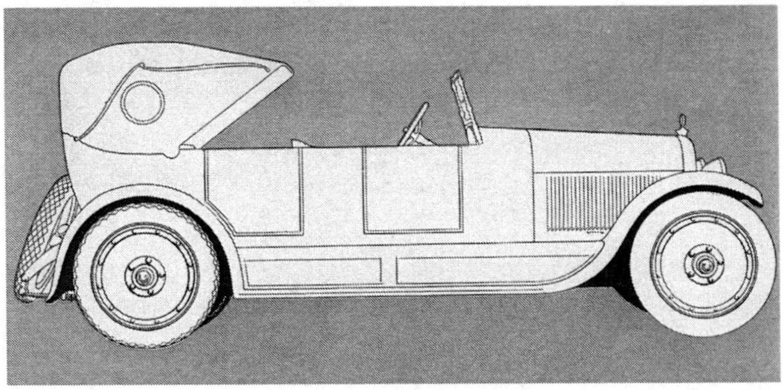

1919 Model F Silhouette Touring with Tonneau Top.

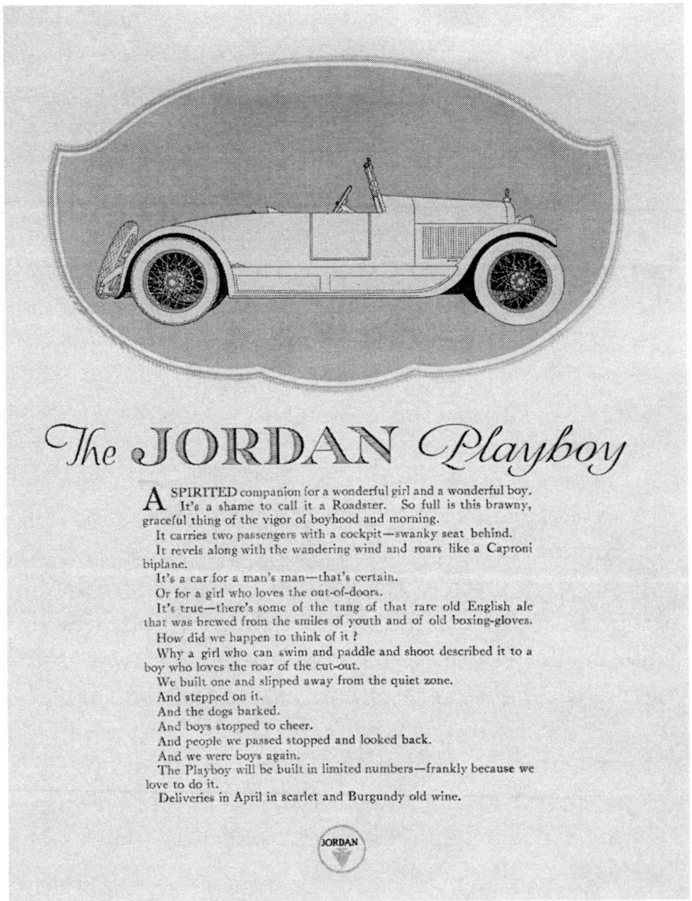

1919 Model F Playboy.

make its appearance, and the name "Playboy" would forever be recognized as the Jordan trademark. Two new Tourings were unveiled: the Silhouette Seven and Four. The Town Sedan and Four Passenger Brougham would be retained, but the Playboy would replace the Sport Roadster. (Jordan advertising spelled it as both Play Boy and Playboy.)

All the new models would be powered by a new six cylinder Continental 9 N engine with bore and stroke of 3½ × 5¼ inches. Wheelbase would still be 127 inches. Special spring shackles to eliminate rattle, spring loaded and self adjusting, were advertised extensively. The two Tourings would be equipped with 32 × 4½ inch Goodyear Cord tires with Firestones being optional. The open cars would now have 29 vertical hood louvers. The new body style showed a European influence, especially French. The open cars were lower and longer with two piece windshields, and the fenders (all double crowned), were fuller at the front.[10]

The new models would be designated as the Model 60 Series F, but that would soon be changed to Model F. Jordan issued an owner's instruction book for the Model 60 Series F and almost immediately issued a nearly identical one for the Model F Series F.

The Playboy was the big news. Ned Jordan described how the Playboy came into existence: "Walking the floor on a Saturday afternoon (1918) waiting for Barger, the Toledo dealer, to come in with a check for two cars he would drive back to Toledo." Jordan finances were tight and they needed the check to meet their payroll. "Barger did arrive and we did meet the payroll.

"Dancing that night with Eleanor Borton, age 19, who remarked, 'Mr. Jordan, why don't you build a car for the girl who loves to swim, paddle and shoot and for the boy who loves the roar of a cut out?' Thanks girl for a million dollar idea."

The next day he caught a train to New York and visited a custom body shop where a swanky roadster was being built for Flo Ziegfeld as a gift for his future wife. Ned got some ideas and sketched an outline on an envelope. Next he visited the American Body Company at Buffalo, New York, where they could punch out the first one on wooden dies, and the Playboy was born.[11]

Eleanor was the daughter of Fred S. Borton, who, along with his brother T. Ernest Borton, owned Borton and Borton, Cleveland stock brokers, who helped Jordan get started in business. Fate must have decreed that Eleanor Borton would have something to do with the birth of the Playboy. She was young, pretty and dynamic, a girl of action. The Playboy suited her well. She later drove her Playboy to Smith College in Northampton, Massachusetts, where she was a student. She left before graduating, and when an interviewer asked if she had trouble with her studies, she replied, "Hell no, I had fun." She later served as an executive for the Girl Scouts of America in upstate New York and later held the same position in Cleveland, Ohio.

She married Rudolph H. Garfield, a stock broker and grandson of President James A. Garfield, in 1925. As a wedding gift, Ned gave the new couple tickets to all the Broadway shows playing that season. Two sons, Rudolph and Borton, were born to this union, and Eleanor was widowed in 1945 after 20 years of marriage. She was active in Republican politics and served two terms as mayor of Mentor, Ohio. She was a dynamic leader in her community for many years and passed away at the age of 95 in 1994.[12]

Eleanor Borton, the girl who inspired the Playboy (courtesy her son, Rudolph H. Garfield.

Meanwhile, Jordan's Brougham (full crowned fenders, four passenger version) had been redone into a five-passenger version.[13] Most models had previously been displayed with wire wheels, but many models were now showed equipped with the Disteel wheel that had been available for some time.

Eleanor Borton (at wheel) with Smith College classmates in a 1919 Model F Playboy (Western Reserve Historical Society).

Jordan had some teaser ads, just before the new models were introduced, showing silhouettes of the new car not containing the word Jordan. The familiar circle was used, but no arrowhead graced it.[14] The first public ad for the Playboy appeared in the May issue of *Vanity Fair*. Ned said the best Playboy ad he ever wrote, though, was the version which appeared in a Jordan brochure.[15]

Ned had flirted with the idea of calling the new roadster the "Doughboy" but decided that was a bad idea because when the boys came home after the war, they would not want to be reminded of their struggle. Girls would be first on their minds with fast cars being a close second. The Playboy would suit them just fine.

Colors were Egyptian Bronze and Burgundy Old Wine for the two Tourings, Brewster Green and Liberty Blue for the Town Sedan and Brougham. The Playboy was available in Scarlet (Red-Orange) and Burgundy Old Wine. There were no dull colors here.[16] These would be the cars that carried Jordan's fortunes for some time, and the Playboy would lead the parade. Weight was from 3,120 to 3,240. Prices for the Silhouette were not given at the time they were released for sale.

On May 17, a new building program was announced by the company.[17] Five main units would be expanded. The assembly plant would be increased by 100 × 300 feet and the paint area by 60 × 90 feet; a two story office building 50 × 250 feet would be constructed; a new power plant would be 40 × 60 feet; and a new engine test building would be 30 × 90 feet. Also, a new restaurant would be installed for the benefit of employees and visitors. Production of 30 cars per day was expected after the new buildings were finished.

On May 22, a series of letters from several satisfied customers was published in *Motor Age* under the title "Sixty Striking Stories of Satisfaction."[18] The first 30 were published on May 22 with 30 more to come later. Testimonials from satisfied owners were always welcome and contributed greatly to their advertising.

The Tale of the Playboy

YOU'VE heard, or maybe you haven't heard, but the secret is out, it seems,
How Jordan has built his Playboy of glory and steel and dreams,
Built for the joy of the building, and the joy of building true,
A brawny thing, and a graceful thing, for the sweep o' the Avenue;
There's a savor of links about it, of laughter and lilt and light,—
There's a hint of old loves and boxing gloves, and folly and faith and fight!
It's a shame to call it a roadster — so full is its thoroughbred frame,
Of boyhood and mirth and morning, and the cross of wild and tame.
It's built for a man's man, certain! And it's built for the lass whose face
Is brown with the sun when the day is done of revel and romp and race.
And whether in cockpit swanky aft, or in leather comfort fore,
You'll breathe more deep at the forward sweep, and the glorious thunder-roar
As you loosen the jaws of the cut-out and hark to the voice of Thor.

—and how that tale will be read.

TONIGHT, in the quiet of home-time, in the land of your heart's desire,
As you lounge in your sleepy-hollow chair, and draw on the rare old brier —
With the folk of your heart about you, and — sh! — from the music-room
A rare old Gaelic melody finds its way thru the stately gloom,—
Perhaps you will know, as never before, the glory of love and life;
Perhaps you will know that, weal or woe, sorrow or joy or strife,
It's good to live and it's good to give and it's good to cram the days
With all of the joys of living, in all of the master ways
That man has wrought with toil and thought, from the sea and the earth and air —
Perhaps the tale of the Playboy will call to the boy in you
As a certain pond and a hook and line and a mongrel used to do!

Inspired by the Playboy and inscribed to
E. S. JORDAN *by* J. MITCHEL THORSEN.

Written by "Pit" of Cosmopolitan
"America's Greatest Magazine"

"The Tale of the Playboy" appeared in the *Jordan Arrow*.

In June, *Automobile Trade Journal* carried an ad stating that Jordans would now be equipped with Guide Headlamps.[19] Guides were made in Cleveland, thus saving shipping costs.

Advertising was going full blast for the Silhouette. This probably was the most heavily advertised car that Jordan would ever produce. Ad headlines included "Imagine a Car Like This," "Sturdy and Substantial but Light," "You Can't Afford to Carry Extra Weight," "Dominant Jordan Features," "For Those Who Know What They Want," "The Origin of the Jordan Idea," and "The Kind of Comfort Europeans Know" along with a dozen others. Ads were carried in most trade magazines plus *Saturday Evening Post*, *Vanity Fair*, *Vogue*, *The American Magazine*, *Literary Digest*, *The Atlantic Monthly*, and many others. Ned had learned while at Jeffery that this was the most effective way to sell automobiles.

The company underwent a restructuring on July 19. It would now be called The Jordan Motor Car Company, Incorporated, and would be chartered in the state of Delaware. The officers felt that the company would be better served by incorporating. Charles L. Bradley, an officer in the Union National Bank and a large Jordan stockholder, would form a syndicate to sell additional stock in the newly incorporated company.[20] Edward S. Jordan would remain president and control the company. T.E. Borton would be vice-president and Paul Zens would be secretary and assistant treasurer with

Otto Miller being treasurer. W.B. Riley, Russell Begg and Charles L. Bradley would make up the Board of Directors. The Delaware address was listed at 900 Market Street, Wilmington. Apparently this was the address of the Delaware Registration Trust Company, a front for many corporations registered in that state.[21]

In July, Jordan was having trouble getting parts, particularly tops. The factory was making 15 cars per day, but shortages were a big problem. Optimistic about the future, Jordan announced that 30,000 feet of new building space would be added for the purpose of keeping more stock on hand.[22]

On September 6, an ad entitled "Jordan Policy" was published. A photo of Ned accompanied by a statement describing the policies of the company was carried by several publications.[23]

On September 19, the fortuitously named Nell Wanderwell left Atlanta, Georgia, on a world tour. She, her brother and two others were driving a stock Jordan chassis with a highly modified body mounted. They intended to tour until 1924. Several organizations were sponsors, notably the American Automobile Association (AAA).[24]

On October 25, Ned and Russell Begg, along with a party of three others, sailed for Europe on the steamer *Adriatic*. The purpose of this trip was to attend the London Auto Show and visit other automobile exhibitions.[25]

The 1920 model year began very strangely. No new Jordan models were announced; they just made their way into the lineup without fanfare. By October, the new Model M had made its appearance.[26] A Five Passenger Sedan and Brougham were added to the Jordan lineup and would soon be joined by a Touring.[27] The Touring was now designated as the Silhouette Five. All body styles would be designated as the Model M and would be powered by a Continental 7 R six cylinder engine with bore and stroke of 3¼ × 4½ inches.[28] All models retained their styling but were 7 inches shorter as the wheelbase had been reduced to 120 inches. The Brougham, which formerly had no hood louvers, now had 29, as did the Town Sedan, which was previously equipped with ten.

The familiar triangle side windows ahead of the windshield were now back on all closed models, having previously been dropped on everything but the Brougham. The bodies were lower and the rear was concave with a spare tilted forward.

Both closed models had cowl ventilators and the hood, on all models, now had 29 louvers. Tires were 32 × 4 inches.

The Model F Town Sedan would continue until January 1920 and the other two previous touring models would continue in the Model F line.[29] The Four Passenger Touring would be dropped soon but the Seven Passenger would continue until the introduction of the Model MX in October 1921. Russell Begg had begun building the Model M prototypes in 1917. He had experimented for two years with five models, and each one had been driven at least 20,000 miles over all kinds of roads and terrain. Testers took one of these cars to Uniontown Hill in Pennsylvania and gave it a torturous test up and down the hill until Begg said, "OK boys! She's ready for production."

The Model M bodies would be supplied by American, Ohio and Bryant. The frames would come from the Hydraulic Pressed Steel Company of Cleveland. Prices were $2,220 for the Silhouette Five Touring. The Brougham and Five Passenger Sedan sold for $3,600.

Ned Jordan at work. Note the "Jordan Policy" on the wall (Art Michnevitz).

1920 Model M Brougham.

A playgirl with her 1920 Model M Playboy.

Model M Five Passenger Touring (courtesy John Conde).

Ester "Behling" Korthals driving her 1920 Model M Playboy. A few accesories have been added: a through-the-windshield spotlight, windwings, cowl lights, bumpers, a toolbox, step plates and what appears to be a running board light (courtesy L.M. Korthals).

1920 Model M Enclosed Special, a Touring fitted with a winter top that could be removed so that a regular top could be installed for warm-weather driving. The winter top was probably made by Art Craft.

The Seven Passenger Town sedan sold for $3,800. The right front seat of the Brougham would still tilt for entrance to the rear and revolve should the passenger want to face rearward.

It is not clear when the new Model M Playboy made its appearance, but it came somewhat later. The Model F Playboy was selling so well that Jordan must have been reluctant to change.

The Playboy sold so well that it did not need to be advertised heavily. Consequently, very few ads for the Model F or M exist. Prices for the Playboy were seldom listed. Playboy models must have sold at a premium though, as all other models were heavily advertised with prices listed.

In December 1919 it was announced that Jordan had purchased the Metal Parts Manufacturing Company, which adjoined the factory, and that it would be used as a new production unit.[30] It is possible that Jordan was now manufacturing some of its small parts.

Somewhere during the Model M's existence, an all-weather car was introduced. It was a touring fitted with a special weatherproof top, for winter driving.[31] When summer came, the owner could remove the top and re-install the summer one. This model was designated the "Enclosed Special," and though it was advertised by Jordan it was never listed in any owner or parts manual. The top was probably made by the General Top Company of Cleveland and called "The Art Craft Top."[32] That company did release a catalogue showing a Jordan fitted with their top.

The Models F and M were called the "Silhouette," and that is unfortunate in a later age for those who collect photos. The cars were typically depicted as silhouettes; it is very rare to find a factory photo of the real car.

The U.S. Congress had passed the Volstead Act on October 28, 1919, banning the sale of alcohol. Ned Jordan, who liked a drink as well as anyone, ordered two truckloads of liquor for company functions but did not want to store it where it might be pilfered. W.B. Riley, sales manager, was a non-drinker and it was decided to store it in his basement. Mrs. Riley nearly went into hysterics but finally relented and Jordan's booze was safe.[33]

With the Playboy selling faster than it could be produced and the rest of the line selling well, Jordan entered 1920 in good financial shape.

FIVE

Surviving the First Pinch, 1920–1922

Jordan entered 1920 with the four body styles of the Model M selling well and the Seven Passenger Model F Touring performing fairly well. The Seven Passenger Town Sedan was supposed to have been dropped, but all evidence points to it staying in the line. As the price of steel began to rise, the company found it necessary to raise prices. All models had an average price increase of $200.[1] The Model M was switched from the grease cup lubrication system to the Alemite, pin type, high pressure system about this time.[2]

Jordan's good fortune of enjoying high demand and strong prices was rapidly coming to an end as the postwar recession began to affect all manufacturing. Company executives decided to cut prices by October 1,[3] wiping out the increase of April. Things would not improve for some time.

Outside the automotive industry 1920 was an eventful year for the United States. For the first time in history the making and selling of distilled spirits was illegal, a noble experiment that would fail resoundingly. Women gained the right to vote and helped elect Warren G. Harding to the presidency of the United States. The first radio broadcast of an official radio station was made by KDKA, Pittsburgh, with the results of that election. In baseball, Babe Ruth joined the Yankees and hit 54 home runs, but the biggest news was the eruption of the Black Sox scandal in Chicago, with eight members of the White Sox being indicted for accepting bribes to throw the World Series of 1919. They were acquitted but banished from the game for life.

The Jordan Motor Car Company was having its troubles too. The recession dragged on all year and sales fell substantially.

On July 31, 1920, *The Chronicle*, a business publication, reported that the Jordan Motor Car Company, Incorporated, and The Edward S. Jordan Company would be merged if stockholders approved at the September 9 meeting. The Edward S. Jordan Company had been formed by Ned as a holding company for his common stock, which amounted to more than 50 percent of all common. Both companies had been chartered under the laws of Delaware, and the merger would not change the name of the Jordan Motor Car Company, Incorporated.

The company advertised heavily during 1920. One of its advertisements landed Ned in hot water with the New York Society for the Suppression of Vice, an organization founded by Anthony Comstock that considered itself a watchdog against the moral corruption of the country. Ned had written an ad titled "The Port of Missing Men" showing a red Playboy parked outside a seashore establishment.[4] The building was dark except for one upstairs window and a young lad was walking by. The ad had appeared in three of the leading family magazines of the day, *The Literary Digest*, *Saturday Evening Post*, and *Country Gentlemen*, and the society viewed it as contributing to the moral decay of America's youth. They wrote Ned a scathing letter chastising him for such ads and admonishing him to refrain from such practices. He apologized and promised to see that the advertising was more closely supervised. In reality he had achieved much more publicity than could have been hoped for, even if it was through adversity, and this would not be the last time he ran afoul of the society.

The famous city series of ads appeared during 1920.[5] Jordan would advertise one of its cars, usually a closed version but occasionally an open one, with its normal ad but would salute one of the leading cities of the United States with a nice street scene at the bottom. One ad even featured London, England.

On August 28, a Jordan ad appeared with a remarque at the bottom.[6] These would be used profusely in later years. The sketches were sometimes better than the main ads, and the combination made some great advertisements.

On September 21, Jordan received a copyright for the Silhouette name, for which it had applied on March 18, 1919, when the company had begun using the name.

On September 30, *Motor Age* reported that Ned had been invited as the speaker for 22 trade organizations within the next three months. These speaking engagements would take him from coast to coast. He was becoming very popular, usually speaking on the need for new and better roads. Better roads meant more cars sold and Jordan would benefit along with everyone else. Most car manufacturers encouraged the dealers and distributors to hear him when he was in their city.

By the end of 1920, business was very slow and Jordan was hoping for better days. Not one new car was introduced during the calendar year. As 1921 dawned Jordan production was running at about 25 percent capacity, and dealers held less than a one month supply of cars.[7] There was but one way to go and that was up. In a year that saw Mae West jailed for appearing in a risqué play called *Sex*, Babe Ruth hit 59 home runs for the Yankees, who would still lose to the Giants in the World Series, and the introduction of Wheaties breakfast cereal and *Reader's Digest*, Jordan's fortunes would begin to brighten.

In order to stimulate sales, Jordan introduced a new car in January.[8] The Landaulet Coupe was shown at the Twenty-First Annual New York Automobile Show. It was a specially bodied version riding on the Model M chassis with the same mechanical specifications as all other Model Ms, but the body was a radical departure from Jordan styling. The maker of this body has never been determined; it has sometimes been attributed to Locke, but this connection is unlikely.

The body of the new car looked somewhat like a box had been fitted to the chassis. The cowl was vented on both sides and top and there were two vents over the windshield, which was fitted with a large visor. The roof also contained a vent and two windows at the rear along with Landau irons behind the doors which were hinged at the rear.[9]

The top from the doors back was made to look as if it would fold, but it is very doubt-

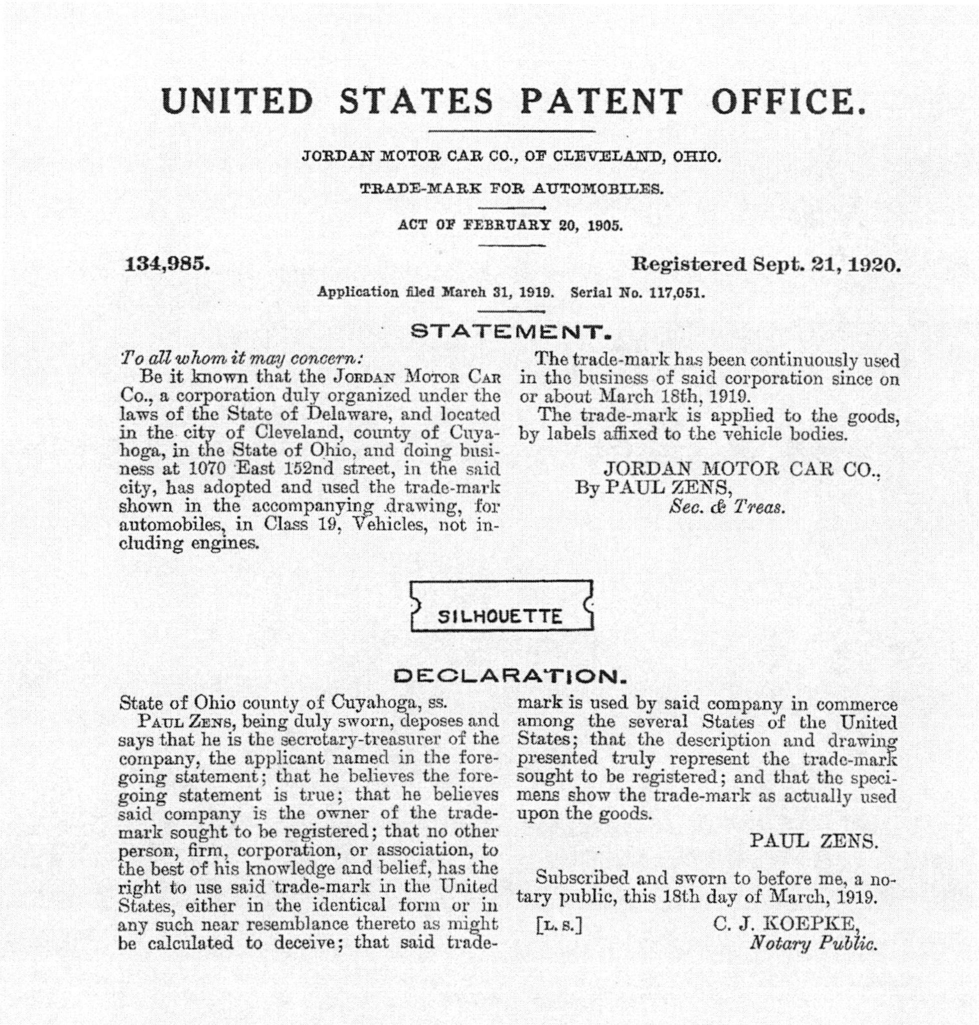

UNITED STATES PATENT OFFICE.

JORDAN MOTOR CAR CO., OF CLEVELAND, OHIO.

TRADE-MARK FOR AUTOMOBILES.

ACT OF FEBRUARY 20, 1905.

134,985. Registered Sept. 21, 1920.

Application filed March 31, 1919. Serial No. 117,051.

STATEMENT.

To all whom it may concern:

Be it known that the JORDAN MOTOR CAR Co., a corporation duly organized under the laws of the State of Delaware, and located in the city of Cleveland, county of Cuyahoga, in the State of Ohio, and doing business at 1070 East 152nd street, in the said city, has adopted and used the trade-mark shown in the accompanying drawing, for automobiles, in Class 19, Vehicles, not including engines.

The trade-mark has been continuously used in the business of said corporation since on or about March 18th, 1919.

The trade-mark is applied to the goods, by labels affixed to the vehicle bodies.

JORDAN MOTOR CAR CO.,
By PAUL ZENS,
Sec. & Treas.

SILHOUETTE

DECLARATION.

State of Ohio county of Cuyahoga, ss.

PAUL ZENS, being duly sworn, deposes and says that he is the secretary-treasurer of the company, the applicant named in the foregoing statement; that he believes the foregoing statement is true; that he believes said company is the owner of the trade-mark sought to be registered; that no other person, firm, corporation, or association, to the best of his knowledge and belief, has the right to use said trade-mark in the United States, either in the identical form or in any such near resemblance thereto as might be calculated to deceive; that said trade-mark is used by said company in commerce among the several States of the United States; that the description and drawing presented truly represent the trade-mark sought to be registered; and that the specimens show the trade-mark as actually used upon the goods.

PAUL ZENS.

Subscribed and sworn to before me, a notary public, this 18th day of March, 1919.

[L. S.] C. J. KOEPKE,
Notary Public.

A Silhouette trademark.

Above: Three views of the 1921 Landaulet Coupe (*Top:* Detroit Public Library, National Automotive History Collection. *Middle* and *bottom:* Applegate & Applegate collection.)

ful that it did. The landau irons probably were added for appearance' sake. The Landaulet Coupe did not sell very well but was carried on into 1922 as a Model MX.[10] The price was $4,200, very steep for a two passenger car, but it was supposed to appeal to those people who wanted something distinctive and who could afford it.

On April 29, the company announced a drastic reduction in prices.[11] The Five Passenger Touring and Playboy were reduced from $2,650 to $2,250, the Seven Passenger Model F Touring from $2,875 to $2,475, and the Brougham from $3,700 to $3,300. The Landaulet Coupe, which started out selling for $4,200, was reduced to $3,300, and the Seven Passenger Model F Town Sedan was reduced from $4,200 to $3,700.[12] *Motor Age* reported the price decrease on May 5 as being $600–$900, but *Automobile Topics* reported that all models were reduced by only $400. The Town Sedan and Landaulet Coupe were not mentioned.[13] The Seven Passenger Model F Town Sedan and Seven Passenger Touring continued in the line and would do so for at least one more year. There was no Model M Seven Passenger Sedan. The price cut stimulated sales, and things began to improve immediately with the economy on the rebound.

Jordan was beginning to become popular in foreign countries. In May 1921 *Vanity Fair* carried an article about body building in Japan, featuring a photograph of a beautiful limousine body, built of wood and mounted on a Jordan chassis. It was built for the use of Baron Den, the governor general of Formosa. The photograph was made in front of the Crown Prince's palace in Tokyo.

A Japanese handbuilt body on a Jordan 127-inch wheelbase chassis, built for Baron Den, the governor general of Formosa (*Vanity Fair*, May 1921, courtesy of Z. Taylor Vinson).

On July 13 it was reported that shipments of new automobiles for the entire industry were running at 60 percent of the figure for June 1920. On July 26, Jordan reported to a meeting of distributors, at the factory, that the plant was now running at capacity.[14] The recession was nearly over, and Jordan was doing better than most other manufacturers.

For the new model year, a completely new line of automobiles, the MX, was introduced.[15] The body was basically the same as the Model M, but nearly everything else had changed. The frame was more rigid and a new Continental 6S engine, exclusive to Jordan, supplied the power. The bore and stroke were 3 5⁄16 × 4¾ but it now had a Morse silent timing chain. Tire size was 32 × 4 and the wheelbase remained at 120 inches. A Timken Detroit transmission and Timken front and rear axles were used. A Sparton radiator, Gemmer steering and Delco electricals completed the mechanics.

A dash with all instruments under glass was a new feature, and barrel type, nickel plated headlights added a pleasing look to the front end. A tool compartment was located in the driver's door of the open cars, and a quick locking gas cap was a new feature. The Alemite high pressure lubrication system which was added to the later version of the Model M was now standard. The steering wheel was redone and a transmission lock was featured. A cowl vent was now employed and hood louvers, which had previously been pressed to the outside, were now pressed to the inside producing better ventilation.

Top: Continental 6S Engine (early version), used in all 1922–1925 MX, H, K, L models. The later version had an inspection plate on the intake manifold that was exclusive to Jordan. *Bottom:* Another view of the Continental 6S Engine.

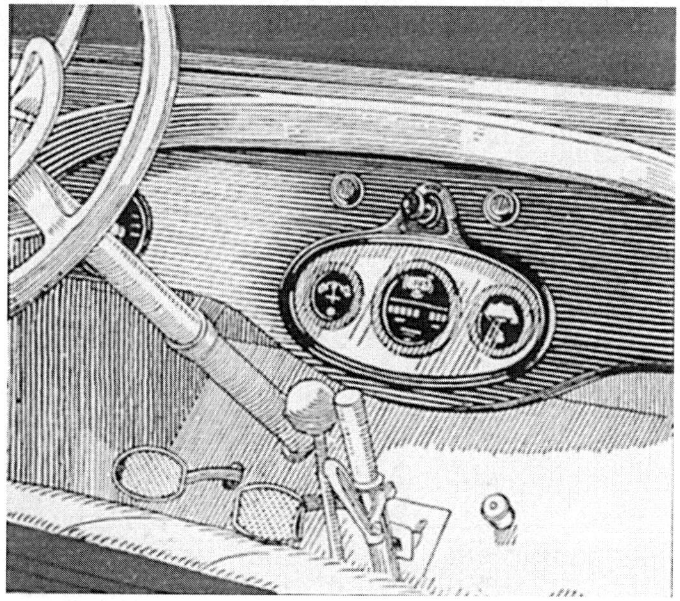

Dash of 1922 Model MX.

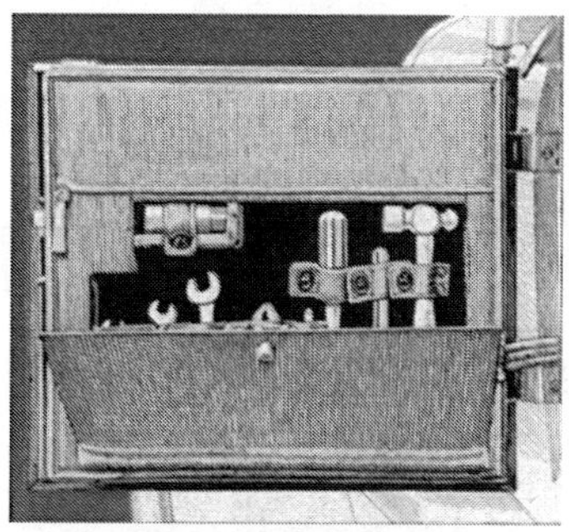

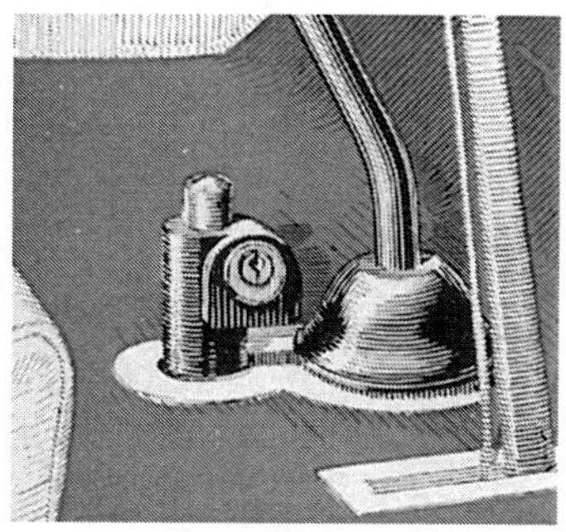

Above, left: 1922 MX Playboy tool kit in driver's door. *Above, right:* MX Gearshift Lock. *Left:* 1922 MX headlight. All early MX models but the Playboy had painted headlight rims. Later MX open models were all nickel; the closed cars retained painted rims.

Ned Jordan at the wheel of 1922 Model MX 5 Passenger Touring (courtesy William Bailey).

MX Gas Cap.

The MX came in five body styles, priced below their Model M predecessors. The Five Passenger Touring and Playboy now sold for $2,095, the Brougham and Five Passenger Sedan were priced at $3,200 and the Landaulet coupe, whose days were numbered, sold for $2,595.

The factory was now running at full capacity with orders for enough cars to stay that way for some months to come. Employment had been increased by 30 percent.

Automobile Topics reported on October 8, 1921, that Jordan would be making a Seven Passenger Sedan and Touring on a 124 inch wheelbase.[16] This statement apparently was in error because no other evidence of any kind has been found to support it. The Model F on the 127 inch wheelbase was still being offered in those body styles. Those who wanted a seven passenger Jordan automobile would have to be content with the Model F for the time being.

When the new models were released to the public, the instruction manual featured the MX models only. It would be another year before the Model H on a 124½ inch wheelbase would be mentioned.

By the end of 1921 the economy had recovered and a bright future lay ahead. The "Roaring Twenties" were beginning to roar. Women were now exercising their right to vote and were demanding independence in other matters. Flappers were appearing everywhere with their short hair and short shirts. New dances were emerging, and one of the popular songs of the day was "I Wish I Could Shimmy Like My Sister Kate." The term "speakeasy" was being used to describe watering holes as the sale of alcohol was driven underground. Louis "Satchmo" Armstrong was popularizing jazz music. The first live radio broadcast of the World Series was made on October 4, as the Giants beat the Yankees. By January 21, 1922, Jordan production was within 6 percent of its highest mark.[17] With buyers newly optimistic about the future, new cars were selling well and Jordan was among those that benefited most. At the Chicago Auto Show, 32 cars were sold at retail and orders for 2,782 were received from distributors.[18] By February, production was 350 percent better than it was in February 1920.[19] Things were looking up and Jordan would maintain this pace for four years.

1922 MX Playboy, early version with split windshield.

The headlights of the new MX cars were of a new design, and dealers were having trouble servicing them. They were modified twice by March. The change was mostly a new way to remove the glass lens and did not affect the basic design of the headlight.[20]

On March 29 a substantial price reduction was announced. The Five Passenger Touring now sold for $1,795, the Playboy for $1,895, the Five Passenger Sedan and Brougham for $2,785 and the Landaulet for $2,695. Prices on the Model F supposedly were not changed,[21] but one day later the Seven Passenger Touring was listed at $2,150 and the Seven Passenger Sedan at $3,250.[22]

The Five and Seven Passenger Sedans were becoming more popular with families and the Brougham was popular with the ladies who could drive their own. The Landaulet was not selling well but those who wanted something distinctive were still buying. Enclosed bodies would be selling almost equally to the open cars by the end of the year. The Playboy, however, remained a favorite of young people and would be Jordan's signature model for many years.

Ross Judson, president of Continental Motors, and his 1922 Model MX Landaulet. The previous year's Model M Landaulet had round rear windows (*Jordan Idea*, courtesy Dan Jordan).

The new 6S engine, which powered the MX with its silent timing chain, was a great success. Although manufactured by Continental, as were all

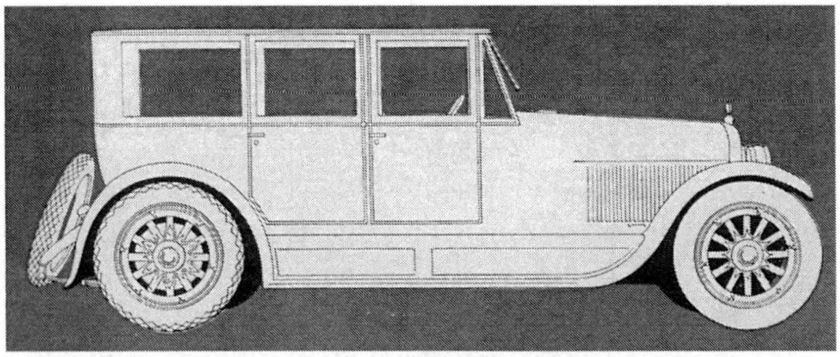

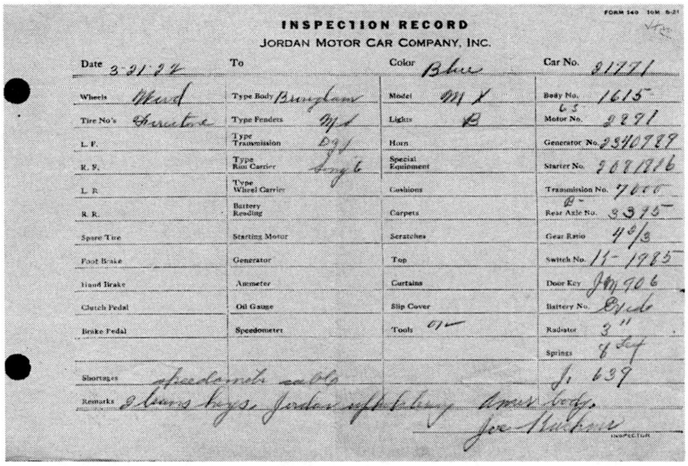

FORM 140 10M 8-21

INSPECTION RECORD

JORDAN MOTOR CAR COMPANY, INC.

Date 3-21-22	To	Color Blue	Car No. 21771
Wheels Wood	Type Body Brougham	Model MX	Body No. 1615
Tire No's [illegible]	Type Fenders [illegible]	Lights B	Motor No. 2291
L. F.	Type Transmission [illegible]	Horn	Generator No. [illegible]
R. F.	Type Rim Carrier Single	Special Equipment	Starter No. [illegible]
L. R.	Type Wheel Carrier	Cushions	Transmission No. [illegible]
R. R.	Battery Reading	Carpets	Rear Axle No. 3375
Spare Tire	Starting Motor	Scratches	Gear Ratio [illegible]
Foot Brake	Generator	Top	Switch No. 11-1985
Hand Brake	Ammeter	Curtains	Door Key JM906
Clutch Pedal	Oil Gauge	Slip Cover	Battery No. Exide
Brake Pedal	Speedometer	Tools OK	Radiator 3"
			Springs 8 leaf

Shortages speedometer cable

Remarks [illegible]

Inspector [illegible]

***Left, top:* 1922 MX Five Passenger Sedan, early version. *Left, middle:* 1922 Model MX Brougham. *Left, bottom:* Vlchek furnished tools for all Jordan cars. *Above:* A 1922 inspection record.**

Jordan engines, it was designed by Jordan and would never be used in any other make.

With business booming, Jordan added 10 new distributors and 75 associate dealers during March and April.[23] By July, production had reached a rate of 1,000 cars monthly[24] and Jordan common stock had risen 135 points on the Cleveland Stock Exchange by August.[25]

Minor equipment changes took place during the model year. By the end of June, the Playboy windshield had been changed to one piece; the Touring, though, would continue to be two piece until the MX was dropped. The Delco lighting and ignition switch were improved and had a much more pleasant appearance.

Bodies were now being built by Ohio Body and Blower Company of Cleveland, Walker Body Company and Bryant Body Company, both of Amesbury, Massachusetts, and possibly American. Bryant was controlled by the Walker family and would later be absorbed by them. Parish & Bingham had made Jordan's early frames, but when the M was introduced it apparently had a frame made by the Hydraulic Pressed Steel Company, also of Cleveland. *Motor* for January 1923 stated that frames for the MX-H were being made by Parish & Bingham.[26]

At the beginning of the 1923 model year, on August 29, Jordan unveiled a new automobile and a sensation it was.[27] The long awaited Blue Boy was a Four Passenger Touring riding on the 124½ inch frame, designated as the Model H. The car was long and low and beautiful. The color was Blue Devil Blue, and the interior was finished in blue Morocco leather. The body had the previous attributes of the MX and a few more.

Late 1922–1923 MX Playboy with solid windshield (courtesy John Conde).

There was a trunk mounted at the rear with a spare tire behind, and the car sported bumpers front and rear. The gas gauge, which had been previously mounted on top of the tank, was moved to the side adjacent to the filler cap as necessitated by the trunk being mounted at the rear.[28] A new walnut steering wheel graced the front cockpit, and new gas and spark controls were added. The large, bulky quadrant from previous models was now eliminated. A one piece windshield with nickel plated wiper was standard equipment. Price was $2,150.[29]

On September 29 Jordan announced some changes in the body style of the Sedan and Brougham.[30] Prices would also be dropped from $2,785 to $2,485 on both models. The top was 2½ inches lower, corners were now slightly rounded, and a large visor graced the front windshield. The Brougham now carried a trunk at the rear. The rear body curvature was changed from concave to convex, and six vertical aluminum strips were added to protect the paint from dings while the trunk was being mounted and removed.

The sedan body was lengthened for better access and more rear room. This small change improved the appearance of the closed cars dramatically. The interior of both models was upgraded to harmonize with the body color, and platinum finished hardware was used. The sedan was now called the Touring Sedan. A new worm type window regulator replaced the old chain type and better service access was made possible by removable door panels.[31]

By the end of September, Jordan production was 100 percent greater than the same nine month period

Top: 1923 Model H Blueboy. *Bottom*: 1923 Model H Blueboy, fitted with windwings, windshield visor, and rear windshield. (Both courtesy John Conde.)

1923 Blue Boy with modified top.

Left and right: 1923 Model H Blueboy (Free Library of Philadelphia).

Far left: 1922 Model MX Touring dash, early version with original style spark and throttle levers and all instruments under one glass. *Left:* 1923 Model MX dash showing new throttle and spark controls.

1923 MX Sedan (Applegate & Applegate collection).

Left and right: **1923 MX Brougham (both Applegate & Applegate collection).**

of 1921.[32] At a distributors' meeting at the Winton Hotel in early December, orders were placed for 4,350 cars. Four hundred dealers and distributors in attendance expressed their confidence that the depressed economic conditions were coming to an end. Jordan reported they would probably manufacture 9,000 cars for 1922.[33] This was an optimistic figure because actual production was 7,803 vehicles of which 5,260 were open body styles and 2,543 closed. The number of Jordan factory employees had now reached 365 and the total payroll for 1922 was $735,035.[34] Having orders for six months' production made for some happy officials.

Reportedly 1922 was the year Jordan stopped building cars with aluminum bodies, not to resume until the model Z appearance in 1930. Jordan entered 1923 with a projection of 80 cars per day. This would be accomplished by a new conveyor system to handle the chassis and an overhead system for handling the bodies.[35]

Six

"Somewhere West of Laramie," 1923–1924

As 1923 dawned, Jordan was riding high. Ned Jordan took just about everyone of importance to the January New York show, and most of the crowd went to the Chicago show as well. At the Chicago show Jordan displayed a cutaway version of the 6S engine, enabling show attendees to see the inner workings. They especially wanted a potential customer to see the timing chain which was new to the 6S engine and MX series.[1]

At the annual meeting of stockholders on March 26, officers were elected. Edward S. Jordan was re-elected president and C.L. Bradley vice president. Paul Zens was re-elected secretary and treasurer with Otto Miller, T.E. Borton, Russell S. Begg and W.B. Riley being re-elected directors. Paul Zens presided at the meeting in the absence of Ned Jordan and reported the factory was shipping cars at a rate of 62 per day with expectations of that figure climbing to 75 per day by April.[2]

One individual in the Jordan organization received very little publicity and wanted it that way. Walt Surrell was a burly former Cleveland policeman whose official title at Jordan was assistant sales manager. His unofficial duties were to look after Ned, who sometimes let his mouth operate too freely. Surrell was his driver and accompanied him on his road trips, always near enough to protect his boss if it became necessary.[3]

Auto sales would soar in 1923, but Ford would remain dominant, selling one of every two cars sold in America. Outside the industry, U.S. Steel cut its work day from twelve hours to eight, *Time* magazine published its first issue, the Yankees beat the Giants in the World Series, President Harding died on August 2, and a massive earthquake killed 100,000 people and destroyed 575,000 buildings in Japan.

Ned Jordan received some personal satisfaction in April as Charles Aronson, a Merrill automobile dealer, sought and obtained a Jordan dealership. The hometown boy was finally getting some recognition from the home folks.

April 21 saw the introduction of a new Brougham into the lineup. The body had been restyled but the fenders, hood and mechanical specifications remained practically the same as the previous model which it replaced. The body now had significantly rounded corners, a large visor over a vertical windshield and four doors. There was no more "crawling over," as Jordan put it, referring to the previous two door version. A trunk and spare tire were carried at the rear. The Brougham seated five passengers and would sell for $2,285.[4]

On May 15, a nationwide policy concerning the resale of used cars by Jordan dealers took effect. All cars would now have to be painted and refurbished mechanically. Any parts found to be defective would be replaced and all others cleaned and inspected. When a dealer received a trade-in, he would being the car up to Jordan standards and apply for a metal plate which would be attached to the car reading "Jordan—The Mark of Service." The company was concerned about its image in the used car market and wanted an owner to be as happy with a used car as he would be with a new one. The country would be divided into six selling zones and the company would set the price of all refurbished cars sold in their respective zones.[5] This good policy gained the Jordan organization much respect. Until that time

Top: **1923 MX Brougham, late four-door, at the Jordan factory (Free Library of Philadelphia).** ***Middle:*** **1923 MX Brougham, late four-door (Applegate & Applegate collection).** ***Bottom:*** **Rear view of 1923 MX Brougham, late four-door (Applegate & Applegate collection).**

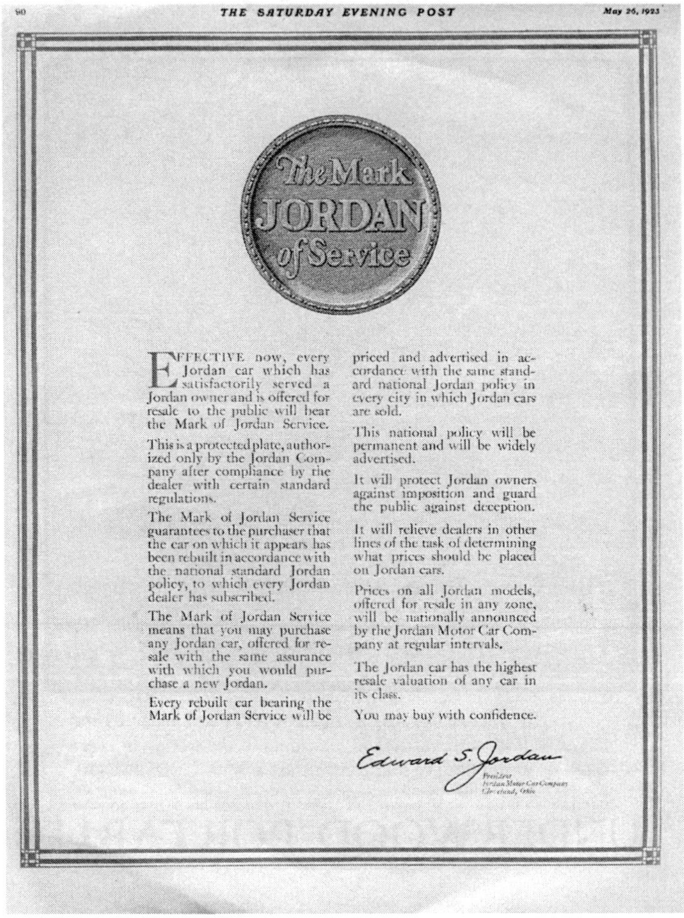
90 THE SATURDAY EVENING POST May 26, 1923

The Mark JORDAN of Service

EFFECTIVE now, every Jordan car which has satisfactorily served a Jordan owner and is offered for resale to the public will bear the Mark of Jordan Service.

This is a protected plate, authorized only by the Jordan Company after compliance by the dealer with certain standard regulations.

The Mark of Jordan Service guarantees to the purchaser that the car on which it appears has been rebuilt in accordance with the national standard Jordan policy, to which every Jordan dealer has subscribed.

The Mark of Jordan Service means that you may purchase any Jordan car, offered for resale with the same assurance with which you would purchase a new Jordan.

Every rebuilt car bearing the Mark of Jordan Service will be priced and advertised in accordance with the same standard national Jordan policy in every city in which Jordan cars are sold.

This national policy will be permanent and will be widely advertised.

It will protect Jordan owners against imposition and guard the public against deception.

It will relieve dealers in other lines of the task of determining what prices should be placed on Jordan cars.

Prices on all Jordan models, offered for resale in any zone, will be nationally announced by the Jordan Motor Car Company at regular intervals.

The Jordan car has the highest resale valuation of any car in its class.

You may buy with confidence.

Edward S. Jordan
President
Jordan Motor Car Company
Cleveland, Ohio

Jordan Mark of Service ad that appeared in the *Saturday Evening Post*, September 26, 1923.

most dealers had paid little attention to the used car market.

On May 28, Jordan cut the price of three models: the Silhouette Five Touring from $1,795 to $1,695, the Playboy from $1,895 to $1,750 and the Blue Boy from $2,150 to $1,995. The new Four Door Brougham was still selling at its introductory price of $2,285. The Touring Sedan was not reduced from its introductory price of $2,585.[6] The Five Passenger Model MX Sedan had been dropped and replaced by the Model H Touring Sedan about the time the Four Door Brougham was introduced. The body corners were more rounded, following the lead of the Four Door Brougham.[7] A seven passenger version of the Five Passenger Model H Touring Sedan had been introduced shortly after the five passenger version became available, but it was nothing more than a Five Passenger Sedan with two jump seats added.

Automobile Topics reported on June 2, 1923, that a new model seven passenger touring was being built on the Model H chassis, but no evidence has been found to verify this. The Model F had been dropped by then, and it is possible that the new Model H version was being offered. It is not listed, however, in any owner's instruction manuals, parts books or advertising literature. The Model H Touring Sedan and Seven Passenger Sedan on the larger frame were advertised extensively, and it would seem reasonable to assume that the touring would have gotten the same treatment. However, nothing has been found to verify or refute the claim.

Although the sedan bodies had been restyled, the slanted windshield and triangular side windows were retained.[8] The new MX Brougham had a straight windshield and would soon be followed by a new Victoria of the same design, but the sedans would not receive such treatment.

Late 1923 Model H Seven Passenger Sedan.

The price cuts and model changes stimulated sales, and the factory was now on a schedule of 1,000 cars monthly until demand had been satisfied.[9]

On June 13, *Motor World* featured a photograph of a Jordan truck. Whether it was manufactured by the company or created by a dealer is not clear. It has the appearance of a touring which has been cut off behind the front doors and a truck bed added. It was equipped with a cloth top, and the styling of the bed makes it very appealing. The design of the headlights suggests that it is based on a Model F or M.[10]

On June 23, Jordan changed automobile advertising forever when the famous "Somewhere West of Laramie" ad (*see page 130 and color page C6*) appeared in the *Saturday Evening Post*. Showing a cowgirl racing a Playboy, it created a sensation and is still considered one of the best advertisements ever written. The ad supposedly originated when Ned was riding a train through Wyoming headed for California. As evening approached he saw a young lady on a sassy pony racing the train. She reminded him of his daughter Jane, an excellent rider who had learned horsemanship at an early age. He took a pen and envelope from his pocket and sketched the scene. Turning to Mr. Austin, an attorney who was accompanying him, he asked where they were. "Oh, somewhere west of Laramie" was his reply and with that remark, one of the most enduring bits of advertising ever created was born. It is still referred to in advertising textbooks and is considered by collectors of automobile ads as a prize possession.[11]

The ad created a demand for the Playboy that was hard to meet and would buy the company prosperity for several years. An exact copy of the *Post* ad ran in *The American Magazine* in August and a different full color version appeared in another leading magazine about the same time.

On July 1, sales figures were released showing that Jordan had produced 10,147 cars from June 1922 until June 1923. Sales totaled $15,029,456.[12]

During the summer months

Jordan service truck from Jordan Worcester Inc., Worcester, Massachusetts. Jordan sold no trucks to the public; this appears to be a Model F or M.

A spoof of the famous "Somewhere West of Laramie" Playboy ad.

when a young man's fancy turns from books and school to great adventure, 16-year-old John Stanlaw "Jack" Jordan and three companions of the same age set out on an ambitious trip. Driving a Model M Touring car which had already covered 35,000 miles, he and his companions covered 17 states and two national parks (Yellowstone and Glacier) in 45 days. This was a publicity stunt for Jordan cars equipped with Delco electrical systems and got prominent notice in an advertisement by Delco during April 1924.[13] The car young Jordan was driving had been modified to carry side mounted spares. It would be safe to assume that it had been refurbished mechanically before the trip, and that every Jordan dealer who was anywhere near their route was ready to give assistance.

On July 2, a Jordan Blue Boy was selected to be the pilot car for a race from Denver to Castle Rock and back. Strictly stock, except for the removal of top and windshield, the car averaged over 60 mph.[14]

Soon after its introduction, the Model H Touring sedan received upgrades that resulted in a markedly better equipped car. Bumpers were added front and rear,

JORDAN IDEA

Jordan Leads Again

NEW ROAD RACE ROUTE

This Jordan Blue Boy, a strictly stock car, was selected as pilot car in the News-Times Pageant of Progress race from Denver to Castle Rock and return on July 2nd.

It started just ahead of the special racing cars—and finished one minute behind the winner.

The course was rough in many places and ran through a number of towns—around curves—and over railroads.

The Blue Boy averaged 60 miles an hour for the entire distance. Actual time for the 61½ miles was 1 hour 5½ minutes.

We didn't build the Blue Boy for speed. We built it for comfort, style, reliability and economy. That's what the average person wants in a motor car today.

Not many people want to go sixty miles an hour—even for a few miles. But they do want to go along mile after mile, year after year, with a minimum of service expense and a maximum of satisfaction.

That's what you get in a Jordan.

A page from the *Jordan Idea*, circa 1923, ostensibly promoting the "comfort, style, reliability and economy" of the Blue Boy.

a trunk rack was added at the rear and the spare tire was removed from the rear to the left front just ahead of the driver's door.[15] The Model H Touring Sedan was now a suitable companion to the Blue Boy. Two side mounted spares could be furnished if the buyer so desired. Bodies were now being made by Ohio Body and Blower, Walker, Bryant and American.[16] Owners of the first version could now order a kit containing all the parts necessary to upgrade their cars if they so chose.[17]

In early September, Ned joined Ross Judson, Continental Motors president, on a fishing trip to the Upper Great Lakes. They flew in Judson's new float plane to all the inaccessible areas of the lakes, the plane creating quite a stir among the Indians who lived there.[18]

Top: 1923 Jordan in San Francisco; Ned Jordan is at center (courtesy Paul V. Osika). _Bottom:_ 1923 Model H Touring Sedan, second version.

Ned spent most of his time traveling around the country promoting his car. If he expected Lottie to stay home and tend to her knitting, he was in for a big surprise. After they settled into the big home at 14923 Grandview Terrace, East Cleveland, she became active in the suffrage movement and in women's clubs and served for a while on the East Cleveland School Board. She was into painting and sculpture but was not the dainty type who preferred coffees, teas and bridge. She loved the outdoors. Sometime in early 1923 she and a friend, Mrs. Edna Brush Perkins, made a 40-day trip across the Sahara Desert on the back of a camel. They were the first women, other than the natives, to make such a trip and were accompanied only by a Bedouin chief and several native horsemen who served as guides. Mrs. Jordan praised the nomads as magnificent specimens of manhood.

This was not their first venture into the sand dunes as they had trekked the Mojave Desert in California in 1920. Mrs. Perkins wrote books about both adventures. Mrs. Jordan described the Mojave as far superior to any other desert she had ever seen.

On September 6, the company declared a dividend of 1¾ percent on its preferred and $5.00 per share on its common stock, to shareholders of record on September 15, to be paid September 30.[19] It was the first dividend on common stock since 1920. The company was now reaping the benefits of hard work and sound financial judgment.

The 1924 model year brought a new body style, the Victoria. Actually it was the old two door Brougham made over and renamed. In appearance, the new body resembled the Four Door Brougham but with only two doors. The large visor over the vertical windshield remained, and a trunk still graced the rear. Exceptionally wide doors allowed easy access to the rear seat. The price was the same as the Brougham, which was selling at $2,285. Colors were Crane Simplex Gray or Jordan Blue.

Top: **1924 Model K Victoria with two-wheel brakes (Applegate & Applegate collection).** ***Bottom, left:*** **Folding front passenger seat in the 1924 Model K Victoria.** ***Bottom, right:*** **Rear seating in the 1924 Model K Victoria. (Both photographs: Free Library of Philadelphia.)**

The mechanical specifications of the 1924 models changed very little, and the MX and H model names carried over. Virtually the only visible difference was a gas gauge mounted on the right side of the dash.[20] There would not be any changes in body designs of the closed cars as they had only been around for a few months.

Stockholders were summoned to a meeting on December 22 to decide whether to vote themselves a nice Christmas present in the form of a 600 percent stock dividend. Directors of the company had decided on December 10 to increase the shares of common stock to 200,000 at no par value. The dividend would be six shares of the new common to every one share of the old common then held. Preferred stock would remain at 12,000 shares.[21] The stockholders voted a recapitalization of the company as recommended by the directors.[22]

The Society of Automotive Engineers was meeting in Chicago on December 14. Ned Jordan was the principal speaker and his subject was "What I Know About Engineers." It had been announced his speech would be titled "What I Know About Engineering," but he changed it because, he said, they were two vastly different subjects.[23]

As 1924 began, Jordan

was experimenting with something new. A Playboy, painted Napier Green, had been fitted with four wheel Lockheed hydraulic brakes and balloon tires. At the New York Automobile Show the new braking system greatly surprised but pleased showgoers. It was intended as an extra which the customers could have installed at their option.[24]

Jordan's changeover from two wheel mechanical brakes was a big gamble, as few automobiles were yet fitted with hydraulics. Many people actually opposed hydraulic brakes, claiming they were dangerous because one might be injured by stopping too quickly. In fact, there was opposition to four wheel mechanical brakes for the same reason. It might have been reasonable to try four wheel mechanical brakes before embarking on such a radical change, but Jordan did not.

The gamble paid off rapidly as the public started demanding the new system. Jordan soon switched its en-

1924 Model K Brougham with four-wheel hydraulic brakes.

1924 Model K Victoria.

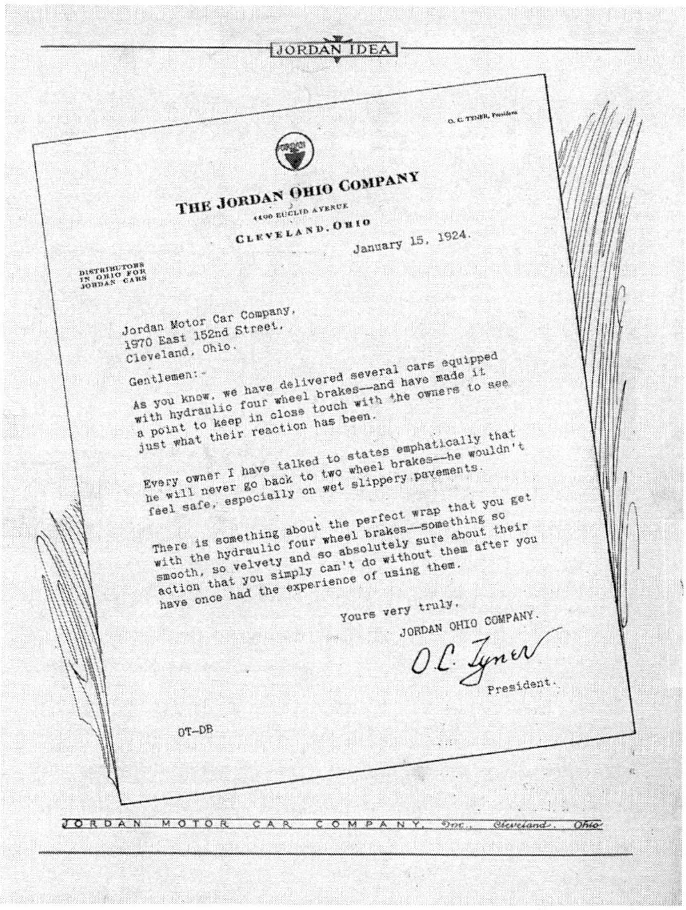

JORDAN IDEA

O. C. TYNER, President

THE JORDAN OHIO COMPANY
1400 EUCLID AVENUE
CLEVELAND, OHIO

DISTRIBUTORS IN OHIO FOR JORDAN CARS

January 15, 1924.

Jordan Motor Car Company,
1970 East 152nd Street,
Cleveland, Ohio.

Gentlemen:-

As you know, we have delivered several cars equipped with hydraulic four wheel brakes—and have made it a point to keep in close touch with the owners to see just what their reaction has been.

Every owner I have talked to states emphatically that he will never go back to two wheel brakes—he wouldn't feel safe, especially on wet slippery pavements.

There is something about the perfect wrap that you get with the hydraulic four wheel brakes—something so smooth, so velvety and so absolutely sure about their action that you simply can't do without them after you have once had the experience of using them.

Yours very truly,
JORDAN OHIO COMPANY.
O.C. Tyner
President.

OT-DB

JORDAN MOTOR CAR COMPANY, Inc. Cleveland, Ohio

Left: **This letter, printed in the *Jordan Idea*, suggests that four-wheel brakes were being sold before the New York show.** ***Right:*** **A May 1924 *Saturday Evening Post* ad for the Model K Playboy.**

JORDAN MOTOR CAR CO.

Balance Sheet, February 29, 1924

Assets	
Cash	$1,087,276
Notes receivable	19,924
Accounts receivable less allowances	563,647
Inventory	990,792
Securities held and other assets	20,508
Land, buildings, machinery, fixtures, etc.	117,200
Contracts, plans, etc.	300,000
Deferred	107,086
Total	$3,911,341
Liabilities	
Accounts payable	$381,065
Accrued accounts	64,064
Dealer deposits	62,372
Reserves	104,150
Capital stock:	
Preferred stock 7% cumulative authorized and issued less treasury stock	1,160,750
Common, no par value, authorized 200,000 shares, 126,000 shares issued.	
Capital surplus	1,868,478
Profit and loss, surplus	270,459
Total	$3,911,341

Jordan's balance sheet as of February 29, 1924, showed the company in fine shape.

***Top:* 1924 Model L Blueboy with four-wheel hydraulic brakes (Skip Weeks). *Bottom, left:* Model L Sedan Interior. *Bottom, right:* Rear seat in Model L Sedan. (Both photographs: Free Library of Philadelphia.)**

tire production to accommodate them; In fact, by the time of the Chicago show in late January, all models had been switched to the new brakes. Model designations changed at this point, with the 120 inch wheelbase car being called the Model K and the 124½ inch wheelbase version becoming the Model L. In fact, Jordan would list the 1924 two-wheel-brake models MX and H as models K and L. The K and L parts manual lists parts for two-wheel mechanical brakes and four-wheel hydraulics. It is fairly safe to say that the 1924 models with mechanical brakes are models MX and H and those with hydraulic brakes models K and L. The new braking system pushed prices on all models up $100, with the exception of the Five and Seven Passenger Sedans.[25]

By late February, the stock option which Jordan directors had recommended and stockholders had approved was oversubscribed. It sold for $31.00 a share and from the proceeds, $200,000 was set aside to retire preferred stock at 110 percent of value.[26] Noyes & Jackson and Lage & Co., both members of the New York Stock Exchange, handled the sale.[27]

The Jordan Company was going strong, having produced 8,857 cars during 1923 with net earnings of $700,000.[28] The number of employees had risen to 450 by the end of December 1923 and Jordan had paid out $867,475. Of the cars produced 4,391 were open models and 4,466 were closed. Jordan applied to list 126,000 shares of common stock on the New York Stock Exchange in late March 1924.[29] The balance sheet showed the company to be in sound financial shape on March 1.[30]

In the automotive field, employees were always looking to better themselves, and in early April 1924 Jordan lost its technical engineer, H.V. Howatt, to the Studebaker Corporation.[31]

Ned's passion for advertising and especially the outdoor theme earned him some money during the month of May. *Field and Stream*, an outdoor magazine, presented him with a check in the amount of $1,000 for the best advertising with outdoor appeal.[32]

Some big plans that had been slowly and quietly taking form during the first few months of 1924 were

Top: **Charles and Clara Bradley of Long Beach, California, with their 1925 Model A Great Line Eight Playboy (Charles Patrick Bradley).** ***Bottom:*** **1925 Model A Great Line Eight Playboy.**

announced to the public on June 26. Breaking a Jordan tradition of six cylinder engines since the company's inception, an all new eight cylinder car was introduced.[33] The largest car Jordan had ever manufactured to this point would be designated the Model A and would have a Continental 9K engine with bore and stroke of 3 × 4¾ and a wheelbase of 125½ inches. Dubbed the "Great Line Eight," it would be offered in five body styles: Sedan, Four Door Brougham, Two Door Victoria, Touring and Playboy. The bodies of some of these cars had been fitted to the 124½ inch wheelbase Model H chassis during 1923 as an experiment. It must have been successful as they were adopted for use on the new model.

All body styles would have nickeled radiator shells and large, drum type, nickeled headlights. The bodies were restyled with a much longer hood to accommodate the eight cylinder engine. The radiator was higher and more square than that of the K and L. The bodies of the closed cars were similar to those of the K and L, with the exception of a two piece windshield which jutted forward at the center with triangular side windows and a large visor, a very distinctive design. Fenders remained in the same profile but now had a raised section for added stability.[34]

The Five Passenger Sedan would sell for $2,975,

1925 Model A Great Line Eight Brougham (Applegate & Applegate collection).

1925 Model A Great Line Eight Victoria (Applegate & Applegate collection).

Left: **1925 Model A Great Line Eight Sedan.** ***Right:*** **Interior of 1925 Model A Great Line Eight Sedan. (Both photographs: *Jordan Idea*, courtesy Dan Jordan).**

Jordan Price Schedule

Effective August 1st, 1924

Silhouette Six

Five Passenger Touring	$1775.00
Blue Boy	$2095.00
Victoria	$2385.00
Four Door Brougham	$2385.00
Five Passenger Sedan	$2585.00

Great Jordan Line Eight

Five Passenger Touring	$2575.00
Playboy	$2575.00
Victoria	$2775.00
Four Door Brougham	2875.00
Five Passenger Sedan	$2975.00
Five Disc Wheels (Extra)	$35.00

Artillery Wheels and Hydraulic Four Wheel Brakes standard on all models

Prices F. O. B. Cleveland, Ohio
War Tax Extra

Jordan Motor Car Company, Inc.

Cleveland, Ohio

1924–1925 Jordan price list (Detroit Public Library, National Automotive History Collection).

the Five Passenger Brougham for $2,875, the Four Passenger Victoria for $2,775 and the Five Passenger Touring and Playboy for $2,575.[35] Orders for 4,892 of the new model were received within five days after the announcement with 347 being sold without the purchaser seeing as much as a photograph.[36] By August 16 the factory was producing them at a rate of 40 per day.[37]

The six cylinder models were now succumbing to the straight eight craze, and the factory was more than willing to oblige. The Model L would still be offered in the Blueboy and Touring Sedan, but all other body styles would be phased out as soon as stocks were depleted. Both models would be carried into the new model year which began in mid–August.

On September 1, an official resale price list of used Jordans for all zones was released.[38]

On November 4, Jordan was granted trademark #191,232 for the Line Eight, having applied on June 30. This trademark would be used for the 1925 Model A and the 1926 Model J as well as the future AA, J1 and JJ. Jordan also applied on October 20, 1924, for a trademark to protect the corporate arrowhead emblem which appeared on the *Jordan Arrow* and *Jordan Idea*. Trademark #196,649 was granted on an unknown date.

Ned embarked on a 60 day trip through the western United States early in November. His purpose was to visit 60 distributors and dealers, spread good will and sell automobiles. He did the same thing in the eastern United States, traveling in his personal Pullman car.[39] Ned was now spending about eight months a year

1925 Model A Great Line Eight Touring (*Jordan Idea*, courtesy Dan Jordan).

Two views of the Continental 9-K engine in the 1925 Model A Great Line Eight.

Jordan's Official Resale Prices

The prices on rebuilt Jordan models, with original equipment, offered for resale in the company's six zones, are as given below, the list becoming effective Sept. 1, 1924:

Model	Resale Price in Zone 1	Resale Prince in Zone 2	Resale Price in Zones 3 and 4	Resale Price in Zone 5	Resale Price in Zone 6
1921 Model M Touring	$ 550	$ 650	$ 675	$ 700	$ 750
1921 Model M Playboy	600	700	725	750	800
1921 Model M Brougham	800	900	925	950	1050
1921 Model M Sedan	800	900	925	950	1050
1922 Model MX Touring	800	900	950	975	1000
1922 Model MX Playboy	900	1000	1050	1075	1100
1922 Model MX Brougham	1150	1250	1300	1350	1450
1922 Model MX Sedan	1300	1350	1400	1450	1550
1923 Model MX Touring	1100	1200	1225	1250	1300
1923 Model MX Playboy	1200	1300	1325	1350	1400
1923 Model MX Brougham (4-Door)	1450	1650	1700	1800	1850
1923 Model MX Brougham (2-Door)	1250	1450	1500	1600	1650
1923 Model MX Sedan	1650	1700	1750	1850	1900
1923 Model H Sedan	1700	1800	1850	1900	2000
1923 Model H Blue Boy	1350	1450	1500	1550	1600
1924 Model K Touring	1400	1500	1525	1550	1600
1924 Model K Playboy	1500	1600	1625	1650	1700
1924 Model K Brougham (4-Door)	1700	1900	1950	2050	2100
1924 Model K Victoria	1800	1900	1950	2000	2100
1924 Model H Sedan	1900	2000	2050	2100	2200
1924 Model L Sedan	2000	2100	2150	2200	2300
1924 Model L Blueboy	1600	1700	1750	1800	1850

Jordan resale price list by zone, September 1924.

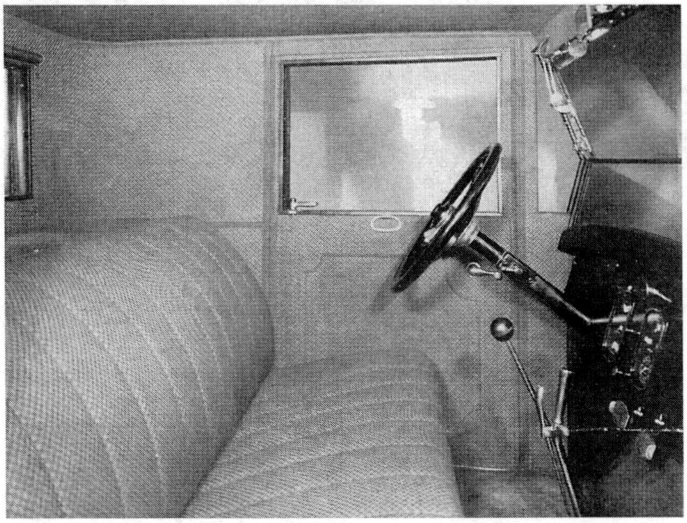

***Top, left:* 1925 Model A Great Line Eight Friendly Three Coupe (Free Library of Philadelphia). *Bottom, left:* 1925 Model A Friendly Three Coupe. *Above:* 1925 Model A Great Line Eight Friendly Three Coupe interior.**

on the road, and his family was being neglected. He tried to spend an extended vacation with them during the summer months, but demands on his time were so great that his wife and children never saw much of him.

On December 20, 1924, a new body style was eased into the Model A Great Line Eight lineup. The Friendly Three had all the mechanical features of the other Models A's but was a three window blindback coupe.[40] Ned stated it would carry two passengers, three if they were friendly. The body was slightly wider than the other closed models with the seat measuring 51 inches. A golf bag door was located to the rear of the right door, and the car carried a spare tire at the rear. Claims have been made that the body was by Judkins, but most evidence points to Bryant Body Co. of Amesbury, Massachusetts. Bryant had made bodies for some of the previous Model A's and was controlled by Walker, so it is logical to assume that the factory would not have changed to a different supplier. This association had been going on since the beginning of the Jordan Company.[41]

Things could not have been better as 1925 approached.

SEVEN

New Models and All Steel Bodies, 1925–1926

Jordan showed up at the 1925 New York Automobile Show, which was being held in the Bronx in an armory rather than in its usual Manhattan location, with a new body style added to its lineup. The Model A Great Line Eight Sedan had all the features of the A, and the wheelbase had been stretched to 132 inches. This extra space would accommodate two jump seats, creating a seven passenger car that would be priced at $3,250. Shortly afterward a partition behind the rear seat, making the car virtually a limousine, was offered for $100 extra.[1]

The recently introduced Friendly Three was on display along with all the Model A's as well as the Model K Victoria and Four Door Brougham. The Blue Boy would be the only representative from the Model L lineup and would continue until the new Model J was announced. The Model K Victoria and Brougham, along with the Touring Sedan, would be dropped soon.

Earnings for the previous year, released on February 14, showed Jordan had done well during 1924. Gross sales amounted to $12,009,596, and the company enjoyed a net profit of $858,469 before taxes. Other than 1923, this would be Jordan's best year to date. The number of employees had fallen to 420 from 450 just a year earlier.[2] All Jordan directors were re-elected at the annual meeting held the latter part of March.[3]

Space was again becoming a problem, prompting a search for additional room. The plant of Briggs Manufacturing Company on Taft Avenue close to 120th Street was leased in mid–May, giving Jordan an additional 185,000 square feet of working space.[4]

On May 23, *Automobile Topics* reported that Nell Wanderwell, the round the world automotive traveler, had arrived in New York City. She was greeted by the

Jordan's exhibit at the 1925 New York Auto Show.

Jordan Price List

Effective February 1st, 1925

Great Jordan Line Eight

Five Passenger Touring	$2575.00
Playboy (Roadster)	$2575.00
Victoria	$2775.00
Friendly Three	$2875.00
Four Door Brougham	$2875.00
Five Passenger Sedan	$2975.00
Seven Passenger Sedan	$3225.00
Seven Passenger Sedan (with glass partition)	$3375.00

Artillery Wheels, Balloon Tires and Hydraulic Four Wheel Brakes standard equipment on all models of The Great Line Eight

Silhouette Six

Blue Boy (four passenger sport)	$2095.00
Victoria	$2385.00
Four Door Brougham	$2385.00

Artillery Wheels, Cord Tires and Hydraulic Four Wheel Brakes standard on the Silhouette Six

Prices F. O. B. Cleveland, Ohio
Add tax and freight

Jordan Motor Car Company, Inc.
Cleveland, Ohio

Price list as of February 1, 1925.

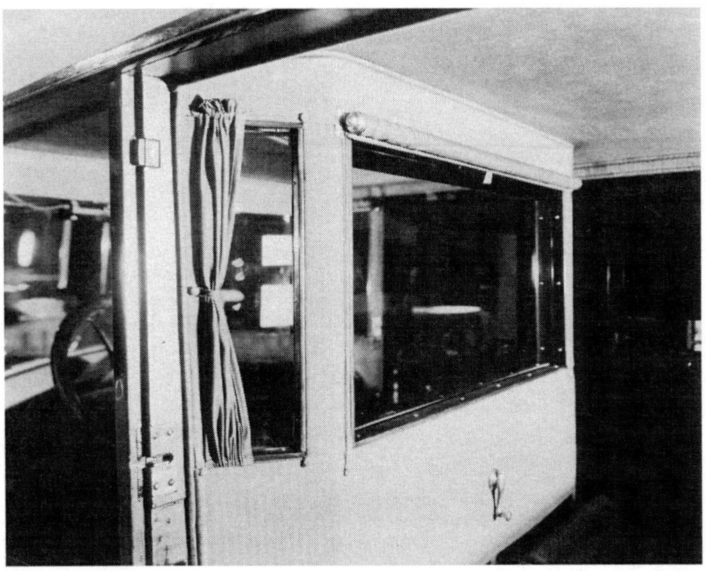

Interior of the 1925 Model A Great Line Eight Seven Passenger Sedan, showing the partition that made it essentially a limousine (Detroit Public Library, National Automotive History Collection).

Nell Wanderwell promotional piece, circa 1923.

press and showed off the Jordan car she was driving. By this time the highly modified body was riding on a Blue Boy chassis. When she left Atlanta, Georgia, on September 22, 1919, the body had been mounted on a 127 inch chassis. The tour was intended to end in 1924 but kept going, and by the time Wanderwell reached New York she had traveled over 200,000 miles.[5]

Jordan vice president Charles Bradley, along with his wife, completed a tour of dealers in the Southern and Western states in late May and would begin a tour of the Pacific Northwest dealers by mid–June.[6]

Always looking for ways to improve its product, the company imported a Citroen taxicab and displayed it in the lobby of the Central Union Trust Company for a few days in late June. The Citroen supposedly would run 32 miles on a gallon of gas and Jordan engineers were seeking to improve their product by studying its design. Why they would display it in a bank is a mystery.[7]

In early August, as the 1926 model year approached, Jordan started running many teaser ads featuring the new models. Prices of the Great Line Eight

Above, from top: 1926 Model J Line Eight Playboy; 1926 Model J Playboy. The Jordan summer home was near Point Judith, Rhode Island. The 1926 Rhode Island dealer plates suggest that this could be the family car. Could this be Jack and Jane Jordan? (courtesy the late Allan MacNicol). _Right, top:_ 1926 Model J Line Eight Playboy. _Right:_ Edward S. Jordan, 1925.

were reduced by $300 on all body styles on August 8.[8] All six cylinder models had been dropped by this time.

Just before the new models were announced, Jordan started touting the virtue of the all steel body. Anyone could guess what was coming, but the teaser ads continued until October 1 when the new Model J was announced. Shipment to dealers had actually begun on September 8, but the car was not presented to the public until October 1.[9]

The new Model J Line Eight was a sensation. The Playboy was a scaled down version of the Model A but the sedan had a facelift in the windshield area. It was powered by a Continental 8-S engine with a bore and stroke of $2\frac{7}{8} \times 4\frac{3}{4}$, and rode on a 116 inch wheelbase. It was nimble and quick, unlike the Model A, and own-

The Continental 8-S engine used in all J and J1 models in 1926 and 1927.

ers loved it. It was also less expensive with the sedan selling at $1,845 and the Playboy at $1,695. The Playboy had a top that was easily and quickly removed and a buffed leather interior.[10] The sedan retained most of the styling of the Model A, but the windshield was now a one piece vertical type with a large overhanging visor which was part of the top. Bumpers were still not standard equipment on all models.

The all steel body which Jordan had been raving about was now a reality. It was made by Budd and was a great improvement over the older styles. Small posts, which made for much better vision, were a great improvement over the previous models.[11]

The Model A line continued as Jordan wanted to see how the all steel body would be received. By October 1, shipments by the factory were up 165 percent over 1924. The new Model J was being produced at a rate of 65 per day.

Ned Jordan made the big time in November as he was featured in *Time* magazine. An article commending his

Above, right: **1926 Model J Line Eight Sedan (Applegate & Applegate collection).** ***Near right:*** **Interior of the 1926 Model J Line Eight Sedan.** ***Far right:*** **Rear seating in the 1926 Model J Sedan.**

Jordan's display at the 1926 New York Auto Show (William Bailey).

The 1926 Model J Victoria had a fancy paint scheme and dash and featured step plates and a trunk as standard equipment (William Bailey).

abilities as the writer of his own advertising gave him some very favorable publicity.[12]

On December 12, it was announced that the Playboy would be equipped with a Glassmobile top and side curtains. This was just a fancy name for a material to replace the old celluloid ones. On this same date a dividend of 75 cents on a share of common stock was declared along with a 1¾ percent dividend on preferred.[13] With 1925 coming to a close, the Jordan factory was running at capacity with enough orders to keep going at that pace for another 90 days.[14]

Jordan entered 1926 on a high note after a strong year.

The New York Automobile Show opened in January with Jordan introducing a new body style. The Victoria, shown in the Model J Line,[15] retained the previous styling of fenders, bumpers, and front end, but the body was definitely a change. A long hood-cowl section was mounted to a short two-door body with a distinctive hump at the top. The long, protruding visor which had been introduced on the Sedan was even more pronounced on the Victoria. The trunk was mounted at the rear with a spare tire behind. However, the trunk would not be standard equipment but an extra.

The interior was Chase Mohair, and paint was Cactus Gray with a red body stripe. The Victoria would sell for $1,895. Unlike the Sedan and Playboy, it did not have an all steel body.

Joining the Victoria at the show were Jordan's complete line of A and J models as well as a working cutaway Model J chassis.[16] The Budd all steel body, used on the Sedan and Playboy, had been received very well.

While in New York, Ned took the opportunity to address the Society of Automotive Engineers on January 14. He gave a rousing speech, declaring that the automotive manufacturing business was the best occupation in the world, and the Society reacted very favorably.[17] Ned Jordan was now at the height of his popularity. He was in constant demand as a speaker and was spending a majority of his time traveling from city to city in his private Pullman car, speaking anywhere he had an invitation and visiting distributors and dealers. He took time out for a Caribbean cruise after the show and sailed from New York on the United Fruit Lines steamer *Pastories*. Charles and Alva Bradley and their families accompanied him on the monthlong journey. The boat was no tramp steamer as the United Fruit Lines owned the Great White Fleet, and some of the finest ships afloat sailed under their flag.

After returning from his cruise, Ned made the Boston Car Show and spoke to the Boston Motor Car Dealers on March 9. His topic was "what to get out of the show and how to get it."[18]

On March 16, Jordan received a patent (#1,577,048) relating to the steering column and the way bushings had been placed in the column to improve its operation. Stanley R. Thomas, a Jordan engineer, had filed for the patent on April 23, 1925, and assigned the rights to the Jordan Motor Car Company.

Also on March 16, the company reported that it earned profits of $790,475 before taxes during 1925. This amounted to a dividend of $5.60 a share on common stock.[19] Jordan was going strong. Having added a new plant for the purpose of painting and trimming bodies, the company projected that 14,000 cars would be produced and that employees would increase significantly.

Price increases were announced for all J models in

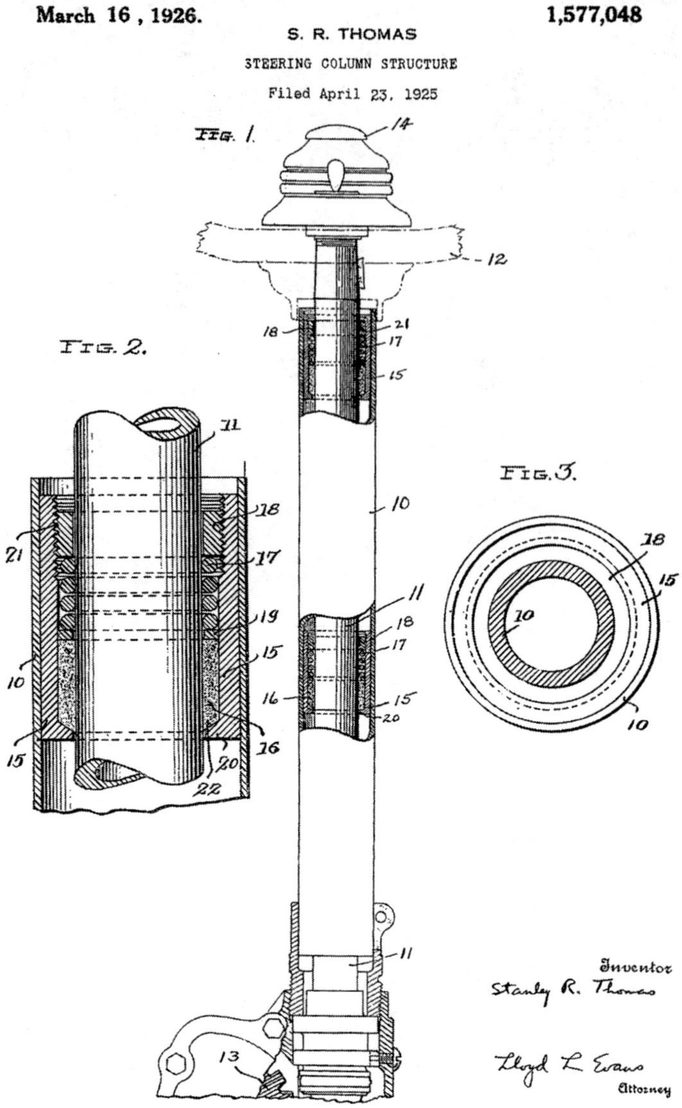

Steering column patent drawing.

early March. The Playboy jumped from $1,695 to $1,895. The Victoria and Sedan would now sell for $1,995, the previous price being $1,895.[20] Prices of the Model A Line would hold until April 5 when the Seven Passenger Sedan would be reduced to $2,675.[21]

On April 6, a campaign to raise $1.5 million for Charity Hospital of Cleveland was started. Ned Jordan, busy as he was, had been persuaded to head the campaign. He furnished cars for the workers, employees from the Jordan Company helped and Ned contributed liberally of his time and money. Charity Hospital was run by the Sisters of Charity and was sorely in need of new facilities and the remodeling of existing ones. Ned worked untiringly for the cause. The fundraising goal was a tall order for a one-week campaign, but when the final tally was completed, a total of $1,520,621.55 had

Jordan Price List

Effective April 5th, 1926

Great Line Eight Series

Five-Passenger Touring	$2275
Four-Door Brougham	$2575
Five-Passenger Sedan	$2675
Seven-Passenger Sedan	$2675

Line Eight Series

Playboy	$1845
Five-Passenger Sedan	$1945
Four-Passenger Victoria	$1945

Artillery Wheels, Balloon Tires and Hydraulic Four-Wheel Brakes standard equipment on all models of both series
Trunk and suit case equipment for Victoria is extra

Prices F. O. B. Cleveland, Ohio
Add tax and freight

Jordan Motor Car Company, Inc.
Cleveland, Ohio

Price list effective April 5, 1926.

May Number

The SPIZERINCTUM

Published Every Month by the LORD MOTOR CAR CO.
Selling and Servicing Automobiles in Los Angeles Since 1906
1240 South Figueroa ~ Los Angeles.

Vol. 1 LOS ANGELES, APRIL 29TH, 1926 No. 9

NED JORDAN'S IN TOWN!

EXTRA! Edward S. Jordan arrives today via Santa Fe just two laps ahead of a Solid Trainload of New Line Eights. Big Demonstration at Station as Ned's Observation Car is Switched alongside a waiting Observation Sedan.

A dealer publication trumpeting a visit by Ned Jordan in April 1926.

been raised. The sisters were overjoyed, the citizens of Cleveland were relieved that a facility which catered to the poor was saved and Ned Jordan was revered as one of Cleveland's finest.[22]

On April 25, a train load of Jordan Model J's left Cleveland headed for Los Angeles. Jordan had been ballyhooing the all steel body and the Santa Fe Railroad had just started using all steel freight cars designed to haul automobiles. Ned Jordan, the Santa Fe officials and Harry Lord, owner of the Lord Motor Company, Jordan distributors for southern California, had gotten together for a publicity stunt. Ned Jordan had left earlier, in his private Pullman car, and arrived at Los Angeles on April 29. His Pullman, adorned with Jordan emblems, was switched to a side track and he was met by Harry Lord, Santa Fe officials and a bevy of good looking young women. With movie cameras rolling and cameras clicking, Ned was presented with a floral piece in the design of the Jordan radiator emblem. A reception was held on the platform for dealers, owners, and Lord Motors employees.

Lord Motors had 31 Jordan cars present, mostly Playboys, each with a banner on the side of the hood which said "Ned Jordan's in Town." The police led a procession of 42 cars (some Jordan owners joined in) from the railyards to Lord Motors where another reception was held. Ned was feted to a dinner at the Los Angeles Athletic Club that night and every Jordan dealer in the territory was invited to attend.

The trainload of Jordans arrived on Tuesday, May 3, at 7:25 p.m.—seven days, 23 hours and 55 minutes after leaving Cleveland. That was a long time by today's standards but about three or four days less than the usual time. The train had only stopped to change engines and crew while en route and at the last stop before Los Angeles, a brand new engine was coupled to the train, making it a completely new, all steel train. The engine

Left: Ned Jordan arrives in Los Angeles. That's Harry A. Lord with the hat and Ned with the dinky cap. Right: California distributors and dealers welcome Ned Jordan.

Ned Jordan arrives in Los Angeles, his private Pullman visible in the background.

was adorned with Jordan emblems, and a banner three freight cars long, promoting the event, was hung on the sides of the first three cars. Ned, Harry Lord and Santa Fe officials met the engineer as he pulled into the yards. There were more festivities and picture taking as everyone wanted to get as much publicity out of the event as possible.[23]

June 11 was a joyous occasion for the Jordan family as they journeyed to Brookline, Massachusetts, to see daughter Jane graduate from the prestigious Choate School for Girls.[24] Jane would take a year off for fun and traveling. She loved the Southwest and horses. She worked the rodeos and would enter the University of Arizona in the fall of 1927 because it was close to the things she loved.[25]

On June 22, two new body styles on the Great Line Eight chassis were offered. They were virtual duplicates of the Model J Sedan and Victoria, only nine and one-half inches longer. All mechanical specifications of the Model A would be retained, but bumpers had been added. Prices for the new models, the Model AA Custom Victoria and Custom Sedan, were $2,675 and $2,495 respectively.[26] The Sedan body was all steel but the Victoria was not. A metal trunk at the rear of the Victoria would now be standard equipment.

The previous Model A Sedan and Brougham would be dropped. Somewhere during the life of the Model A, Jordan had supposedly begun offering a Seven Passenger Touring. It too, would now be dropped but would be available on special order. No evidence has been uncovered to indicate that Jordan indeed made this car.[27]

On June 24, Ned addressed the delegates to the Associated Advertising Clubs of the World then meeting in Philadelphia.[28]

The new Fedco numbering system made its appearance on the AA models, and all other models would fol-

A trainload of all steel bodied Jordan Model J Playboys and Sedans bound for the Lord Motor Car Company in Los Angeles.

***Left:* Dealer Harry A. Lord congratulates the engineer. *Right:* Santa Fe officials greet the Jordan train.**

low suit. Other automobile manufacturers had been using the plate for a few years.[29] The Fedco system was a fancy plate with the number embossed into it and mounted on the dash in a manner which made it almost impossible to remove. It was registered with the Burns Detective Agency and was supposed to reduce theft of automobiles. It probably had some deterrent effect but was not an absolute safeguard.

The company did not pay a dividend on its common stock which was due in September, citing financial obligations due to a new development program then beginning.[30] That development program was the small car then being designed. Also, Jordan had produced more cars than could be sold. This excess would be the start of financial problems to come. In fact, most car makers overproduced during 1926. The big makers could cut their prices and absorb their losses, but the smaller makers did not have that luxury.

Two new body styles were added to the line on September 1, though in truth they were not substan-

1926-1927 Model AA Great Line Eight Custom Victoria (Applegate & Applegate collection).

1926-27 Model AA Great Line Eight Custom Sedan (Applegate & Applegate collection).

tially new. The J Model Sedan and Victoria had been fancied up with special paint jobs, deluxe interiors and new instrument board. A trunk, which had been an option on the previous Victoria, would be standard on the new model. Both the Sedan and Victoria would now be called "Custom" and would be designated as J1 models. The Sedan body would remain all steel and the Victoria composite. Being released in September, they would be 1927 models at a price of $2,195 for either one.[31]

Ned Jordan was in San Antonio, Texas, for the unveiling of the 1927 line as a guest of the Crockett Automobile Company, the Jordan distributors for southwest Texas. Five thousand people attended the gala affair at the Municipal Auditorium. Mayor John Tobin was present when the curtain was raised and William Stum-

A REWARD IS OFFERED FOR THE RECOVERY OF A
1927 Jordan Playboy Roadster,
Motor #85-14197
Registration #DN487L
Owned by Mrs. M. E. Light,
2543 Scottwood Ave.,
Toledo, Ohio.
Stolen from rear of 817 Lakeside
Place, Chicago, Ill.
Between 30th of May and June 1, 1928.

If recovered wire or 'phone Claim Department,
Kemper Insurance, 4600-Block, Sheridan Road,
Chicago, Ill. Telephone - Longbeach 8000.

#584

A Reward will be paid for the recovery of a 1929 Jordon Coupe, Tomboy Model, Motor 14-E-1104, Serial DE-344-D, Transmission Gear Case #3318, Body #86-B-153, Rear Axle #34240-F-28, Door Key #644, Switch Key #937, License L-14872 N.Y. Color of the car is green Car is equipped with Firestone Tires, and Six wire wheels. Color of wheels is black. There are tire covers on two spare tires. Car was Stolen on Feb. 26, 1929, between 8:00 P.M. and 12:30 A.M. from between S. Warren and Peace Sts. on Lafayette St. Trenton, N.J.

TELEPHONE OR TELEGRAPH: HERBERT V. LIGHTHIPE
56 PINE STREET NEW YORK CITY TELE: JOHN-3646

The Fedco numbering system may have discouraged automobile thefts, but it did not prevent them.

bardt, President of the Crockett Company, drove a new Jordan to center stage accompanied by movie star Seena Owen.[32] Ned made a speech and a great musical program was performed.

On September 21, Russell S. Begg, Jordan's chief engineer, was granted three patents relating to running gear construction and especially concerning springs and spring shackles. Jordan had been using the spring loaded shackles for several years and some other automobile companies had been doing the same. The original patent (#1,600,953) had been filed on December 16, 1920. The second (#1,600,954) was an amended version of the first and was applied for on May 12, 1924. The third (#1,600,955), a further amendment, was applied for on December 14, 1925. All three patents were assigned to the Union Trust Company of Cleveland, for reasons that are not entirely clear. Perhaps the Union Trust Company was a majority stockholder or was in a better position to defend the patents should litigation become necessary.[33]

Sometime in late November or early December 1926, without fanfare, a new sport coupe was eased into the J1 lineup. This was a beautiful car. It was equipped

Sept. 21, 1926. R. S. BEGG 1,600,955
RUNNING GEAR CONSTRUCTION
Original Filed Dec. 16, 1920 4 Sheets-Sheet 1

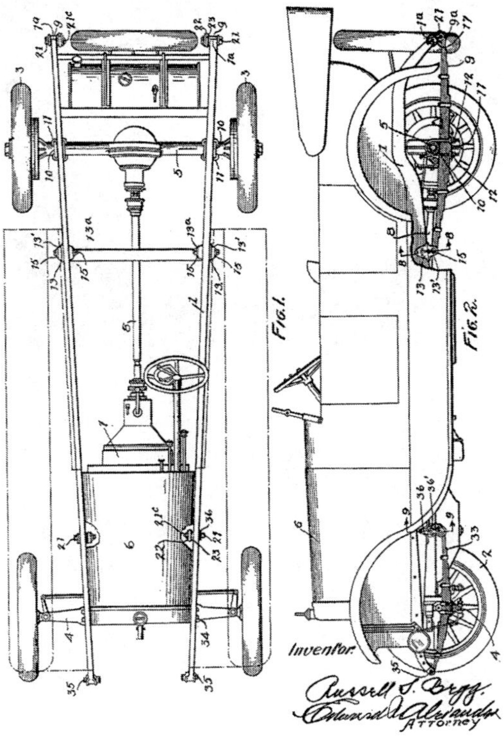

Sept. 21, 1926. R. S. BEGG 1,600,955
RUNNING GEAR CONSTRUCTION
Original Filed Dec. 16, 1920 4 Sheets-Sheet 2

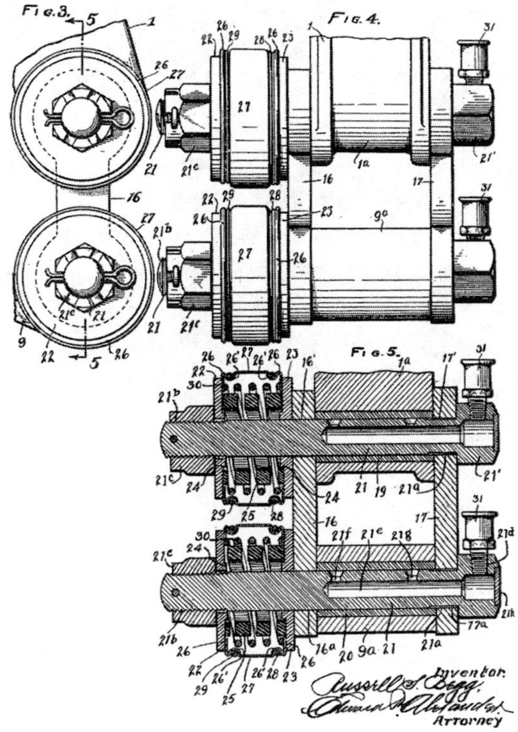

Sept. 21, 1926. R. S. BEGG 1,600,955
RUNNING GEAR CONSTRUCTION
Original Filed Dec. 16, 1920 4 Sheets-Sheet 3

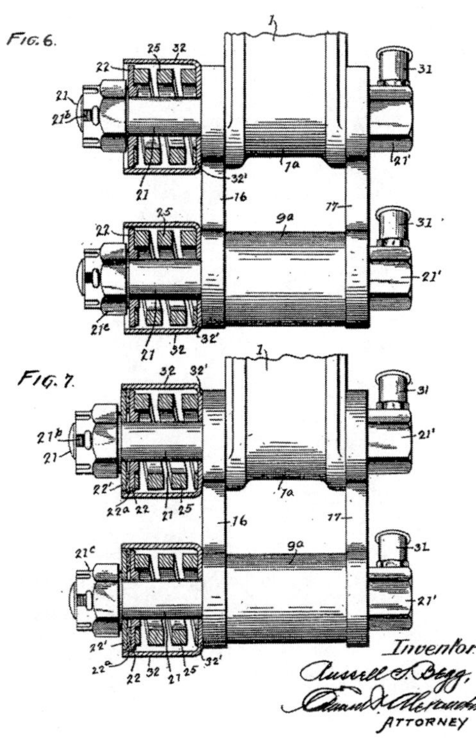

Sept. 21, 1926. R. S. BEGG 1,600,955
RUNNING GEAR CONSTRUCTION
Original Filed Dec. 16, 1920 4 Sheets-Sheet 4

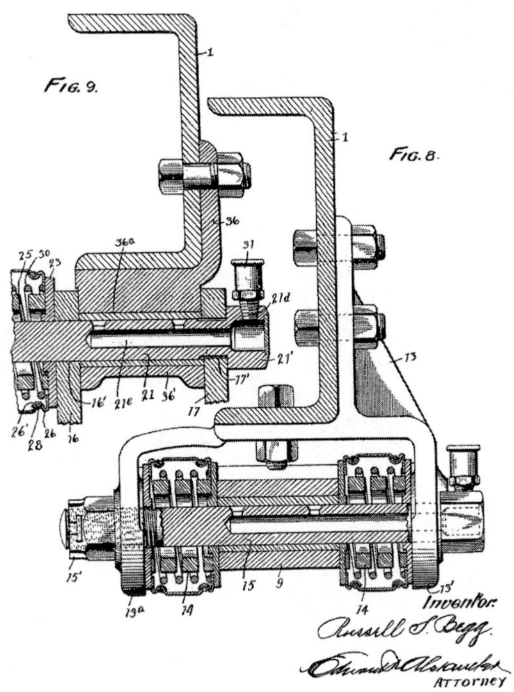

Patent drawings showing improvement to running gear and springs.

1926-1927 Model J1 Seven Passenger Sedan on a 132-inch wheelbase.

A 1926 Model AA Seven Passenger Sedan that has been in the Fye family since new (courtesy John and Margie Fye).

with a hard leather top and a large windshield visor, landau irons graced the rear, a golf bag door was added to the trunk just ahead of the rear fender and a rumble seat for two finished the exterior appointments. The interior could be had in Laidlaw broadcloth or green gray mohair. For the buyer who wanted something truly deluxe, a leather interior was available at $50 extra. The body was finished in Cameron Heath and Argyle Gray or Bosky Green and Lush Green with Lark Green trim. Nickeled bumpers, black fenders and splash aprons added a touch of elegance to the new creation. The price was $2,195.

Although the body from the dash forward was made by Budd and stamped as the all steel body, in reality the body was a composite of steel and wood with the latter being used profusely. Very little advertising was done for this car. That is a mystery, because by its looks it should have been one of Jordan's best sellers.[34]

Sometime during the production of the Model J 1, a new Seven Passenger Sedan was announced. Jordan released a pamphlet giving all the particulars, but no other advertising has ever been found. All the J 1 Model specifications applied to the new body style, but the wheelbase was stretched to 132 inches to make room for two jump seats. Photographs of the new car look surprisingly

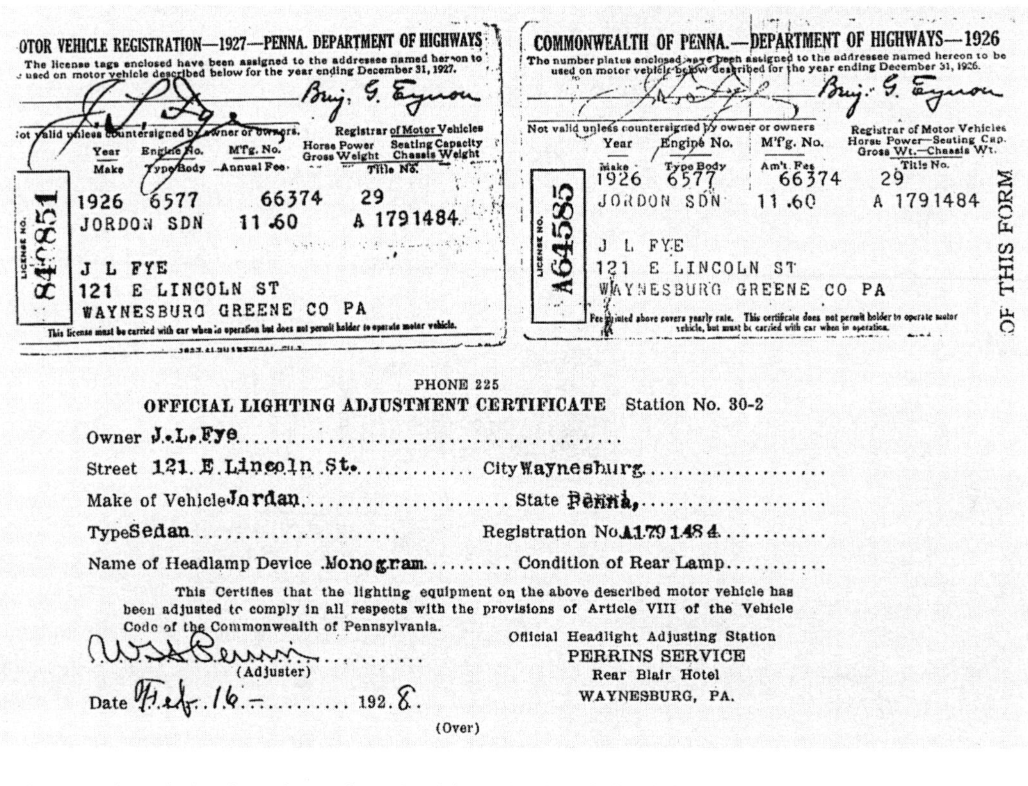

OTOR VEHICLE REGISTRATION—1927—PENNA. DEPARTMENT OF HIGHWAYS

1926 6577 66374 29
JORDON SDN 11.60 A 1791484
J L FYE
121 E LINCOLN ST
WAYNESBURG GREENE CO PA

COMMONWEALTH OF PENNA.—DEPARTMENT OF HIGHWAYS—1926

1926 6577 66374 29
JORDON SDN 11.60 A 1791484
J L FYE
121 E LINCOLN ST
WAYNESBURG GREENE CO PA

PHONE 225

OFFICIAL LIGHTING ADJUSTMENT CERTIFICATE Station No. 30-2

Owner J.L.Fye
Street 121 E.Lincoln St. City Waynesburg
Make of Vehicle Jordan State Penna.
Type Sedan Registration No. A179 1484
Name of Headlamp Device Monogram Condition of Rear Lamp

This Certifies that the lighting equipment on the above described motor vehicle has been adjusted to comply in all respects with the provisions of Article VIII of the Vehicle Code of the Commonwealth of Pennsylvania.

(Adjuster)

Date Feb. 16. 1928.

Official Headlight Adjusting Station
PERRINS SERVICE
Rear Blair Hotel
WAYNESBURG, PA.

(Over)

J.L. Fye's original registration for his 1926 Model AA Seven Passenger Sedan (courtesy John and Margie Fye).

JORDAN PRICE LIST AND COLOR OPTIONS

Effective September 1st, 1926

Line Eight Series

Model J

Standard Five-Passenger Sedan........$1945

Colors—Jordan Blue. Buckingham Gray. Grenada Maroon.

Model J

Standard Four-Passenger Victoria......$1945

Colors—Buckingham Gray. Two-tone Liberty Blue and Peerless Gray. Two-tone Cameron Heath and Argyle Gray

Trunk $25.00 extra
Suitcases $10.00 each, extra

Model J

Playboy.............................$1845

Colors—Carmine. Buckingham Gray. Two-tone Liberty Blue and Peerless Gray. Two-tone Bosky Green and Lush Green

Line Eight Series—Custom Style Models

Model J-1

Five-Passenger Sedan................$2195

Colors—Two-tone Cossack Brown and Zarina Biege. Two-tone Labrador Smoke and Sandoval Green

Line Eight Series—Custom Style Models

Model J-1

Four-Passenger Victoria..............$2195

Colors—Two-tone Pelham Blue and Larchmont Blue. Two-tone Helmet Gray and Manor Green

Trunk without suitcases, standard equipment
Suitcases $10.00 each extra

Great Line Eight—Custom Style Models

Model A-A

Five-Passenger Sedan................$2495

Colors—Two-tone Crockett Brown and Boone Brown. Two-tone Coromandel Maroon and Grenada Maroon

Model A-A

Four-Passenger Victoria..............$2495

Colors—Two-tone Cameron Heath and Argyle Gray. Two-tone Lush Green and Bosky Green

Trunk without suitcases, standard equipment
Suitcases $10.00 each extra

Artillery wheels, balloon tires and hydraulic four-wheel brakes—standard equipment on all models
Five Disc Wheels $15.00 extra
Five Wire Wheels $100 extra
All prices f. o. b. Cleveland. Add tax and freight

Jordan Motor Car Company, Inc.
CLEVELAND, OHIO

Price list and color options as of September 1, 1926.

like the J Sedan; in fact there is no discernible difference.[35] It is possible Jordan simply used the Five Passenger Sedan photos because the car had not been built at that time. If insufficient interest was shown to make the new model financially feasible, it may never have been built.

A Seven Passenger Model AA Sedan was produced sometime during the latter half of 1926, but no photos or brochures are known to exist. The car itself does exist as a beautiful example and is owned by a couple in Illinois. It retains all of the styling of the AA Custom style sedan, just in a longer form.

Jordan would enter 1927 with great expectations, but already storm clouds were on the horizon.

EIGHT

Litte Car, Big Blunder, 1927–1928

Jordan went to the 1927 New York Show with its lineup of AA, J and J1 models, plus something radically new.

Prototypes of the Little Custom Jordan were on display. This was something entirely new as big cars had always been Jordan's bread and butter.[1] The advertising department had blitzed the automobile trade publications with news releases and lavish ads in the first week of January. They had started the campaign in late December but with no name then attached to the new car.

The small car had sweeping fenders, a high, nickel plated radiator shell, two rows of vertical hood louvers, and Edmund and Jones bullet shaped aluminum headlights. Riding on a 107 inch wheelbase, it was powered by a Continental 12-E six-cylinder engine with a bore and stroke of 3¼ × 4. Bodies would be built by Murray, but the most radical feature of the new car was the worm drive rear end.

At first only three body styles were offered, with a fourth being added later.[2] These were a cabriolet, known as the Little Custom Playboy, a Little Custom Sedan and a Sport Salon. The Sport Salon was a very fancy two door Victoria with landau irons at the rear and a deluxe interior. Someone soon realized that the Little Playboy name was not fitting and it was changed to Little Tomboy. All models would be designated the Model R.

Jordan had overproduced in 1926 along with most of the industry and now had a large stock of unsold cars which it had to market at reduced prices. It took a financial bath as a result, with the balance sheet as of December 31 reading $1,303,035 lower than at the same time in 1925. The picture would not improve, and problems getting the Little Custom into production added to the company's troubles.[3]

Jordan's own figures suggest that they produced from three to four thousand more cars than they sold during 1926 (assuming all figures are correct). They were practically forcing dealers to take them. If the Little Custom had been released, dealers would have wanted the new car and the older models would not have sold. This was the start of the downfall of the Jordan Motor Car Company. Some dealers began to look to other manufacturers, and when the new car did appear it was too late.

Jordan's advertising again gained notoriety with an ad which appeared in the January issue of *House and Gardens* magazine entitled "In the Middle of the Night" (*see color page* C8). Someone brought it to the attention

On this page and the next are three views of the Model R Little Custom Playboy prototype at the New York Automobile Show. The name was changed to Tomboy before the car went on sale (courtesy William Bailey).

1927 Model R Little Custom Sedan prototype at the New York show. This example is equipped with the rarely seen disc wheels (courtesy William Bailey).

1927 Model R Little Custom Sport Salon prototype at the New York show. Prototypes had Edmund & Jones bullet type aluminum headlights and no air horns (courtesy William Bailey).

of John S. Sumner, secretary of the New York Society for the Suppression of Vice, and he wrote the advertising department another editorial, admonishing them to refrain from the practice of corrupting American youth.

> The automobile, like most other things, has its uses and its abuses and one of the abuses commonly attributed to it is the private petting party far removed from any restraining influence or observation. The inducement held out in your advertisement is that this particular closed car can be used "in the middle of the night" away from the observation of "tiresome chaperons" by youth after the dance.
>
> In the picture the car is presented with no passengers apparent. Whether or not it is in motion is a debatable question. This situation with the wording, lends an added suggestion to the printed matter and I think that the point raised by the person who brought the matter to our attention is apparent. In other words, there are sufficient inducements for youth to do what they would not do under the observation of "tiresome chaperons" without such suggestion appearing in an advertisement in a magazine indiscriminately circulated.

Jordan Motor Car Company, Inc.

Balance Sheet December 31, 1926

ASSETS

Current:			
Cash			$ 95,987.49
Accounts Receivable			130,531.77
Merchandise Inventory (At cost or market, whichever is lower)			1,202,610.60
			$1,429,129.86
Real Estate, Plant and Equipment, etc.		$1,842,011.58	
Less—Reserve for Depreciation		636,520.00	1,205,491.58
Other Assets			34,812.96
Contracts, Plans, Specifications, etc.			300,000.00
Deferred Expenses			131,897.17
			$3,101,331.57

LIABILITIES

Current:			
Current Accounts Payable / Taxes, Payrolls & Sundries Accrued, Not Due / Accrued Taxes—Federal Income and Excise			421,657.27
Reserve for Contingencies			40,000.00

CAPITAL AND SURPLUS

Capital Stock:			
Preferred—7% Cumulative:			
Authorized	$1,200,000.00		
Less Treasury Stock	274,750.00		
Outstanding		925,250.00	
Common—No Par Value:			
Authorized	200,000 Shares		
Issued	126,000 Shares		
CAPITAL SURPLUS		1,714,424.30	2,639,674.30
			$3,101,331.57

Statement of Income for the Year Ended December 31st, 1926

Sales of Automobiles and Parts		$11,632,083.94
Cost of Goods Sold	$10,191,807.77	
Depreciation	233,753.04	10,425,560.81
GROSS PROFIT		$ 1,206,523.13
Selling, Administrative, and General Expense		1,109,729.28
NET PROFIT		$ 96,793.85

Statement of Capital Surplus

Balance December 31, 1925		$ 2,157,536.18
Net Profit for the Year		96,793.85
		$ 2,254,330.03
Less:		
Adjustments		
Pertaining to 1925	285,785.59	
Dividends Paid	254,120.14	539,905.73
Balance December 31st, 1926		$ 1,714,424.30

Balance sheet from Jordan's 1926 year-end report to stockholders.

JORDAN MOTOR CAR CO.

Balance Sheet, December 31, 1926

Assets	1926	1925
Plant, equipment, etc.*	$1,205,491	$1,235,431
Contracts, etc.	300,000	300,000
Accounts receivable	130,532	185,116
Cash	95,987	‡628,510
Inventories	1,202,611	1,640,599
Other assets	34,813	17,420
Deferred assets	131,897	397,287
Total	$3,101,331	$4,404,366
Liabilities		
Preferred stock	$925,250	$943,700
Current liabilities	421,657	1,288,130
Contingency reserve	40,000	15,000
Capital surplus†	1,714,424	1,868,478
Earned surplus	......	289,058
Total	$3,101,331	$4,404,366

* After depreciation.
† Represented by 126,000 no-par shares.
‡ Includes government bonds.

This financial statement, published in March 1927, tells the tale of the start of the Jordan decline.

This was the second time Jordan had been in hot water with the society, but this time Ned did not apologize.

When the Little Custom finally reached dealer showrooms in mid–May, the damage had been done. Over five months had elapsed since the car had been announced. The public had grown tired of waiting and many of them had purchased other brands.[4] Meanwhile a few changes had been made to the car. Someone realized the E&J headlights did not add to the appearance of the car and replaced them with more conventional bullet style, painted headlights with nickeled rims. Air horns were also mounted on the right cowl. The Sport Salon which at first was shown without a trunk at the rear now had been fitted with one.[5]

Ned Jordan had an eventful spring. On April 3 he was banged up in a car wreck in Cleveland Heights. He was bruised and shaken when the car in which he was riding slid into a utility pole but did not require hospitalization.[6] Not letting the accident slow him down, he traveled to Dallas, Texas, to speak to the Texas Automobile Salesmen on May 16. While on this trip he visited San Antonio, Houston, and several other Texas cities.[7]

On May 2, the Jordan Worchester Company of Worchester, Massachusetts, was made a direct distributor of Jordan automobiles. With the Little Custom not doing as well as expected, something needed to be done and quickly. By June 22, a new body style had been added to the Model R Little Custom Line.[8] A touring car with a folding windshield mounted behind the front seat was shown. All mechanical features of the Model R were retained. This would be the

Top: 1927-28 Model R Little Custom Tomboy. Production models had different headlights from the prototype and air horns had been added (Free Library of Philadelphia). Bottom: 1927-28 Model R Little Custom Tomboy.

only car Jordan ever named the same as a previous model. It would be called the Little Custom Blueboy and would sell for $1,757.

Two more new models were introduced on July 15: a Playboy Roadster and a Sport Coupe, both in the AA Line.[9] The experiment of the small car was not going well, but the decision to expand the 125½ inch wheelbase Model AA line is hard to understand. The Model J Playboy was still in production, with a J 1 coupe having joined the line in late 1926. The Friendly Three was a coupe, but a rumble seat could have been added to make it a sport coupe. Very little is known of these two models, and no manual or advertising material has ever been found. The Playboy would sell for $2,345 and the Coupe for $2,495.

In June, the company sponsored a slogan contest to promote the Little Custom with the first place winner receiving a new car. Of the many entries received, the winner was Mr. R.L. McGean, whose contribution was "A Glorious Challenge to an Eager Generation—The Little Custom Jordan." Some of the other contenders were "A Tomboy with Six Appeal," "The Little Custom Jordan—A Young Man's Fancy and an Old Man's Delight," "The Little Custom Jordan Rides Like a Lincoln and Parks Like Its Poor Relation." Numerically, "Roll, Jordan Roll" was the favorite.[10]

Despite its troubles, Jordan did manage a profit of $86,773 for the second quarter of 1927. In July, Ned denied rumors of a merger with several other automobile companies. He acknowledged that discussions had taken place but insisted they had not gotten beyond the conversation stage.[11]

On August 15, a leak to the trade journals revealed that Jordan would soon release a new car powered by a revolutionary engine. The new engine had been in development for several months with Jordan, Continental Motors, and Stromberg Carburetor Company having pooled their knowledge in the endeavor. Carburetion would be similar to an airplane engine and

Top, left: 1927-28 Model R Little Custom Sedan. *Top, right:* 1927-28 Model R Little Custom Sedan (Applegate & Applegate collection). *Middle, right:* 1927-28 Model R Little Custom Sport Salon (Applegate & Applegate collection). *Bottom, right:* 1927-28 Model R Little Custom Blueboy (Free Library of Philadelphia). *Bottom, left:* German movie star Harry Hardt poses with a 1927 Model R Little Custom Sedan in Budapest, Hungary (courtesy Brooks Brierley).

1927-28 Model R Little Custom Blueboy.

Interior of the 1927 Model R Little Custom Blueboy.

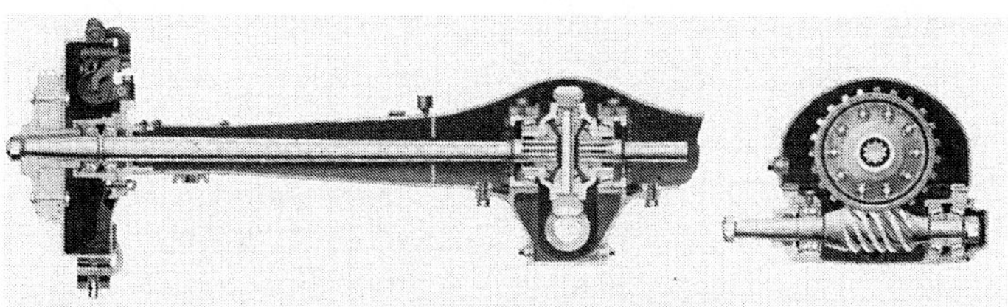

Columbia worm drive rear axle used in Model R.

the weight would be less than conventional auto engines. It was said to produce 33 percent more horsepower and give greater fuel economy.[12]

On August 23, an export department was formed. Jordan had been selling automobiles in several foreign

Two views of the Continental 12E six cylinder engine used in the Model R.

countries but had never had a formal export branch. The ostensible purpose was to handle the increased demand for the company's product overseas, but the real reason was that Jordans were not selling and the company was trying desperately to find new markets for them.[13]

The company was now building 12 different automobiles on three different chassis: the Model AA, J1 and R. On September 15, a fourth model was introduced. A virtual copy of the Model R, only larger, the new car retained the 116 inch wheelbase of the J1 and was powered by the newly developed engine, a Continental 14-S eight cylinder with a bore and stroke of 3 × 4¾. Horsepower would be increased by 33 percent owing to a split intake manifold and better carburetion.

Car Price Changes and New Models

	Old Price	New Price
Erskine		
Tourer	$945	$915
Business Coupe	$945	$895
Sport Coupe	$995	$965
Custom Sedan	$995	$965
Sport Roadster	New M.	$965
Essex		
5-p. Sedan	$795	$835
Jordan		
Blue Boy (R)	New M.	$1,745
Playboy (AA)	New M.	$2,345
Sport Coupe (AA)	New M.	$2,495
Lincoln		
Coupe	$4,400	$4,600
Locomobile		
Brougham (8-70)	$1,895	$1,975
Sedan (8-70)	$1,895	$1,975
Brougham (8-80)	New M.	$2,900
McFarlan		
Sport Phaeton (St. 8)	New M.	$3,180
7-p. Sedan (St. 8)	New M.	$3,680
Suburban Sedan (St. 8)	New M.	$3,780
Suburban Sedan (TV)	$7,110	$6,920
Moon Series A		
Collapsible Coupe	New M.	$1,795
Special Sedan	New M.	$1,545
Nash		
Coupe (Std. 6)	$925	$875
Sedan (Std. 6)	$925	$895
Sedan (Spec.)	$1,485	$1,335
Spec. Sedan (Adv. 121)	$1,695	$1,545
7-p. Touring (Adv. 127)	$1,490	$1,440
Victoria (Adv. 127)	$1,790	$1,595
Coupe (Adv. 127)	New M.	$1,775
Amb. Sedan (Adv. 127)	$2,090	$1,925
Sedan 7-p. (Adv. 127)	$2,090	$1,990
Reo A		
Brougham	$1,595	$1,685
Stearns-Knight G-885		
7-p. Limousine	$4,850	$4,950
Sedan Limousine	$4,950	$4,850
Studebaker Std. 6		
Business Coupe	New M.	$1,245
Sport Coupe	New M.	$1,345
Velie Std. 50		
Met. Sedan	New M.	$1,325

Jordan added the Little Custom Blue Boy on August 1, 1927. Without fanfare, the AA Playboy and Sport Coupe were also added.

1928 Model JE Air Line Eight Five Passenger Sedan (Free Library of Philadelphia).

1928 Model JE Air Line Eight Five Passenger Sedan.

Unlike the Model R, the JE would have a conventional, Hotchkiss type, differential.[14]

The model designation was Model JE, and Jordan called the new car the Air Line Eight, taking advantage of the airplane craze since Lindbergh had flown the Atlantic earlier in the year. It came in four body styles, a Five Passenger Sedan, Victoria, and a Four Passenger Coupe with permanent or collapsible top. Surprisingly, there was no touring car. Unlike the Little Custom, the sedan sported a small windshield visor. Headlights were modified bullet type, painted, with nickeled rims.

The bodies were built by Murray, which also bodied the Model R, and all models sold for $2,195.[15]

Jordan introduced the Model JE Air Line Eight because their styling was getting stale. The JE was a good car and styling was adequate. The new engine and carburetion system gave it plenty of pep. A weak spot, however, was the hydraulic contracting brakes, which were barely adequate at best.

Early in October, Paul Zens was in Europe exhibiting the complete line of Jordan cars at the Paris, London and Berlin automobile shows. He had been promoted to vice president in charge of sales when the Little Custom was announced.[16]

In November, owners of the J and J1 Models were offered the Air Line Eight cylinder head as a replace-

1928 Model JE Air Line Eight Victoria (Applegate & Applegate collection).

Rear view showing "roomy trunk" of the 1928 Model JE Air Line Eight Victoria.

ment. It was touted as drastically increasing horsepower on those models, for a complete installation cost of $44.40.[17]

Sometime in late 1927, two new cars were quietly eased into the Jordan lineup. In reality the only significant thing about them was the engine. A Five Passenger Sedan and a Sport Coupe which had previously been a Model J1 had new engines installed—the Continental 14-S, the same engine which was used in the Air Line Eight—and were renamed as the Model JJ. No advertising material is known to exist, but a company parts book referring to the JJ is known. In all probability Jordan had excess J1 bodies left over when the Air Line Eight went into production and decided to make use of them.

By September the J Models had been phased out. The Playboy was moved to the J1 lineup, which consisted of the Sport Coupe, Custom Sedan and Custom Victoria.

1928 Model JE Air Line Eight Playboy Coupe with collapsible top.

1928 Model JE Air Line Eight Playboy Coupe with permanent top.

Despite a line of automobiles to please anyone, Jordan's fortunes would continue to worsen as they entered 1928. At the opening of the New York Automobile Show a price cut was announced. All models of the JE were reduced from $2,195 to $1,995. The Little Custom Blue Boy Model R was reduced from $1,745 to $1,495 and the Sport Salon from $1,595 to $1,295. The Tomboy and Sedan would be reduced from $1,595 to $1,395. The J1 Series prices would remain unchanged.[18]

On January 30, 1928, a four page letter sent to all distributors, dealers, owners and stockholders denied that Jordan was trying to merge with another company[19] and attempted to rally support for the company's policies. The next day, it was announced that no dividend would be paid on Jordan stock.[20]

By the time the Chicago Automobile Show had opened, Jordan had given the JE Models a facelift. Spare tires on wire wheels (one or two) were now side mounted, and a luggage rack with trunk now graced the rear of the Victoria and Sedan. The Playboy Coupe with collapsible top had a rack but no trunk. No mention was made of the business coupe, which probably

Interior of 1928 Model JE Air Line Eight Victoria (Free Library of Philadelphia).

The Continental 14 S engine used in early and mid-period JE models.

The complete line of Jordan is now as follows:

Model "R"	Price
4 p. Blue Boy	$1,745
4 p. sport salon	1,595
2-4 p. Tomboy	1,595
5 p. sedan	1,595
"J-1"	
4 p. Playboy	1,545
2-4 p. sport coupe	1,695
5 p. custom sedan	1,695
4 p. custom victoria	1,695
"JE" (Airline)	
5 p. sedan	2,195
5 p. victoria	2,195
4 p. collap. coupe	2,195
4 p. perm. coupe	2,195
"AA"	
2-4 p. Playboy	2,345
2-4 p. sport coupe	2,495
4 p. custom victoria	2,495
5 p. custom sedan	2,495

Jordan's complete 1928 line, with prices.

Rear seating in 1928 Model JE Air Line Eight Five Passenger Sedan (Free Library of Philadelphia).

A 1928 Model JE Air Line Eight Sedan, second version.

was dropped due to lack of sales. It would not appear in any factory literature after this date.[21]

On March 6, the *Cleveland Plain Dealer* reported that three new executives had joined the Jordan Motor Car Company. Edward Ver Linden, former president of the Peerless Motor Car Company, was named chairman of the executive committee. This fueled speculation that a merger of the two firms might be in the making, but it never materialized though such an action had been discussed. Joining Ver Linden as vice president would be John McArdle, a former Chrysler executive who had recently been with the Murray Body Company of Detroit. A.F. England, another former Murray executive, was named secretary and treasurer. These new executives were brought in to get Jordan moving again, but they would accomplish very little.

On March 8, W.B. Riley, Jordan's outgoing secretary and treasurer, announced that business was increasing steadily.[22] Riley had been elevated to the new position from sales manager after Paul Zens was moved up to vice president. Riley himself was out by the time the announcement made the papers.

On March 31 Jordan was hit with a bombshell. Russell Begg, chief engineer, left the company for a position as chief engineer with the Budd Wheel Company. He would also be associate chief engineer of Budd Manufacturing Company.[23] In addition, Paul Zens saw the handwriting on the wall and started making plans for his own exit. In July of 1928 he was named a director for the Northern Finance Company.[24] Zens saw no place for himself in the new structure of the company, and in August he was elected a director and named vice president of the Continental Brake & Equipment Company of New York, in charge of the Cleveland office.[25] He would not stay there long but would follow Russell Begg to the Budd Company where he was named treasurer in 1930.[26]

By April 4, business was supposedly going well, according to Ned, who said it would be difficult to produce enough automobiles to meet the demand. Dealer stocks were lower than 500 units for the entire United States at that time.[27] It really made little difference how many cars the company produced: how many it could sell was the bottom line.

1928-29 Model RE Cross Country Six Tomboy.

1928-29 Model RE Cross Country Six Sedan (Free Library of Philadelphia).

1928-29 Model RE Cross Country Six Sport Four (Applegate & Applegate collection).

Logo used on 1928-29 Model JE Air Line Eight, second and third versions.

This mixture of the Little Custom and Cross Country Six has a Motometer and a modified version of the Little Custom bumper with the side mounts of the Cross Country Six (Detroit Public Library, National Automotive History Collection).

The Little Custom was not selling and needed drastic action. On April 26, unlike the JE which had received a facelift, the Model R received a major overhaul.[28] It was now powered by a Continental 14-E engine with a bore and stroke of $3\frac{7}{8} \times 4\frac{1}{4}$, under a hood lengthened by two inches with two rows of horizontal louvers. The Motometer, which had been a Jordan feature since the beginning, now disappeared. The headlights were also reworked, and the Sedan got cowl lights. Spare tires were now side mounted, and a trunk was mounted at the rear. The restyling was designed to make the car look larger, and it did. The former Sport Salon was now called the Sport Four, and both it and the Sedan had a visor over the windshield. Other than the engine, all mechanical features remained the same. The price also held steady. All these changes made for a much better looking car but did little to increase demand.

The Little Custom Blue Boy supposedly got the same treatment as the other models, but that is debatable. It never showed up in any advertisements after the new models were announced, and no literature has been found to confirm that it continued. All body styles of the redesigned Model R would be known as the Model RE Cross Country Six.[29]

Contrary to any denials, Jordan had been in negotiation with Pierce-Arrow concerning a merger between the two firms. On May 31, Pierce-Arrow directors met to discuss the merger. No definite conclusions were reached, but negotiations would continue.[30] Pierce-Arrow was having nearly as much trouble as Jordan, and a merger probably would not have helped either of them. In any event, Jordan was left out in the cold when Studebaker gobbled up Pierce a couple of months later.[31]

June 8 was a big day for the city of Cleveland as the Sisters of Charity Hospital hosted an open house to show off their new facilities and have a formal dedication. The *Cleveland Plain Dealer* gave it generous coverage. All of the important people of the Cleveland Catholic Diocese were there as well as from other parts of the United States. City Manager Hopkins, Police Chief Jacob Gravell and Fire Chief George A. Wallace as well as hundreds of dignitaries were in attendance. It was a special day for Ned Jordan, for he had been the chairman of the committee which raised $1,500,000 to make it all possible.

As a well deserved token of appreciation, the Sisters named the gymnasium and auditorium in his honor. Ned, as busy as he was, devoted much time and energy to the success of the drive during 1926. He organized volunteers, provided automobiles for transportation and gave liberally of his own funds to insure that this endeavor would be successful. A resident of Cleveland for 10 years, Jordan had become well known in society and financial circles. He was very popular as a speaker and faced more demands on his time than he could fulfill. Jordan was a generous and caring person when it came to charitable causes.

Around the time the Little Custom was redone, the Model JE Air Line Eight got similar treatment, as the previous upgrade had done little to stimulate sales.[32] Most significantly, it gained a new engine, a Continental 15-S eight cylinder with a bore and stroke of 3 × 4¾ that raised the horsepower from 80 to 85. The hood was not lengthened, but two rows of horizontal louvers replaced the vertical ones and the headlights were now fully nickeled. As with the Cross Country Six, there would be no Motometer. Side mounts and a trunk had been previously added; now a small visor graced the windshield of the closed cars and all models got cowl lights. If the business coupe had not been dropped earlier it was definitely now gone. Despite the engine change, the JE Air Line Eight did not receive a new model designation.

On Thursday, June 14, the company threw a big bash for its dealers and distributors at the factory. Everyone who had anything to do with Jordan was invited. The real reason behind all this was to drum up enthusiasm for the new RE and JE series. A new car was available for inspection also, as a Landau Brougham had

1928 Model JE Air Line Eight Sedan, third version (Applegate & Applegate collection).

Dashboard of the 1928 Model JE Air Line Eight (courtesy of Art and Dee Worledge).

1928 Model JE Air Line Eight Coupe, third version (Applegate & Applegate collection).

been added to the JE lineup and dealers were getting the first look. It would not be announced to the public until late in August. This was also a driveaway day as every dealer who was within driving distance was going to drive his purchase home. Food and drink were in abundance, and a multitude of games were played. A prize of $50 in gold was given to the dealer who would drive his purchase the farthest. The winner was George France of Des Moines, Iowa. A prize of $25 in gold went to the dealer with the largest feet—Ed Angell, of Cleveland, whose size was 14½. A prize for the person with the smallest feet went to Chester Quinn of Lakewood, Ohio. His victory was disputed by several people who saw him switching shoes with one of the

1928 Model JE Air Line Eight Victoria, third version (Applegate & Applegate collection).

1928 Model JE Air Line Eight Landau Brougham.

1928 Model JE Air Line Eight Landau Brougham.

Jordan office girls, but nonetheless he took home a bottle of 10-year-old whiskey.[33]

With some of the older Model R and JE cars still unsold in inventory, the factory threw another big bash on Thursday, July 26. A style show, carnival acts, rodeo, singing and side shows—26 acts in all—were enjoyed by all. Most were performed by company employees, distributors and dealers. This was topped off by a free lunch for everyone.

All these promotions were designed to sell cars. Desperation was gripping the Jordan Company, which was now trying everything possible to save itself from bankruptcy. In times when you could sell an Eskimo a snowball, the company was going broke.

On August 27, the new body style which the dealers had viewed in June joined the JE series. The Five Passenger Landau Brougham was just a larger version of the Cross Country Six Sport Four, retaining all the mechanical specifications of the New Series Air Line Eight. Two doors, a padded top, landau irons and a trunk at the rear made this a decent looking automobile, and it sold for the same price as the other models at $1,995.[34]

Jordan was now in deep trouble. The Little Custom debacle had taken its toll, and the JE, though a good car, was not selling in great numbers. Something had to be done in a hurry.

On September 19, stockholders were given the option to purchase 74,000 shares of no par value common stock at $8.00 per share. Actually, they were practically forced to participate, as any amount not subscribed would be taken by a banking syndicate. A new board of directors had taken over and the bankers and brokerage houses now largely controlled the company.[35] J. Arthur House, president of the Guardian Trust Company of Cleveland; Joseph G. Fisher, vice president of the Marine Trust Company, Buffalo; Roger Sherman of the Tenney-Harding-Sherman and Rogers investment house of Chicago; and T.E. Borton of Borton and Borton, Cleveland, were now in control.[36]

Edward S. Jordan was still president of the company (they wanted the name) but those who controlled the money were now controlling Jordan and Ned was along for the ride. Apparently deciding at this time to get out, he selected Harrison B. McGraw, a Cleveland lawyer, to pick the safest investments as a permanent trust for his family and started liquidating his assets in the company.[37] Ned had started a $100,000 trust for his

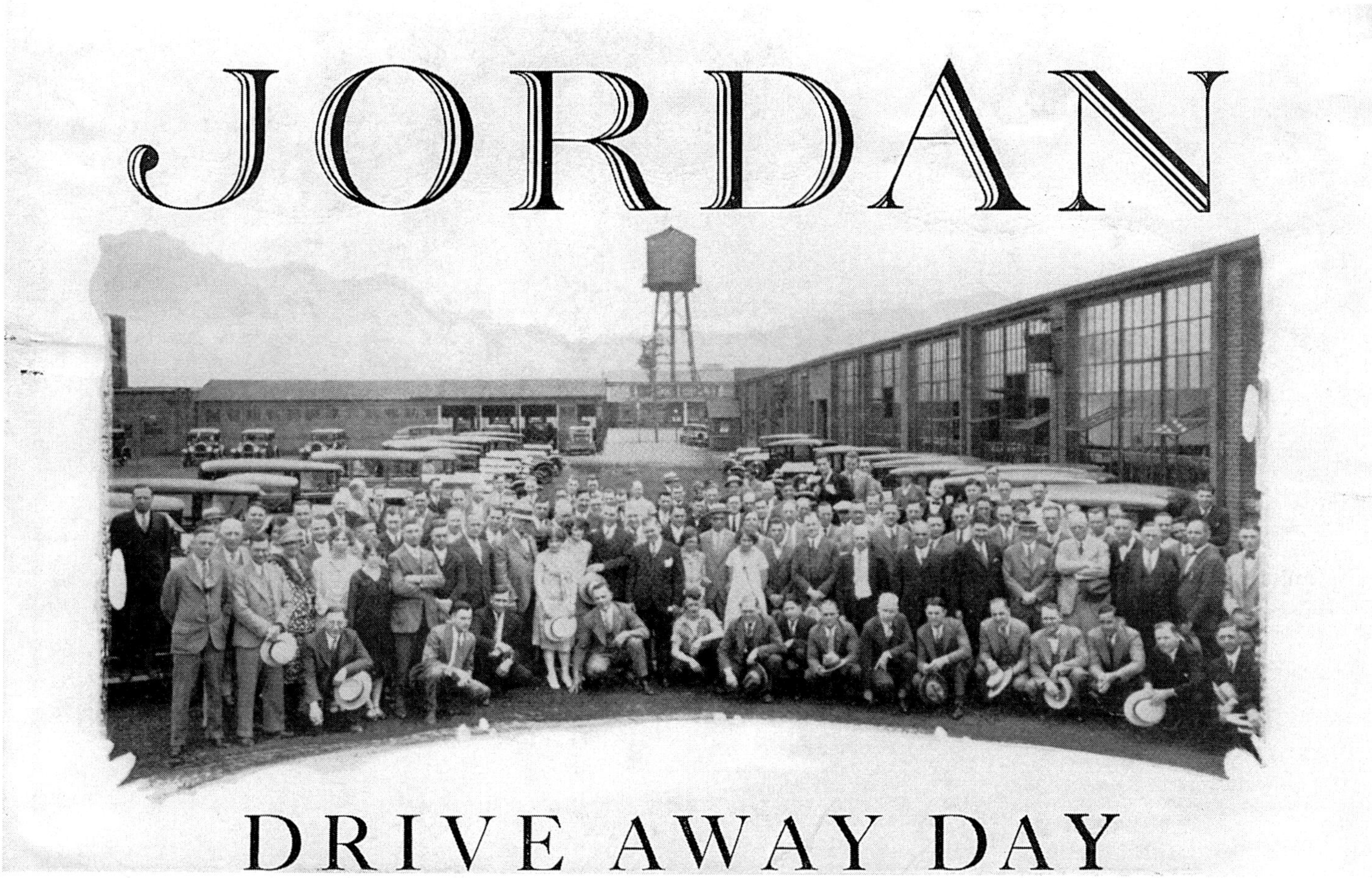

Some 175 dealers with their wives or girlfriends attended Drive Away Day at the Jordan plant on June 14, 1928.

children on December 31, 1924, with the provision that it could be increased if he so desired. He advised his old friends and original stockholders, whose investments had paid 1800 percent by that time, to quietly start getting out too. After this he would be nothing but a figurehead.

On November 2, 1928, Ned addressed the National Automobile Chamber of Commerce Advertising Committee, of which he was the chairman, meeting at the Cleveland Hotel. His subject was "What's Wrong with Automobile Advertising"—a very appropriate subject as Jordan had virtually ceased to advertise except by its own flyers which were printed on low quality paper and with very few illustrations.

By December 31, the stock issue had been 95 percent subscribed and bankers had taken the rest. *Automotive Industries* reported that 100,000 shares at $11.00 per share had been sold. It is unlikely that this was the right figure, but the company did raise a considerable amount of money and ended up with $1,500,000 in cash.[38]

Jordan would enter 1929 with two lines of cars and their finances in decent shape.

NINE

Dashed Hopes of Recovery, 1929

January 1929 arrived with Jordan having weathered the worst storm in its history. Finances were not strong but were adequate to recover should business improve. The engineering department, stylists and everyone else at Jordan had been working feverishly to build something that would sell. The result of that work was then taken to the New York Automobile Show which opened in early January.

The Cross Country Six and the reworked Air Line Eight had been selling poorly and a change was definitely in order. That change would see the Jordan undergo a complete makeover. Styling, which had been suffering in the past few years, was now greatly improved.

The two new models which graced the Jordan space at the show were well received. As in the past few years, two chassis lengths and two engines (a six and an eight) were offered. The larger of the two, riding on a 125 inch wheelbase, was designated as the Model G. It was powered by the Continental 15 S eight cylinder engine that was being used in the current version of the Model JE Air Line Eight. The engine had been modified to accept an engine driven fuel pump but all other specifications remained unchanged. The bore and stroke remained at 3 × 4¾.

With finances being precarious, it was necessary to expend as little as possible on development, and the choice of the existing engine would mean money saved for body and chassis refinement. Those funds were well spent, resulting in a very good looking body mounted on an excellent chassis. The height of the new models had been reduced by two inches from the previous models by springs with less arch and a frame designed to ride lower than previous models. Long sweeping fenders with side mounted wire wheels (wood wheels were standard but seldom installed), bumpers, cowl lights and chrome plated radiator shell with thermostatically controlled louvers made for a great looking car. Twelve inch chrome plated, semi-bullet style headlights by Tilt-Ray, mounted on posts and connected by a crossbar with the Jordan emblem in the center, enhanced front end styling. A luggage rack dressed up the rear.

1929 Model G Sedan.

The Five Passenger Sedan and Coupe were the only closed cars shown. The coupe was equipped with a rumble seat and had a padded top with chrome landau irons. Both closed models had deluxe upholstery and appointments.

Two magnificent Model G open styles Jordan displayed in New York attracted the attention of many who attended the show.[1] The Playboy was a very graceful model

1929 Model G Coupe.

and, in addition to all the attributes of the closed models, was equipped with a folding windshield and pole mounted spotlight. It was long and low with a rear-mounted trunk that visually stretched it even further. The post mounted spotlight would shortly be gone, replaced with one mounted on the windshield frame, and the change would improve on the Playboy's already good looks.

But Jordan's other open Model G offering eclipsed the handsome Playboy. One of the most beautiful styles from any manufacturer to grace the show was the Speedboy. Superb styling and a daring paint scheme made the Speedboy one of the most striking automobiles of any day. It was finished in silver gray aluminum and jet black. Fenders, splash aprons and rear body sections were finished in silver gray. A chrome strip began at the front center of the hood and gracefully sloped down across the cowl section into the front door and made a sweeping curve back to the cowl. This section was painted in silver gray also.

1929 Model G Playboy. Shown is an early version; later models did not have the pole mounted spotlight.

1929 Model G Speedboy, early model without lights on front fenders (courtesy William Bailey).

Dual cowls with folding windshields, a rear mounted trunk contoured to fit the body, and a post mounted spotlight finished off the dazzling bodywork. Unlike all the other models, the Speedboy did not have cowl lights. Wood wheels were standard on all models except the Playboy and Speedboy. Painted steel wire-spoke wheels were standard on those two models with chrome being an option.[2] Twin side-mounted spares with covers were standard equipment also.

When the Chicago Automobile Show opened on January 25, the Speedboy Phaeton had already had a facelift. Small lights had been added atop the front fenders and the rear body section which had previously been painted silver gray was now black. Those two small changes made a distinct improvement in the appearance of the already good looking phaeton.

Prices were $2,195 for the Model G Sedan and

1929 Model G Speedboy—second version with rear body painted black and lights added to front fenders. This car retains the post mounted spotlight, however.

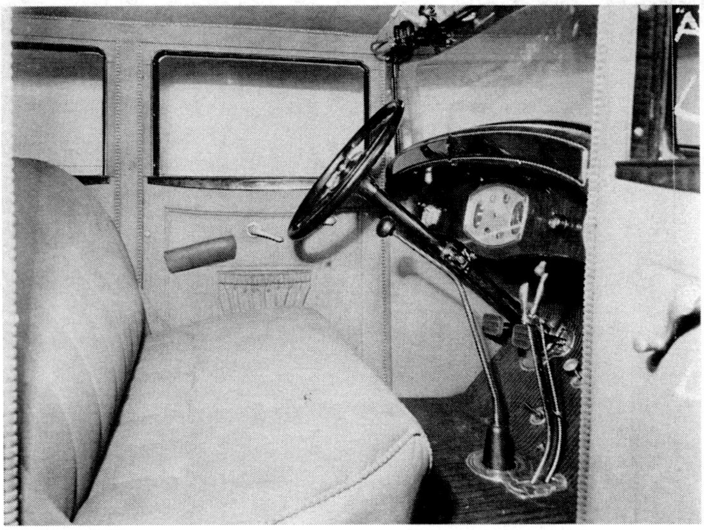

Interior of 1929 Model G Sedan (Free Library of Philadelphia).

1929 Model E Sedan.

1929 Model E Coupe.

Model E front end.

Coupe, $2,695 for the Playboy and $2,895 for the Speedboy. These four styles were the initial offerings but others would be added soon.

The mechanical features of the new Model G had not been neglected either. Rubber and steel spring shackles, a gas tank suspended in rubber lined straps, Marles type ball bearing steering and double action hydraulic shock absorbers made for a smooth ride and good handling. But the change most welcomed by drivers was the brakes. Previous models had been equipped with outside contracting hydraulic brakes which were minimal at best. The new Model G was equipped with double expanding, hydraulic type brakes, fitted to 14 inch drums. Here was a car that not only rode and steered well but could be stopped without fear.[3]

Trying to cover as much of the buying public as possible, Jordan also brought something to the show to please the economy minded. A new six cylinder Model E featured styling that closely resembled the Model G, on a shorter 116 inch wheelbase. The engine was a Continental 18C with a bore and stroke of 3⅜ × 4⅝.

The Model E differed visually from the G only in subtle ways. Upon close examination one found that the headlights were smaller and mounted on a bar only, unlike the G which had posts and a bar. As on the G, the bar between the headlights displayed the Jordan emblem in the center. All brightwork was now chrome, following the lead of the G. Unlike the Model G, the Model E did not have radiator louvers. The Coupe had a rumble seat and padded top, but the landau irons were a combination of chrome and black.[4]

Factory engineers had worked hard to improve the

looks and performance of the new models and had taken a lesson from Henry Ford along the way. Many mechanical and body parts were now interchangeable. Fenders, bumpers, luggage racks, gas tanks, tire carriers, and many other parts could be used on either car. Even the splash aprons had their mounting holes punched alike and the G aprons could be used on the E by trimming nine inches from the rear.

Wood wheels were standard on the Model E but could be upgraded to wires for a fee. Also, the upholstery, which was not as elegant as that of the Model G, could be improved for a modest sum.

Mechanically, the Model E six cylinder power plant was the big difference in the two models. Cranking out 70 horsepower, the engine was a great improvement over the previous Cross Country Six.

Prices for both the Coupe and Sedan were $1,795. The Model RE and JE would still be made and carried in the line until at least July.[5]

On January 12, at a meeting of distributors and dealers, John McArdle stated that Jordan was planning to sell from eight to ten thousand cars in 1929. He also stated that six months earlier the company was $1.5 million in debt but now had $1.5 million in the bank and no debts. The sunny rhetoric was undoubtedly designed to keep stockholders, distributors and dealers happy. McArdle also stated that the company had representatives in 32 foreign countries and that foreign shipments were 115 percent better in 1928 than in 1927 and expected to increase substantially in 1929. L.F. Murphy, who had replaced W.B. Riley as sales manager and acted as toastmaster for the event, stated that about 200 cars would be manufactured in January and that a schedule of 60 cars per day was anticipated in February.[6]

Finished chassis were always available from Jordan so that the customer who wanted to fit a custom body could do so. They came complete with the front end (hood, fenders, cowl, windshield), running boards and rear fenders. One company that built beautiful examples of custom bodies was the Joseph Wildanger Company of Red Bank, New Jersey. This company specialized in hearses, ambulances, funeral cars, buses and fire trucks. However, their best work was station wagons which they called "Suburbans." Mr. Wildanger built a beautiful example of a station wagon on a Jordan Model G chassis for his own use and pleasure. The business was family owned and survived until 1984.

Jordan underwent more personnel changes in 1929. On February 23, 1929, Harvey R. Buckner was promoted to works manager. He had previously been division superintendent for Willys-Overland before coming to Jordan as superintendent.[7] In late December, R.C. Reichel was appointed as sales manager. He replaced L.F. Murphy, who had joined Jordan Distributors, Inc., as vice president and general manager of the new division located in New York City. Reichel had previously been with Buick, Chalmers and Chrysler.[8]

1930 Model G Great Line Ninety station wagon (Suburban) bodied by the Joseph Wildanger Company in Red Bank, New Jersey (courtesy Edward G. Wildanger).

Interior of the Wildanger-bodied 1930 Model G Great Line Ninety station wagon. Note the roll-up windows, very advanced for a body of this type (courtesy Edward G. Wildanger).

On March 2, the new selling organization designed to market the company's products on the East coast was formed in an attempt to get the Jordan selling again. With the new models now available it would be moderately successful.

The stockholders meeting which was scheduled for March 18 was postponed due to lack of a quorum. It was rescheduled for May 21. On April 5, however, Ned announced that a stockholders meeting would be held on April 24 for the purpose of asking permission to increase the shares of common stock from 300,000 to 500,000. This was an attempt to raise $1,345,000 in order to keep Jordan solvent. Apparently the company could not wait until May 21 as had previously been announced. Stockholders would be offered the new stock at $12 per share. As the new stock would not be underwritten, all monies raised would go directly to the company.[9]

Great Lakes biplane.

For the first two months of 1929, Jordan earned only $3,000, but in March the profit was $54,695. By May the net profit was up to $143,404 and, financially, things were looking a little better. For the same period in 1928 Jordan had lost $355,000.[10]

On May 9, the *Cleveland Plain Dealer* reported that Charlotte Jordan and her youngest daughter Joan had both been honored at the May show of the Cleveland Museum of Art. First prize for sculpture was awarded to Mrs. Jordan for her work entitled "Young Woman" and daughter Joan took home a first for a group of relief cuts entitled "Calf," "Figure," "Elephant" and "New York." Mrs. Jordan was an accomplished sculptor, having studied under Henry G. Keller at the Cleveland School of Art and under E. Ambrose Webster at Provincetown, Rhode Island, and having also studied in New York and Europe. Joan Jordan, 19, had also studied under Webster at Provincetown and was a student of the Art Students League of New York. She would soon begin studies in Paris.

Ned Jordan himself meanwhile remained busy with a range of activities both inside and outside the company. He was always pushing for more and better roads which would in turn help the automobile industry. Flying was another of his interests, and he worked hard to see it become more popular. He had invested in Allied Motor Industries, Inc., which owned the Great Lakes Aircraft Corporation, and on March 7 he had been made a director of the company, recognizing his importance to the industry.[11]

On May 14, Ned presided over a meeting of the national Automobile Chamber of Commerce Advertising Committee of which he was chairman. His topic was "Advertising—What Are You Going to Do About It?" He should have had the answer as he was recognized as one of the best.[12]

On June 18, Ned met with Jordan distributors and dealers in St. Louis, Missouri. That night he spoke to the St. Louis Automobile Dealers Association at the Missouri Hotel. His topic was "Salesmanship and Services, a Great Combination." A crowd of 600 was expected for the meeting and eagerly awaited Ned's appearance.[13]

A three-page report on the status of the company was mailed to distributors, dealers and stockholders on June 30. Compared to 1928 things looked much better and there was hope for the future. Unlike all former communications, which were signed by Ned Jordan, this one was signed by John McArdle, vice president and general manager.

By July 1, Jordan had decided to offer a new model, expand its Model G line by five new body styles and drop the JE and RE models from the lineup. Distributors and dealers came to a big party at the factory. A large tent was set up on the Jordan grounds to host the activities and display the new models.

The previous Model G would now be designated as the Model G, Great Line 90. Only a few changes were made from the previous Model G. The engine would now be mounted on rubber, a three-lens oval taillight with a backup light was standard and all-vision windshield wipers were added. The Speedboy and Play-

A SIMPLE STORY OF PROGRESS . . . . .

PROGRESS is taken so much for granted in America today that we often do not stop to analyze an accomplishment that seems at first glance to be only normal.

Something more than normal, however, has happened in the financial situation of the Jordan Motor Car Company—and we feel that you will be intensely interested in a detailed analysis of it.

About one year ago, Edward S. Jordan gathered around him a new group of operating executives, a new board of directors, and a number of young, aggressive distributors and dealers from the more important centers.

New plans were made. New models were started—and with new blood and new enthusiasm, the old Jordan idea of "building a chassis of finished mechanical excellence and equipping it with a series of custom style bodies," was given new impetus. From that day Jordan has gone steadily forward.

What happened is now history—but it is interesting history—and history still very much in the making.

JORDAN

Above and following two pages: A letter sent to reassure dealers, distributors and stockholders, circa July 1929.

A glance at the following comparative figures for the first six months of 1928 and the first six months of 1929 tell the story briefly and convincingly

	As of June 30, 1929	As of June 30, 1928
Current Assets	1,862,731	1,179,952
Current Liabilities	258,469	1,626,914
Ratio	7.2 to 1	Liabilities Exceed Assets
Total Assets	3,336,720	2,600,392
Increase	28%	
Total Liabilities	735,770	1,844,870
(Excluding capital and surplus)		
Decrease	60%	
Bank Loans	None	225,000
Capital and Surplus: Net Worth	2,600,950	755,522
Increase	244%	
Earned and Paid in Surplus	1,278,794	Deficit 2,038,205
(Incl. in above)		
Increase	3,316,999	
FIRST SIX MONTHS		
Net Profit	151,138	Loss 473,372
(After depreciation, interest, etc., but before Federal Taxes)		
Increase	624,510	

That is the story—up to date

WHERE a year ago we had a dead inventory of considerable proportions, our inventory today is clean and active. Receivables are all good. Reserves are ample. Permanent assets have been liberally depreciated, bringing them considerably under appraised values. Orders are satisfactory—and everything points to even better business in the last half than in the first half.

Today every man in the Jordan organization is looking forward. What has been accomplished will serve only as an inspiration to accomplish more.

With a steadily growing dealer organization—a steadily growing appreciation of the new cars—a steadily growing respect on the part of owners, bankers, dealers, and public for the soundness of the Jordan Company and its business policies—a permanent and satisfactory place in the industry is assured.

John McArdle

VICE PRESIDENT *and*
GENERAL MANAGER
Jordan Motor Car Company, Inc.
Cleveland, Ohio

JORDAN

Complete Jordan Line

SERIES 90

Model	Equipment	List
7-Pass. Limousine	With glass partition at back of front seat, leather front seat upholstery, wood wheels	$2,795
7-Pass. Sedan	Wood wheels	2,695
5-Pass. Sedan	Wood wheels	2,395
Sport Sedan	Wood wheels, trunk	2,695
Standard Coupe	Wood wheels	2,395
Convert. Coupe	Wood wheels	2,595
Speedboy Phaeton	Lacquered wire wheels and lacquered radiator shutter. Price includes two spare wheels with tires, tire covers, trunk and bumpers	2,895
7-Pass. Touring	Wood wheels	2,995
Playboy Roadster	Lacquered wire wheels and lacquered radiator shutter. Price includes two spare wheels with tires, tire covers, trunk and bumpers	2,695
SERIES 80		
5-Pass. Sedan	Wood wheels	$2,095
Std. Coupe	Wood wheels	2,095
SIX		
5-Pass. Sedan	Wood wheels	$1,795
Std. Coupe	Wood wheels	1,795

Price list covering Jordan's complete line as of August 1929.

boy were now minus the pole mounted spotlight, which had been removed some time previous, but a windshield stanchion mounted spotlight could be had if desired.

The Model G, Great Line 90 now comprised nine body styles.[14] A Convertible Coupe (Cabriolet) and a Sport Sedan had been added to the 125 inch wheelbase frame, and seven passenger limousine, sedan and touring bodies were offered on a 131 inch wheelbase frame.

The Convertible Coupe had all the mechanical features of the other models but was equipped with folding cloth top and landau irons with a luggage rack at the rear.

The Sport Sedan had a padded top and landau irons. The "blindback" body had no windows behind the rear doors and had been shortened to accommodate a rear mounted trunk contoured to fit the body.

The Seven Passenger Sedan was just a stretched version of the Five Passenger Sedan with two jump seats added, and the Seven Passenger Limousine was noth-

A factory event on July 1, 1929, introducing the 1930 Model G Great Line Ninety and Model T Standard Line Eighty (Free Library of Philadelphia).

Inside the Jordan tent, July 1, 1929 (Free Library of Philadelphia).

1930–32 Model G Great Line Ninety Convertible Coupe (Cabriolet) (Free Library of Philadelphia).

ing more than a Seven Passenger Sedan with a glass partition added behind the front seat. However, it did have leather upholstery in the front compartment.

The Seven Passenger Touring was not something entirely new to Jordan. They had made them early on, but not since the Model AA. (Jordan supposedly did make a seven passenger version of the AA, but no solid evidence has been found to verify this.) With the Speedboy seating five passengers, Jordan had decided to cover the field for those who still preferred a large open touring. Like most of the Jordan line, it carried a luggage rack at the rear. Like the previous Blueboy, the new car had a solid windshield, but unlike the Speedboy it did not have wind wings.

Jordan's all new model, designated the Model T Standard Line 80, was a scaled down version of the

1930–32 Model G Great Line Ninety Sport Sedan.

1930–32 Model G Great Line Ninety Seven Passenger Sedan on the 132-inch wheelbase (Free Library of Philadelphia).

1930–32 Model G Great Line Ninety Seven Passenger Limousine (Free Library of Philadelphia).

Great Line 90. Riding on a 120 inch wheelbase frame, it fit neatly between the E and the Great Line 90. It was equipped with a Continental 17-S eight cylinder engine with a bore and stroke of $2\frac{7}{8} \times 4\frac{3}{4}$. The only visible difference (other than the wheelbase) between the

1930–32 Model G Great Line Ninety Coupe (Free Library of Philadelphia).

1930–32 Model G Great Line Ninety Seven Passenger Touring.

1930–32 Model G Great Line Ninety Speedboy (Free Library of Philadelphia).

1930–32 Model G Great Line Ninety Playboy.

Front view of 1930–32 Model G Great Line Ninety Coupe (Free Library of Philadelphia).

1930–32 Model T Standard Line 80 Coupe (Applegate & Applegate collection).

1930–32 Model T Standard Line 80 Sedan (Applegate & Applegate collection).

Front view of 1930–32 Model T Standard Line 80 Coupe.

Model T Standard Line 80 and the Great Line 90 was a round taillight identical to the one used on the former 1929 Model G and E. A Five Passenger Sedan and Coupe with rumble seat were the only body styles offered.[15] As with all previous closed cars, wood wheels were standard but wire spokes could be had as an option.

Jordan now had three models riding on four wheelbases: eleven distinctive automobiles with a price range from $1,795 to $2,995. (The Model E was reportedly dropped in July but it stayed around for a while as dealers sold off those remaining in stock after production ceased.)[16] There was something for everyone, but everyone wasn't buying.

It is unclear who made the bodies for the Model G, T, E and Great Line 90. Murray had been making the JE and RE bodies and it would seem logical that they would have continued to do so. Trade magazines that listed the body maker in their specifications attributed the bodies to Murray. It is also possible, though, that Jordan built their own bodies. The building on Taft Avenue, which also housed the Facto Body Company, was easily large enough to have housed the equipment necessary to build bodies on a scale such as Jordan needed. No body tags or other identification have been found to confirm or deny the Murray versus Jordan theory. Until such evidence surfaces, it will remain a mystery. Another element of uncertainty is Facto, which could have been a Jordan subsidiary and may have been building all their bodies starting in 1929. They did built the Z bodies which were introduced in 1930.

When vice president and general manager John McArdle and export manager C.A. Glentworth sailed for Europe in October to take in the overseas auto shows,[17] calamity was not far off. At year's end Jordan had sold only 2,231 cars. Among the well-known manufacturers only Cord, Gardner and Stutz had sold fewer.[18] Ford had sold 1,310,119 and the Chevrolet Division of General Motors had sold 780,042.

The company's finances had remained shaky while the economy was booming. Now the near total collapse of the American economy in November 1929 had hit while Jordan was already weak, effectively sealing the company's fate. As the Depression began to cause even the big corporations problems, the small ones would soon be on the outside looking in.

TEN

Last Gasps, 1930–1932

The U.S. economy was in a tailspin as 1930 opened. Corporations, businesses, and individuals were going broke faster than could be counted. Only the strong would survive, and many of them would have a rough time of it.

Jordan nevertheless went to the New York show with two new automobiles in addition to the Great Line 90 and Standard Line 80 Model T. The Model E had not been selling at all and was dropped in July 1929. About the same time Jordan supposedly began making a fancy version of the Great Line 90 called the Great Line 93. The exterior was the same but the interior was supposed to be luxurious. No factory documentation can be found to verify the car's production, but it was reported in one of the trade magazines. At a time when Jordan was trying anything possible to sell cars, a fancy interior would not have been beyond their imagination.

Prices had been reduced on the Model T and Great Line 90, a desperate attempt to keep the company in business.[1] Both body styles of the T were selling for $300 less at $1,795, and the Great Line 90 had been reduced by $100 on all body styles. There were no changes to either model. All available resources had been used designing the new Line 70 Sunshine Sedan, sometimes referred to as the Model U (as it was listed in Jordan's report to the NACC) and the Model Z Sportsman and Speedway Ace.[2]

The Sunshine Sedan was basically a Model T chassis with a new body. It was powered by a Continental 17 S eight cylinder engine with bore and stroke of 2⅞ × 4¾, the same engine that had been used in the T. In fact, other than the body, steering, and mechanical brakes, the Sunshine Sedan was basically a Model T.[3]

One major mechanical change was of great importance. The brakes of the Line 70 Sunshine Sedan were

1930 Model U Line Seventy Sunshine Sedan (Free Library of Philadelphia).

Front view of 1930 Model U Line Seventy Sunshine Sedan (Free Library of Philadelphia).

Rear view of 1930 Model U Line Seventy Sunshine Sedan (Free Library of Philadelphia).

1930 Model U Line Seventy Sunshine Sedan (top down) (John Conde).

1930 Model U Line Seventy Sunshine Sedan, shown with top up and landau irons added (courtesy Dan Jordan).

1930 Model U Line Seventy Sunshine Sedan, again featuring landau irons (courtesy Dan Jordan).

Front interior of 1930 Model U Line Seventy Sunshine Sedan (Detroit Public Library, National Automotive History Collection).

cable controlled, two shoe Bendix units. This was a step backward, but Jordan wanted a car which would sell in the lower price range and therefore had to cheapen something.

About the time the Sunshine Sedan was shown, specifications were drawn for a Custom "8" and Master "8," neither of which would be manufactured. The Custom "8" was to have a wheelbase of 138 inches and be powered by an engine with bore and stroke of 3⅜ × 4½. The car was to have cable controlled four-wheel mechanical brakes with 15 inch drums. It would have wooden wheels with two side-mounted tires on rims or, at an extra cost, six natural finish or painted wheels. For a little more one could have six wire wheels. Auto-Lite would furnish all the electrical components and Tillotson would supply the carburetor. All other components were about the same as previous Jordan models.

The Master "8" would have a wheelbase of 125 inches and be powered by an engine with the same bore and stroke as the custom "8" (3⅜ × 4½). All components would be supplied by the same manufacturers as were the Custom "8." Brakes would still be cable controlled but the drums would be 14 inches.

It is not known what body styles these cars would have had, but apparently Jordan was planning a line of lower priced models to offset weak sales of the existing models.[4]

The body of the Sunshine Sedan was a radical departure from anything Jordan had previously offered. It was a four door sedan with a collapsible top. The windows would roll down, with the post collapsing to create a convertible. One could collapse the top and leave the windows up, enjoying the pleasures of a closed car and a convertible simultaneously. One factory brochure exists but reveals little about the car, consisting mainly of hype.

The fenders and hood-cowl section were not much of a change from the T and Great Line 90. Miniature style headlights were mounted on top of the fenders for a European look, and twin sidemounts, held in place by two leather straps, added a touch of class to the front end. In a departure from the previous style, the hood louvers were vertical and fewer in number. Bumpers and wire wheels were standard.

Paint treatment resembled that of the Speedboy. Starting at the top-center of the hood a trim strip gradually swept downward across the hood, cowl and front door ending just a few inches from the rear of the door. Jordan had taken another step backward and hinged the front door at the rear, a design known commonly as suicide doors. The section of the hood, cowl and door below the trim was painted the same color as the fenders.[5]

The windshield was slanted slightly and the collapsible top had an oval window at the rear. The prototype version had the rear of the top breaking at an absolute vertical angle but someone supposedly decided that moving the top corner forward and adding landau irons would yield a better looking car. That may have been the case, but more likely the change was made to give the top more rigidity and improve ease of folding. With a nice metal covered trunk at the rear, the Sunshine Sedan was a fairly attractive car, but no matter how good it looked or what the selling price was, it would not sell. Only a few, perhaps as few as two, were made. So far as is known, the Sunshine Sedan was never put into production, though a letter from Jordan to a client stated that it could be purchased.[6]

The other new model, the Model Z, was such a sensation that viewers at the New York show had to stand in line for extended periods of time just to see it.[7] Only two body styles were offered, but they were something to behold. Styling equal to that of custom body designers was now to be offered on a production model.

Mechanically, the Model Z rode on a 145 inch wheelbase frame. The engine was a Continental 12K eight cylinder with bore and stroke of 3⅜ × 4½, said to produce 114 horsepower. The carburetor was by Schebler, of a dual throat design, fed by an engine driven fuel pump, and ignition was dual point–dual coil type. Top speed was reportedly over 100 miles per hour. The engine was one of Continental's stock units which was offered to several other manufacturers. Jordan was not in a position to spend money for research and development of powerplants. Warner Gear supplied the four speed transmission, and the clutch was a single disc of eleven inches. The differential was of the standard Hotchkiss design and brakes were four wheel hydraulic with 16 inch drums. Marles type Gemmer steering was used and four wheel, double acting, hydraulic shock absorbers were standard.

Bodies were characterized by unusual lines. The Five Passenger Close Coupled Sedan, or Sportsman, had a slanted windshield, D shaped rear door and a bustle at the rear which contained a medium size trunk space. The hood was long and straight from windshield to the radiator shell, which was chrome plated with thermostatically controlled louvers. The radiator filler cap was now inside the engine compartment and the hood had three horizontal louvers. Fenders were sweeping, with the front reaching practically to the bumper, and had an inverted V ridge profile over the entire length. Running boards were airfoil type which did not connect to either fender and sported aviation type red and green navigation lights.

Woodlite headlights mounted on a bar, with miniature copies mounted on top of the fenders, graced the front along with two chrome plated trumpet horns. Chromed front bumpers and rear bumperettes set off the front and rear. One or two spotlights, large taillights which were a copy of the headlights, wire wheels with chrome plated locking rings and large plated hub-

***Three photographs above:* 1930 Model Z Sportsman Sedan (Free Library of Philadelphia).**

Two views of the front end of 1930 Model Z Sportsman Sedan (Free Library of Philadelphia).

caps, rear mounted spare and a pleasing application of paint and trim set the sedan off as one of the most beautiful cars ever made.

The interior was no less appealing. Plush carpeting and luxurious cloth upholstery with elegant trim was standard. The front compartment was something to behold. The dash resembled that of an airplane as all instruments were centered. In addition to the usual speedometer, ammeter, gasoline and oil pressure gauges, the Model Z dash included a tachometer, compass, clock, altimeter, and vacuum gauges. All were finished in chrome trim. Slightly to the right of the instrument panel were the radio controls.

The throttle, spark and choke controls were centered in a mounting on the lower center of the instrument cluster. They had short handles, topped by a round knob and stood vertically out of the chrome plated mount. The gearshift lever was long and curved, chrome plated and was topped by a round knob made from the same material as that of the spark, throttle and choke controls. The spotlight handle was of the same material and shape. Several other elegant appointments finished off the front cockpit.[8]

Body color was an ivory white or solid black and there was one slight difference in the way the bodies were built. Cars painted white apparently had the center door hinges placed slightly lower than those cars finished in black. It is not known how many sedans were built or whether there were more than two colors.

Front interior of 1930 Model Z Sportsman Sedan (Free Library of Philadelphia).

1930 Model Z Sportsman Sedan, showing higher door hinge positioning (courtesy Dan Jordan).

1930 Model Z Sportsman Sedan (John Conde).

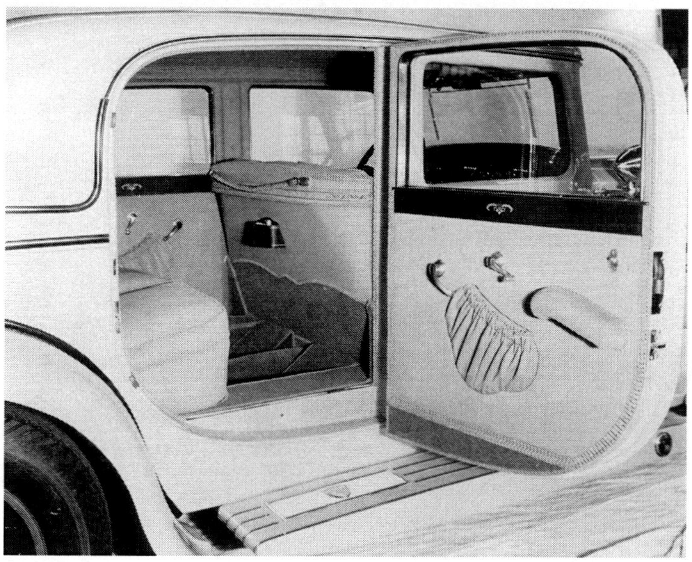

Although surviving photographs show the hinge discrepancy, color may not have had anything to do with it.[9]

The second Model Z bodystyle, the Speedway Ace, shared all its mechanical specifications with the Sportsman and most of the other Jordans. The front end, hood, cowl and fenders were identical to the sedan, but there the resemblance stopped. The body from the cowl back was low and long and could have been a convertible, but instead it was a rumble seat roadster. Doors were hung on an angle with concealed hinges. Entrance to the rear seat was gained by sliding the front passen-

Left, center: Rear interior of 1930 Model Z Sportsman Sedan. *Left, bottom:* Rear interior opening of 1930 Model Z Sportsman Sedan. (Both photographs: Free Library of Philadelphia).

1930 Model Z Speedway Ace (Applegate & Applegate collection).

1930 Model Z Speedway Ace (courtesy William Bailey).

1930 Model Z Speedway Ace (John Conde).

1930 Model Z Speedway Ace at the 1930 New York auto show (courtesy William Bailey).

1930 Model Z Speedway Ace (courtesy Dan Jordan).

Front end of 1930 Model Z Speedway Ace (courtesy Dan Jordan).

Sweeping fender and hood louvers of the 1930 Model Z Speedway Ace (courtesy Dan Jordan).

***Above:* Two views of the dash of the 1930 Model Z Speedway Ace (courtesy Dan Jordan).**

Instrument panel in the dash of the 1930 Model Z Speedway Ace (courtesy Dan Jordan).

Interior of the 1930 Model Z Speedway Ace (Free Library of Philadelphia).

ger seat forward, raising the rear cowl, which was hinged in the middle, and then raising the rumble seat lid which then became the back cushion of the seat. Upholstery was fine leather in the purchaser's choice of color.[10]

The one-piece slanted windshield, unlike the Sportsman's, was straight at the bottom and had chrome plated posts and frame. Chrome plated vacuum wiper motors were mounted at the bottom and rubber hoses with a loop insured that the windshield could be tilted out at the bottom or folded completely down. Single or twin spotlights were mounted on the wind-

Spotlights on the 1930 Model Z Speedway Ace (courtesy Dan Jordan).

Front view of the 1930 Model Z Speedway Ace (courtesy Dan Jordan).

Two rear views of the 1930 Model Z Speedway Ace (courtesy Dan Jordan).

shield posts and wind wings were cut in such a way as not to interfere with their operation. The spare tire was mounted at the rear and a trunk compartment just behind the rumble seat finished off the roadster. Surviving photographs show the Ace as being made in only one color, ivory white.[11]

Supposedly a total of 14 Model Z's were made and of that number 12 were Sedans and two were Roadsters. One surviving example of the Speedway Ace, #0014, remains today and is undergoing a complete restoration at the time of this writing. Various parts of a Sportsman exist but no complete example has ever been found. Factory photos demonstrate that at least three Sportsmen and three Aces were built.

Being restrained by a lack of funds to develop the Model Z, Jordan used as many parts from the Great Line 90 as possible. The frame was the same, just stretched out by cutting two 132 inch frames and welding them together. Extra cross members were added to insure rigidity. Springs were the same length, radiator shutters were identical and the radiator shell was the same except it had no filler cap at the top. The windshield and posts of the Ace were copies of the Speedboy and Playboy.

Most of the mechanical components were supplied by the same firms that had been doing business with Jordan for many years. One exception was the carburetor, which was furnished by Schebler. This was a departure from Jordan's use of Stromberg's carburetors from the beginning. The Z and U would be the only Jordans ever built with anything other than a Sromberg carburetor.

The Ace has never been seen with a top, and it is doubtful that one was ever designed. The windshield posts have fittings at the top to accommodate one and there are snaps for side curtains, but as these were borrowed from the Speedboy and Playboy, their presence is not surprising and may not be meaningful.

The Z was apparently finished just in time for the show. To the casual observer it might have appeared to have a temporary exhaust system. However, the chrome finished, flexible pipe was threaded over the exhaust pipe to enhance its appearance as the battery box interfered with the routing and it could be seen between the fender and the running board. It actually was routed under the running board for a short distance at one point.

Automobile Topics reported on January 11, 1930, that the Z evolved jointly between John McArdle, vice president and general manager of Jordan, and W.C. Colburn, president of the Facto Auto Body Company.[12] The only known piece of Jordan advertising on the subject states that the bodies were by "Coburn."[13] Over the years, automotive writers have seized on this discrepancy to claim that there was no "Facto" or "Coburn." Apparently W.C. Coburn's name was misspelled in the news release by the magazine itself.

There was indeed a Facto Auto Body company, and its president was William Chester Coburn. The secretary and treasurer was William H. Marlatt and the address was 12910 Taft Avenue, Cleveland. Other principals were Morgan P. Guenther, Frank A. Gosnick, George B. Folk and E.M. Shields. The Facto company was incorporated on February 19, 1929, occupying a building that had been owned by Chandler Motor Car Company and later by Hupp, which purchased Chandler on December 22, 1928. Apparently this company was formed for the express purpose of making the Z bodies, perhaps by Jordan's own doing or by some officer of the company.

The two Model Z's which were taken to the New York Show had the body tag affixed to the cowl just in front of the door and about one inch above the running board. The Sportsman, which was painted black, also had this body tag. No other example of either body style has been seen with this identification.

Facto may have also made the body for the Model U Sunshine Sedan. Only a couple of that model were known to exist and it is reasonable to assume that this could have happened. The Facto Company was dissolved on December 20, 1932. After W.C. Coburn's death in 1974, there were found in his personal effects photographs of both the Model Z and the Model U Sunshine Sedan, reinforcing this idea that they did make both the Model Z and U bodies.[14]

The Z did not sell at all as the $5,500 price was just too steep. Anyone who had money was not about to pay that sum for an automobile made by a company that was going broke. The extent of the Depression had not been fully realized and those who had money left were very cautious. The car's failure was unfortunate, as the Model Z might have ranked with the finest automobiles ever made. It is appropriate that the model designation was Z, as this was Jordan's final offering.

No catalogs or brochures picturing the Model Z or Line 70 Sunshine Sedan are known to exist. Jordan stated in a letter to a client that the Z would be sold from photographs only. Also, no operator's manual or parts books have ever been found; probably none were printed. By this time Jordan advertising had all but stopped. Very few newspaper ads and no magazine ads had appeared since August 1929. An occasional flyer was handed out by dealers, but that was it.

Jordan was granted trademark #266,783 on February 4, 1930, for the new logo design which was being used on the Model G and Great Line 90. The application had been submitted in somewhat more hopeful times on April 1, 1929. The arrowhead was still used but in a different design surrounded by a shield. This was a further revision of the two earlier arrowhead trademarks.

While the company was sliding into ruin, Ned Jordan's personal circumstances were equally bleak. His and Lottie's marriage had essentially been over for several years. He stayed gone most of the time, as did she. He seemed to prefer work, women and booze (not necessarily in that order). She preferred art (painting and sculpture) and entertainment. Lottie had taken an apartment at 111 E. 10th Street, New York City, a few years before while Jordan's future still looked bright.[15] She became miffed when, upon her return from Paris on November 16, 1929, Ned did not meet her at the pier. She had been visiting their daughter, Joan, who was studying art. All the children were grown by this time with Jane being a student at the University of Arizona and Jack working with Dr. Elmer A. Sperry of gyroscope fame, helping to perfect the Sperry Rail car which would detect faults in the rails of America's railroads.[16] Incensed at Ned's inattention, Lottie packed off for Reno, Nevada, and established a legal residence there. Essentially all that was necessary to establish a residency was to rent a room or apartment.

BIRD H. MC GARVEY
PRESIDENT

W. M. GOODNOW
VICE-PRES.

GLOBE SECURITIES COMPANY
CITY BANK BUILDING
18TH & GRAND AVENUE
KANSAS CITY, MISSOURI

August 14, 1930

Mr. J. L. Elbert
Holden
Missouri

Dear Sir:

Mr. A. K. Swomley, service manager for the Warwick Jordan Motor Company, has told us that the Jordan factory wrote him that you had made an inquiry of the factory about Jordan cars, and Mr. Swomley thought that possibly we might be interested in the letter.

The Jordan distributor got into some kind of trouble several months ago and was forced to close, and we had to take half a dozen cars on which we had loaned him the money with which to put the cars on his floor. We have sold all of these cars but three, and the three remaining are all 1930 straight 8 sedans of the 80 and 90 models, and have never been sold or used. If you are interested, we will sell you one of these cars at a very low price, as all we are trying to do is to get as near as possible to the amount that we loaned on the cars. Please let us hear from you if you have anything in mind, or if you know someone that might buy one of these cars we will allow him a very large discount and also pay you a commission.

Mr. Swomley thinks that you are interested in the Speedway and Sunshine series, but we are told that none of those models are available at the present time.

Yours very truly,

GLOBE SECURITIES COMPANY

BHMcGarvey

President

BHMcG:S

The recipient of this letter, J.L. Elbert, was 15 years old and wrote to many companies asking for photographs and literature. As this letter reveals, dealers were suffering too in 1930 (courtesy Charles Boles).

Jordan trademark #266,783.

Jordan trademark variation as used on literature and hubcaps.

On March 28, 1930, having attained the required three months' residency, Lottie Jordan filed for divorce. Reno was the divorce capital of the United States at that time, the place to go to end a marriage. Two days later, on March 30, 1930, the marriage was dissolved by the district judge of Washoe County, Nevada. Lawyers for Ned and Lottie had gotten together on March 1 and settled on the terms, which were not disclosed. Lottie went back to New York and Ned to Cleveland.[17]

Although Ned had neglected his marriage for years, he was devastated. The spacious and beautiful home at 14923 Grandview Terrace, East Cleveland, where they had lived since 1919, went up for sale. Supposedly one-half of everything went to Lottie, and she wanted her part.

Meanwhile the Jordan Company was muddling along and Ned had nothing to say about it. Other people were now running the show and he was president in title only. Ned took another hit in June when his sister, Minnie Estelle Jordan Miller, who had been residing in San Francisco, California, passed away on June 22, 1930.[18]

The company had lost $652,408 in 1929 and the

hemorrhage was continuing. Early in October, a new corporation, Jordan Motors Corporation, Inc., was formed for the purpose of taking over the Jordan Motor Car Company, Inc.[19] The plan was to offer five shares of preferred stock in the new company for one share of preferred in the old. One share of common would be offered for each ten shares of old. Total capitalization was to be 500,000 shares of common of no par value. In addition, 150,000 shares were to be sold at $10 per share, thereby raising needed capital with stockholders being given first preference. The plan was approved by stockholders in mid–December, but apparently no new capital was forthcoming and the new corporation never materialized.[20] On December 4, Jordan reported a loss of $677,083 for the first nine months of 1930.[21]

The ad offering the Jordan home for sale.

Jordan's engineering department must have been busy trying to design a new car. At least they were busy at something according to a letter sent to a manufacturing concern. No new cars had been announced since the Sunshine Sedan and Model Z made their appearance at the New York Show. The Model T and Great Line 90 would continue unchanged into the 1931 model year. By the beginning of 1931, Jordan was just about history. Very few if any cars were being made.

In early April another attempt was made to salvage the company, but little became of it. The Brotherhood of Locomotive Engineers was to purchase 30,000 shares of common stock at $10.00 per share. This was supposed to be a good will gesture on their part but it has never been explained why they would want to become involved or what their connection to Jordan was. In any event, no other capital was forthcoming and the deal never materialized.

Jordan entered into voluntary bankruptcy on May 8, 1931, upon the application of the Electric Auto Lite Company, a creditor. John McArdle, vice president, and former judge Adrian G. Newcomb were named as receivers by Judge Dempsey of the Common Pleas Court, Cleveland. The plant and equipment were valued at $900,000 and total debts at $422,800.[22]

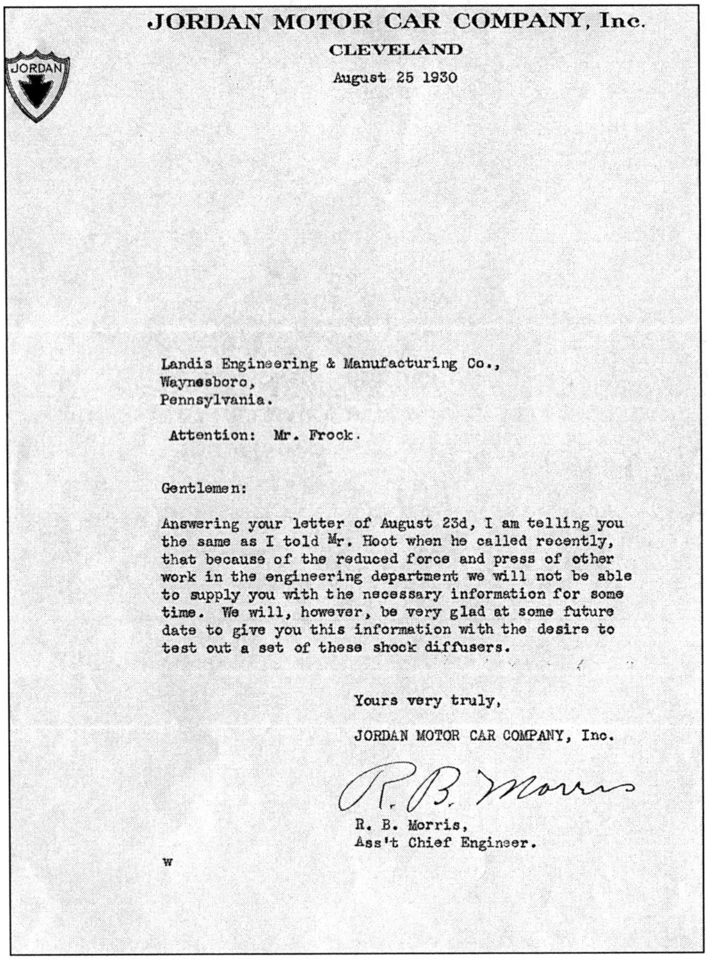

JORDAN MOTOR CAR COMPANY, Inc.
CLEVELAND

August 25 1930

Landis Engineering & Manufacturing Co.,
Waynesboro,
Pennsylvania.

Attention: Mr. Frock.

Gentlemen:

Answering your letter of August 23d, I am telling you the same as I told Mr. Hoot when he called recently, that because of the reduced force and press of other work in the engineering department we will not be able to supply you with the necessary information for some time. We will, however, be very glad at some future date to give you this information with the desire to test out a set of these shock diffusers.

Yours very truly,

JORDAN MOTOR CAR COMPANY, Inc.

R. B. Morris

R. B. Morris,
Ass't Chief Engineer.

W

This letter seems to offer evidence that the Jordan engineering department had been active to some extent well into 1930.

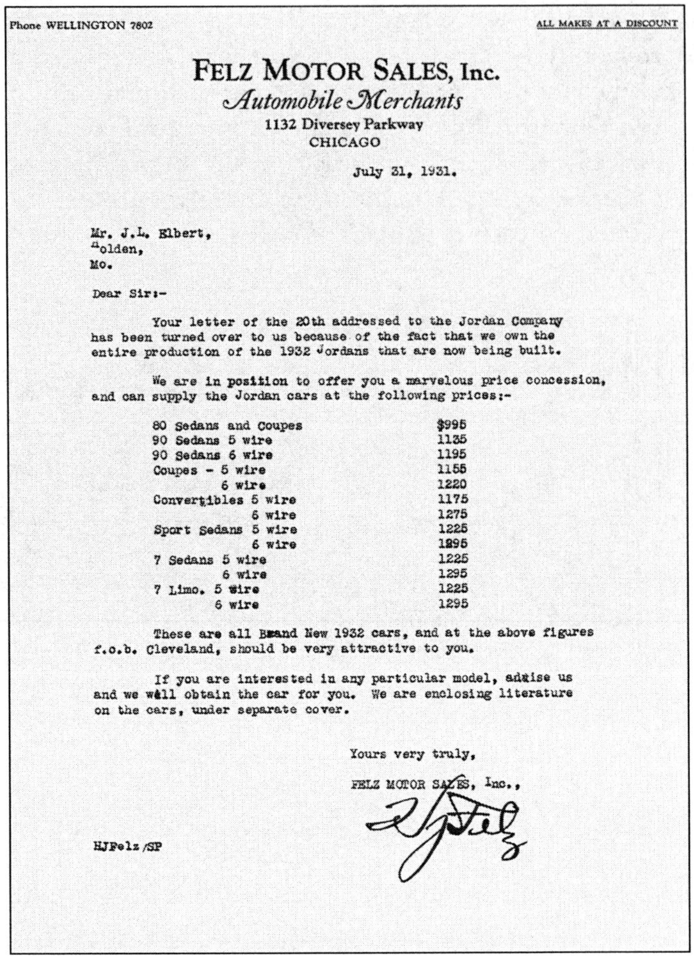

Phone WELLINGTON 7802 ALL MAKES AT A DISCOUNT

FELZ MOTOR SALES, Inc.
Automobile Merchants
1132 Diversey Parkway
CHICAGO

July 31, 1931.

Mr. J.L. Elbert,
Holden,
Mo.

Dear Sir:-

Your letter of the 20th addressed to the Jordan Company has been turned over to us because of the fact that we own the entire production of the 1932 Jordans that are now being built.

We are in position to offer you a marvelous price concession, and can supply the Jordan cars at the following prices:-

80 Sedans and Coupes	$995
90 Sedans 5 wire	1135
90 Sedans 6 wire	1195
Coupes - 5 wire	1155
6 wire	1220
Convertibles 5 wire	1175
6 wire	1275
Sport Sedans 5 wire	1225
6 wire	1295
7 Sedans 5 wire	1225
6 wire	1295
7 Limo. 5 wire	1225
6 wire	1295

These are all Brand New 1932 cars, and at the above figures f.o.b. Cleveland, should be very attractive to you.

If you are interested in any particular model, advise us and we will obtain the car for you. We are enclosing literature on the cars, under separate cover.

Yours very truly,

FELZ MOTOR SALES, Inc.,

HJFelz/SP

Felz did purchase the last of the Jordans, as this July 31, 1931, letter attests (courtesy Charles & Marlene Boles).

On July 28, Common Pleas Court Judge John B. Harris permitted the receivers to borrow $100,000 for the purpose of assembling 262 automobiles which were left over when the plant closed. Any money received would pay off the loan and the rest would go to creditors. Felz Motor Sales, Inc., of Chicago had contracted to purchase all the Model T and Great Line 90s which would be assembled. Felz specialized in this type of business and would sell the Jordan at a greatly reduced price.[23]

Since its inception Jordan had produced between 65,000 and 80,000 cars. According to Ned, they had produced more than 80,000. Even the higher figure was tiny compared to some other companies, but Ned Jordan's way of doing business left an indelible impression upon the industry forever. Jordan was only one of many worthy companies to meet a sad end in the Depression.

John McArdle and several other Jordan executives purchased the Jordan name and all remaining parts and inventory of the now defunct company. Their intentions were to form a new company which would be known as Jordan Motors.[24] In the meantime they formed the Jordan Automobile Parts and Service Company and continued to sell replacement parts and give service out of the original factory. They lingered in Cleveland until 1934 and then moved to Indianapolis, where they merged with a similar company selling Stutz and Velie parts. This lasted until at least 1938 and then they were gone. Stutz and Velie were not bad companies but they had suffered the same fate as Jordan.[25]

On September 22, 1932, the plant and assets of Jordan Motor Car Company were sold to Apex Electrical Manufacturing Company of Cleveland for the sum of $150,880. The Apex factory was directly across the street from the Jordan factory, and the company had been looking for a larger building to house their expanding business.[26]

The receivers had been in court trying to halt the

collection of past due real estate and personal property taxes, but Judge Samuel E. Kramer overruled these attempts and ordered that all past taxes would have to be paid before creditors received any money.[27] Creditors did eventually receive 15 cents to the dollar on their claims.[28]

Late in 1932 John McArdle, along with former judge Adrian G. Newcomb, a receiver for the old company, and several other former Jordan executives did attempt to revive Jordan Motors, Inc., as a manufacturer, intending to keep a plant in Cleveland and build medium priced automobiles, starting with a 1933 model. Also involved were former Jordan treasurer A.F. England and production manager Harvey Buckner, who were slated to keep their former positions in the new company. Joseph C. Little was to be a director along with John F. Sweeney. Sweeney was a partner in Sweeney & James Co., advertising agents, who did the old company's advertising and who would handle the new account, and for whom Ned Jordan was then working. Nothing was said about what Ned would have to do with the new company, if anything.

Parts and service catalog, 1931.

Having purchased the Jordan name, factory tools and equipment along with the parts inventory, they would have been in excellent position to continue the company, but business conditions were so bad that investors could see no future in a new automobile business, and the company never materialized. This was the last attempt to save the formerly great automobile manufacturer.[29]

The saga of Ned Jordan is not unlike that of many others. He started with nothing, became a millionaire and ended up with nothing. What he did in between is significant.

On the personal level Ned could be as warm and gentle as a spring breeze but could also be belligerent and aloof. Ned adored his children and was at first a good father and husband. It was not until the company became successful and he spent most of his time away from home that those relationships began to deteriorate. The children had many warm accounts of Christmas, hunting and fishing, watching the circus parades and driving to their summer home in Rhode Island. Success has its rewards but it sometimes brings agony. So it was with the Jordan family.

Ned was considerate of his employees and associates, displaying great acts of charity and kindness. He was an aspiring poet and had a great sense of humor, was honest to a fault and always strived to produce the best automobile for the price possible. He was an excellent salesman, an advertising genius and a good public relations man.

So why did Ned's marriage and company fail? No one large problem but a series of smaller ones caused its demise. Ned traveled about eight or ten months out of the year. He neglected his family, packing the children off to private schools. The few summer months he spent with them could not overcome the many months of neglect. While Ned was away, Charlotte too, was traveling the world. Months away from home don't do much for domestic bliss. Ned started drinking heavily. Too many meetings and customer relations bashes began to take their toll. He reputedly had a great fondness for the ladies, a combination that does not mix well with business.

Jordan's best year was 1925. The company tried to expand during 1926, but the automobile market was becoming saturated and the large manufacturers were beginning to put pressure on the smaller ones. Jordan was stuck with several thousand cars they could not sell. Jordan got through its first mistake, but the decision to produce a small car would have disastrous consequences. The Little Custom was announced in late 1926, but production was held up for months and dealers did not get deliveries until May 1927. Whether this was a calculated act to allow the 1926 models to be sold or was a genuine production delay made little difference as the results were catastrophic. The small car would not sell and Jordan's line of large ones (the Model JE, first version) wasn't doing well either. A redesign of the Little Custom into the Cross Country Six and changes to the JE had little effect.

Things were going downhill fast. Someone took stock of the situation and began efforts to stabilize the company. New money was brought in but with it came the bankers who would also take control. They brought in their own people to run the company and Ned was shuffled aside. He was still president but had little to say about the decisions which were being made. By late 1928 things were looking a little better, and for 1929 two new cars were designed. The Model G incorporated all the latest in automobile engineering and the smaller six cylinder Model E would be virtually the same. By July the Model G had been improved and called the Great Line Ninety and a smaller eight cylinder version would be announced as the Model T. These changes did perk the finances up a bit, but when the Depression hit in November it was the death blow. The Model U and Z, introduced for 1930, never sold at all and only added to Jordan's already troubled financial situation.

Jordan might have survived had the economy not collapsed. But the economy did collapse and many of their suppliers were in trouble too. Without a steady source of supply, it becomes very hard to manufacture an assembled car. New suppliers would not extend credit to a company that was already broke.

The company might have survived in some capacity, had it merged with Peerless or Pierce Arrow.

The Great Line Ninety was probably the best car Jordan ever made. The engine was sufficient and steering, ride and brakes were superior to anything they had made previously. By the time of its introduction, though, Jordan was too small and too weak, financially, to weather the Depression. They joined a long list of other automobile manufacturers who suffered the same fate.

Top, left: Sport Marine ad from 1918. *Top, right:* The first Playboy ad for the motoring public, attributed to *Vanity Fair*, May 1919. *Above:* 1919 Model F Seven Passenger Touring (courtesy George and Lana Kline).

Top, left: The first color ad for the Blue Boy appeared in November 1922. *Top, right:* A colorful ad from 1923. *Above:* The 1923 Model MX Playboy owned and restored by the author (courtesy *Car & Parts* magazine).

Front view of the author's 1923 Model MX Playboy (photograph by Jack Hearld).

Top: 1923 Model MX Playboy owned by Gary Hein (courtesy of owner). *Above, left:* Dashboard of the author's 1923 Model MX Playboy. *Above, right:* Driver's door toolkit in the author's 1923 Model MX Playboy (courtesy *Car & Parts* magazine).

Top, left: A 1924 ad from *House and Garden* showing the Model K Playboy. *Top, right:* The "Land of Fire" ad from 1924 showed Jordan advertising at its finest. *Above, left:* Cover of a 16-page brochure for the Model A Great Line Ninety, circa late 1924 or early 1925. *Above, right:* A 1926 brochure for the Line Eight Sedan.

Clockwise from top left: 1924 Model L Touring Sedan owned by Ray Unsworth (courtesy the owner); 1925 Model A Great Line Eight Touring (courtesy Barbara Hughes); 1926 J Playboy owned by the late Allan MacNicol with Skip Loose at the wheel, Bob Boyd in the passenger seat and Allan MacNicol in the rumble seat (courtesy Allan and Shirley MacNicol); 1926 Model J Sedan owned by Jules and Terry Baron (courtesy the owners); second version of the "Somewhere West of Laramie" ad, August 1923.

Top, left: 1926 Model J Sedan owned by Jess and Peggy Jordan (courtesy the owners). *Top, right:* 1926 Model J Sedan owned by Les and Tracy Lunceford (courtesy the owners). *Bottom:* Model J Victoria ad, circa 1926–1927.

Top, left: A May 1927 ad for the Little Tomboy. *Top, right:* 1927 brochure for the Line Eight Playboy. *Above, left:* A November 1927 ad for the Model R Little Custom Jordan Sport Salon. *Above, right:* The 1927 ad that inspired a second complaint from the New York Society for the Suppression of Vice.

Top: 1927 Model R Little Custom Tomboy (courtesy Dale and Jill Robinson who owned the car at the time the photograph was taken). *Bottom:* 1927 Model J1 Custom Victoria, sporting three-tone paintwork, owned by Dan and Tracy Jordan (courtesy of owners).

Top: 1927 Model J1 Playboy with Janie Bentley at the wheel (courtesy Olan and Janie Bentley; car now owned by Lee Korthals). *Bottom:* 1928 Model R Little Custom Jordan owned by Joel and Sunnie Andress (courtesy of owners).

Jordan's last ad, for the 1929 Model G Great Line Ninety Playboy, August 1929.

Top: 1929 Model JE Sedan, owned by Art and Dee Worledge at the time of this photograph and now owned by Caroline Kline (courtesy Art and Dee Worledge). *Bottom:* 1929 Model G Playboy Roadster owned by Art and Dee Worledge (courtesy of owners).

Top: 1929 Model G Sedan (courtesy George and Lana Kline). *Right:* 1928 Model J1 Sedan (courtesy Horst W. Jordan, Bochum, Germany). *Below, left to right:* Dealer's promotional bell, early hubcap, Jordan part box (all courtesy Duey and Alice Anderson).

Top: 1930 Model G Great Line Ninety Speedboy owned by Anson "Skip" Loose and Jackie Loose (courtesy the owners). *Bottom:* 1930–31 Great Line Ninety Coupe with Irvin C. Leach at the wheel (courtesy Irvin C. and Wilma Leach).

Cover of Model Z advertising brochure.

Top: Dash of the 1931 Great Line Ninety owned by Anson "Skip" and Jackie Loose (courtesy the owners). *Bottom:* 1932 Model G Great Line Ninety Coupe owned by Howard Sorensen (courtesy the owner; photograph by Joel Andress).

Eleven

Aftermath

When the Jordan Motor Car Company went broke, Ned himself was in a sad financial condition and his mental state was just as bad. He had reputedly spent the last few years tending to extracurricular activities and paying little attention to anything else. His marriage was over, the mansion he had called home for 11 years was gone, his family had all but abandoned him, the automobile empire he had worked so hard to make successful had collapsed and his personal fortune had dwindled to practically nothing.

He finally decided to leave Cleveland and headed to Tucson, Arizona, where his daughter Jane (now Mrs. Jane Graham) and her husband lived. She was expecting Ned's first grandchild and he stayed around until after the birth of his granddaughter, named for her mother, on April 16, 1931. Having grown bored at having nothing to do,[1] Ned became acquainted with Ben Tinker, a big game hunter from Tucson who knew a lot about Mexico, and decided to go hunting and fishing. Ned had hunted and fished most of the United States and Canada but never Mexico. Tinker knew someone in El Paso, Texas, who owned a plane but had no money with which to fly. Ned put up the money and away they flew to Chihuahua, Mexico. They hunted, fished, and hobnobbed with the natives and with the Mormon people who had settled there until Ned again became restless and they headed back to Arizona.[2]

Ned took Jane, her husband and the baby to Hollywood, California, for a vacation and they toured the movie city and surrounding area for a few weeks.[3] Ned was again becoming restless at having nothing to do. While bumming around the Los Angeles area he met a broker who had lost his fortune but managed to keep his yacht. Ned put up the money for groceries and gas and they headed down the California coast, fishing as they went. They ended up in Ecuador, then sailed over to the Galapagos Islands and eventually back to California.[4]

After playing golf on every course in the Los Angeles area, Ned became bored again and decided to head for New York City. He caught a plane at Glendale but was grounded by a snowstorm in Salt Lake City. Ned and a salesman for the Grasselli Chemical Company wrangled a ride on a mail plane headed for Cheyenne. Weather again grounded them, this time at Rock Springs, Wyoming. Disgusted, Ned called Carlie Downing of Cody, took a train, went up and spent the winter at Buffalo Bill's old ranch. He stored a lot of his personal belongings and memorabilia in a building at the ranch, which supposedly later burned, explaining why he had nothing left in later years.[5]

When spring came Ned headed for Billings, Montana, where he caught a plane bound for Chicago. Chicago was only a short stop before he headed for Cleveland.[6] On April 1, 1932, he was the speaker for the luncheon of the Cleveland Advertising Club meeting at the Hotel Statler. He had returned to Cleveland to take a job with Sweeney & James, the advertising agent that had handled much of the publicity for the Jordan Motor Car Company.[7] What money he had left after the collapse of the Jordan company was now exhausted, forcing him to return to earning a living by working for someone else. The position at Sweeney & James lasted for a couple of years; then, on December 15, 1934, Ned was named a special sales representative of the Studebaker Sales Corporation of South Bend, Indiana.[8]

Ned's sister, Minnie Estelle Jordan Miller, who had resided in San Francisco for only three months, had died on June 22, 1930. On September 18, 1834, her remain were returned to Merrill, Wisconsin, for internment. Her sister Anne, who also lived in California, accompanied the remains to Merrill. After the burial in the family plot at the local cemetery, Anne journeyed to Chicago and stayed with friends while she made plans for her return to California. On Friday, October 5, she was suddenly stricken by a fatal heart attack. Her remains were returned to Merrill where she was buried in the same plot as her family.[9] Another sister, Blanche Edith Jordan Berndt, died on November 9, 1951. She had lived in San Rafael, California, for several years.

Ned worked at Studebaker Sales for only a short time before heading for New York to take a job with the Warren McArthur Corporation. Warren McArthur and his brother Charles had been Jordan dealers in Arizona during the good years of the Jordan Motor Car Company. Subsequently Warren McArthur had gotten into the manufacturing business and was a maker of stylish aluminum furniture.

On May 29, 1935, Ned and Apolina Anderson Wilson, M.D., were married.[10] They had met while Ned was employed at Studebaker in South Bend. Born in Newfoundland, where her father was Superintendent of Schools, she was Assistant Superintendent of Healthwin Hospital in South Bend when she and Ned met.[11] She had received her medical training at the University of Edinburgh, Scotland, and had a year of training at the Women's Medical College of Philadelphia.[12] Ned and Apolina resided in New York for at least four years. They were blessed with the birth of a daughter, Kate Wilson Jordan, on April 21, 1939.[13]

Ned and his young daughter Kate, circa 1942 (courtesy Kate Jordan Wallace).

The McArthur Corporation got into the production of aluminum aircraft seats during World War II and had a factory in Bantam, Connecticut. The Jordan family ended up living at nearby Litchfield while Ned worked at the factory in Bantam.

Ned wrote a small book, *The Inside Story of Adam and Eve*, during the summer of 1945. The book was published by Howard Coggeshall of Utica, New York.[14]

Sometime in 1945 Ned and Apolina separated, and she filed for divorce March 14, 1946. On January 10, 1947, after a hearing of the Superior Court for Litchfield County, a divorce was granted. Ned apparently was working for Howard Coggeshall at the time as his address was Utica, New York.[15]

Apolina and Kate remained in Litchfield but Ned ended up in New York City where he worked for McArthur Advertising Corporation, owned by Charles H. McArthur, brother of Ned's former employer Warren McArthur. Charles had helped pioneer 3-D advertising, and Ned supposedly did some great promotion work while employed there. McArthur Advertising supposedly had the first contract for advertising in Grand Central Station and had their headquarters there. Ned was employed by McArthur as late as 1952.[16]

Ned started writing a column entitled "With Ned Jordan" in *Automotive News* on March 27, 1950. It was largely chit-chat about scattered but mostly automotive topics. Occasionally his column contained some good information about his youth and all that transpired during the time he went to college, worked as a newspaper reporter, worked for Jeffery and ran the Jordan Motor Car Company. This column continued weekly for several years and then appeared infrequently for a while, as late as May 1958.[17]

Ned and daughter Jane both lived in New York City during the 1950s and saw each other frequently.

Jane had been employed as an executive in public relations by the U.S. Army and the Office of Price Administration during World War II. She later handled membership promotion for the National Association of Manufacturers. In 1951, she was appointed public relations director of the National Organization for Public Health Nursing. Then on February 25, 1952, she was named the public relations director for the American Nursing Association (ANA), headquartered in New York City.[18]

Ned and Kate with pet rabbit, circa 1942 (courtesy Kate Jordan Wallace).

Jane's daughter, whose name was also Jane ("Jane Jr." was Ned's name for her), went to London on an acting scholarship in the 1950s. There she met Bernard Horsfall, an aspiring Shakespearean actor, whom she married. They had three children. They still live in London and have homes in several countries.[19]

Ned was occasionally invited to speak at automotive functions. He addressed the Antique Automobile Club of America at their annual meeting in Philadelphia on February 17, 1951, and thrilled the crowd with his tales of newspaper reporting and automobile manufacturing.[20] On Sunday, January 27, 1952, Ned was the speaker for the Ohio Region Antique Automobile Club of America's annual dinner at their midwinter meeting held in Cleveland. He and the others assembled for the meeting were guests of the Thompson Antique Auto Museum at a gala event on the Saturday night preceding the meeting.[21] On April 5, 1952, Ned was toastmaster for the 50th Anniversary Celebration of the Automobile in Kenosha. Nash Motors, the successor to Rambler-Jeffery, threw a big party for their employees and dignitaries. Ned was in fine form according to one report.[22]

After that the invitations to speak were few and far between. Ned continued to write his column for *Automotive News* but did little else. His drinking, which he had controlled for a few years, started getting worse and he lived in cheap hotels in the run-down part of the city.

The man who had been so full of life, who worked his way through high school and college, who set trends in advertising which endure to this day and who rose to prominence as the head of his own automobile empire, had bottomed out.

He had a series of strokes which began to incapacitate him and entered into the care of the Bert S. Coler Hospital on Welfare Island, New York, on May 22, 1956. He was in and out of the hospital for a while but soon entered for good. By then the wheels had all run down, the leaves had all turned brown and the "gazoom-pah"—Ned's work for having what it takes—was gone. He passed quietly away on December 30, 1958. In compliance with his wishes, his daughter Jane had his remains cremated.[23] A few automobile publications and some newspapers reported the passing.

His memory lives on with every Jordan car that survives. The Jordan Register, a group of enthusiasts who are devoted to the collecting, preservation and restoration of Jordan automobiles, is very active in the twenty-first century.

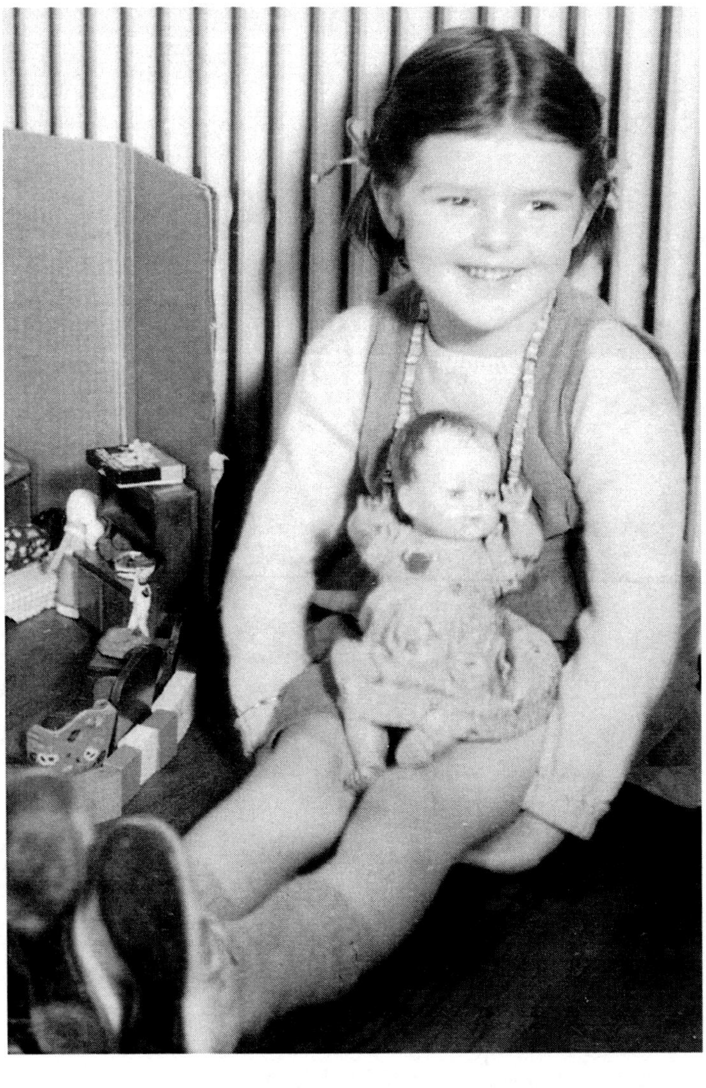

Kate with doll and toys, circa 1942 (courtesy Kate Jordan Wallace).

Ned and Kate mowing the lawn, circa 1942 (courtesy Kate Jordan Wallace).

The Model Z has been recognized as a true classic by the Classic Car Club of America for many years. Recently, through the efforts of Anson "Slip" Loose of Manheim, Pennsylvania, the Model G and Great Line Ninety have been accorded that status also. A fitting tribute to Ned Jordan.

The author started a search for Ned's survivors in the 1970s with little success. By the 1990s some progress was being made, but it was not until the Internet had become popular that the search yielded results.

Janie Jordan Bentley of Washington Court House, Ohio, became interested in the genealogy of the family and we started comparing notes. The author traced Ned's daughter Kate to Wellesley, Massachusetts, but

Kate Jordan Wallace in 2002.

had trouble finding her. Janie Bentley came up with a phone number for someone who we thought might be the right person.

After calling several times with no answer the author finally succeeded in making the connection. Kate Jordan Wallace's husband is a professor at Wellesley College, but Kate resides in the Dominican Republic where she gives tours for tourists who journey there to see the many species of birds native to that area. Richard Wallace gave the author her e-mail address, and with great nervousness, we wrote to explain who we were and what we were doing. The e-mail ended with the statement, "I have been looking for you for thirty years." Two days later came a reply: "I have been waiting for thirty years."

After Kate's mother and father were divorced she and Apolina stayed on in Litchfield, Connecticut. Kate entered Viewpoint School in Amenia, New York, at an early age and graduated in 1956.

She occasionally visited her father who was working for McArthur Advertising in New York City. She graduated from Bryn Mawr College in Bryn Mawr, Pennsylvania, with a degree in art history in 1960 and received her master's degree in education from Wheelock College in Boston in 1977.

She married Richard Wallace on December 16, 1962, in Rome, Italy. Richard William Wallace, Ph.D., is now a professor of art history at Wellesley College in Wellesley, Massachusetts. Kate and Richard have two children, David Andrew Wallace and Maria Susan Wallace, and are the grandparents of Caspian Oake Wallace.[24]

Kate was planning to fly to the United States in August 2002, and a get-together was planned. After arriving at Wellesley she was planning to drive cross country to see their son in Corvallis, Oregon. The author and his wife met her at the home of Olan and Janie Bentley in Ohio. Kate proved to be a lovely person and very outgoing. She knew very little of the Jordan Company and had only seen one Jordan car in her lifetime.

After staying with the Bentleys for a few days and seeing their Playboy she journeyed on to Oregon. Leaving Oregon by way of California she visited with Art Worledge at Yuba City and Dan Jordan at Chino Hills. Both have Jordans (Dan has many) and she got a ride in several. Then she pushed on to New Orleans where she presented a paper before a convention of ornithologists. After riding out a hurricane she journeyed to the home of the author and his wife in Huntington, West Virginia, where she spent several days.

Plans were then made to get her to the AACA show at Hershey, Pennsylvania, on October 12. On that Saturday morning she rode with pride onto the field in Skip Loose's 1930 Jordan Speedboy. That night she was the dinner guest of the officers of the Jordan Register. She has now returned to the Dominican Republic to resume her career.

Charlotte (Lottie) Eva Hannahs Jordan lived to the age of 98 and died at South Kingstown, Rhode Island, on June 4, 1981, not far from the summer home she and her family shared during the good years of the Jordan Company.

Apolina Anderson Wilson Jordan lived to the age of 84 and died on January 14, 1981, at Canaan, Connecticut.[25]

John Stanlaw "Jack" Jordan, along with his sisters, Jane and Joan, had attended the Hathaway Brown School in East Cleveland. He later graduated from Shaw High School in East Cleveland and went on to college at the Massachusetts Institute of Technology, graduating in 1928 with a degree in electrical engineering. He later worked for the Pullman Company and had a career in railroading. He married and had two sons, Patrick Edward and Dennis Allan. Jack passed away on October 18, 1982, in El Paso, Texas.

Jane Jordan went on to high school at Choate School in Brookline, Massachusetts, graduating in 1926. Having been afflicted with tuberculosis as a child, she spent a lot of time in the Southwest because the climate was favorable to her health. There she learned to love horses, Indians and rodeos. She entered the university of Arizona for the fall semester in 1927. She later married her Cleveland boyfriend, Robert Graham. They had two children, Jane and Robert. Their marriage ended in divorce and she later married Curtis C. Rogers, but this marriage would also end in divorce. Jane was employed in the New York area in the 1940s and would stay there until she moved to London where she passed away in February 1980.

Joan Jordan followed her sister Jane to Choate School and later studied art. In the fall of 1929, she eloped and married William McCaw the day before she sailed for Paris where she was to pursue her career in art. She took her Model G Speedboy along. Her husband stayed behind to finish his senior year at Dartmouth. Joan returned to the United States the following spring, resumed her marriage and had two daughters, Sandy and Kathryn (Kitty). She passed away on June 20, 1981, just 16 days after the death of her mother. Her husband William lived until September 26, 1987.[26]

The author has made contact with some survivors from Ned's first marriage, who supplied much of this information. They did not wish to have their privacy invaded and those wishes will be respected.

TWELVE

Advertising

Much has been made of Jordan advertising, and justly so, but in the beginning their ads were as bland as everyone else's.

Months before the first car was successfully launched, the trade magazines were giving Jordan a steady stream of free publicity. This was by design as such publications depended on advertising for their existence, and favorable treatment of a manufacturer in the news sections substantially increased the likelihood of receiving paid advertising.

The first ad appeared in *Motor Age* and *The Automobile* on July 6, 1916. Automobile dealers, repair garages, parts and accessory manufacturers were the readers of these publications. As Jordan needed distributors and dealers as soon as possible, this was a good way to attract them.

The first ad gave no indication as to the identity of the new company, but the Jordan Arrowhead was prominently displayed in bright red and readers could write for details in care of either magazine.

The next week's ad was practically the same but on July 20 *The Automobile* carried an eight page insert entitled "The Realization of a Great Ideal" and this time the Jordan name appeared in the circle with the arrowhead.

The trade ads appeared frequently until September when the *Saturday Evening Post* carried the first ad designed for the motoring public. Black and white was the standard mode of printing in 1916 and Jordan was no different from anyone else. The *Post* ad gave a glowing description of the new car, its qualities and price. Also mentioned were the manufacturers of the parts from which the Jordan was built.

The first ad listed only three open models, and it would be three months before the closed cars made their appearance. On November 18, 1916, the Sedan, Coupe and Limousine joined the Seven Passenger Luxury Touring, Sport Four and Roadster in the lineup. The *Post* carried the news that an addition to the factory, as large as the original building, would soon be built.

The *Post* dominated Jordan publicity for the first 16 months, but the *Literary Digest* would soon supplant it for the next year and a half. After that, advertising would be spread around among several publications. The company was making money by now and could afford to be more liberal in their publicity.

The first ad to break the black and white mould would appear in a January 1918 issue of an unknown magazine and in *The Atlantic Monthly* for February 1918. The Sport Marine made its appearance in full color at that time but thereafter would be doomed to the black and white fate. Factory brochures would be of the same color and content.

New models would be shown as they were introduced, with some getting an amazing amount of publicity, but full color advertising would be four years away with only halftones with full color thrown in occasionally.

On April 17, 1919, the New Silhouette cars made their appearance in *Motor Age* in a teaser ad with no Jordan name attached. This four color ad would soon be followed by a similar one introducing the Playboy Roadster and the rest of the Jordan lineup, but the ads would eventually revert to black and white for several more months. About this time a full color ad attributed to *Vanity Fair* announced the Playboy, which was displayed in a bright red-orange color with excellent accompanying text. Ned said this was his best ad and the author would not disagree. By now Jordan was using several publications to carry their advertising,

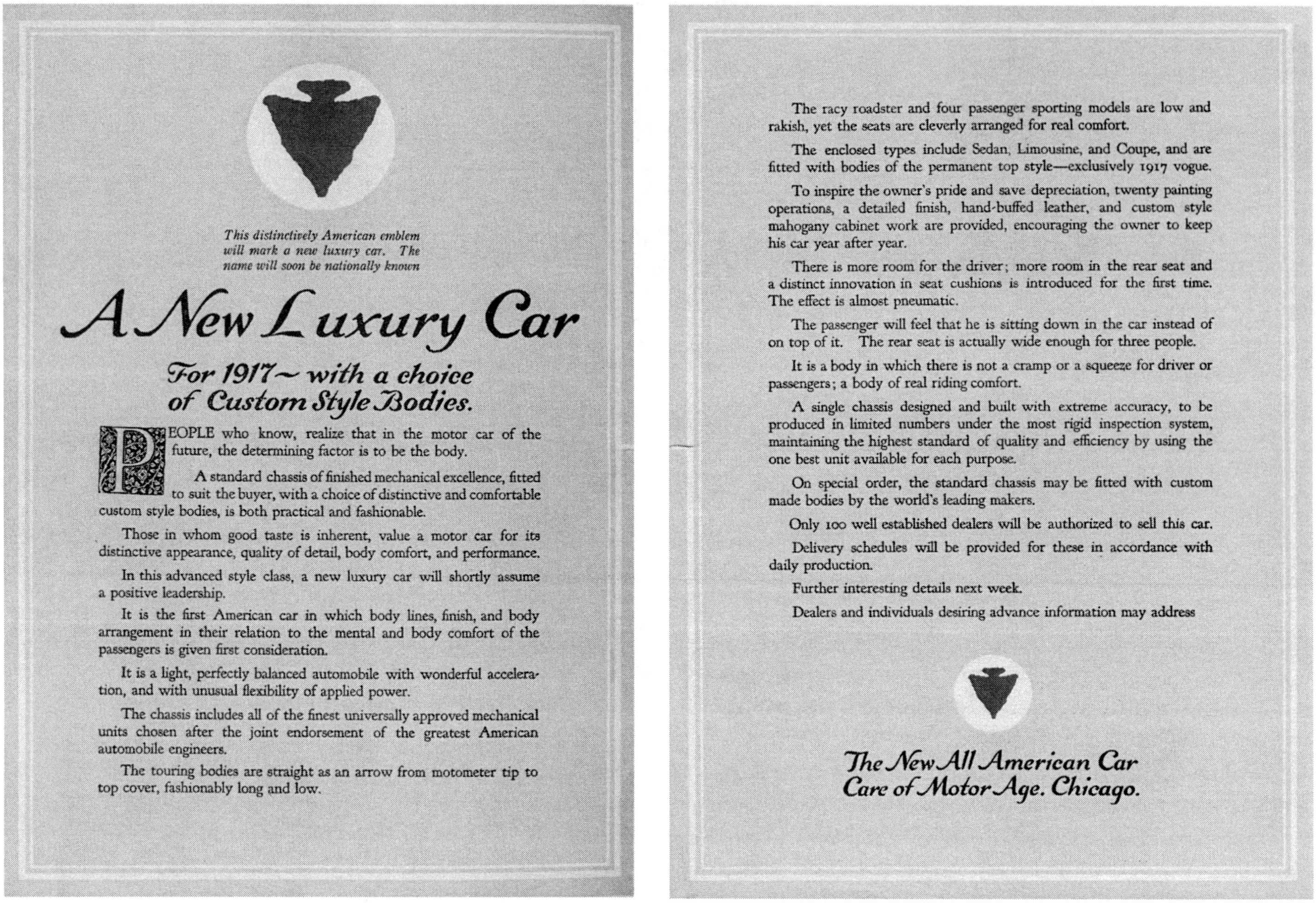

Jordan's first ad, from July 1916.

but the *Saturday Evening Post* was the major beneficiary.

At this time a series of ads for the Silhouette started appearing in four colors. The car would appear in silhouette form with an aqua or blue background. At the bottom of the page would be a drawing of a street scene from a major American city (or in one case London). New York's Fifth Avenue, Chicago, San Francisco, Philadelphia, Washington, D.C., Cleveland, Detroit and Boston would all be featured.

Several beautiful full color advertisements appeared in *Vogue* during 1919, but it would be 1922 before full color would again be featured.

One of Jordan's most infamous ads appeared in November 1922. The ad titled "Port of Missing Men," featured in the *Literary Digest*, *Saturday Evening Post*, and *The Country Gentleman*, landed Ned in hot water with the New York Society for the Suppression of Vice. He promised to reform but six years later he would again be called on to tone down his work.[1]

Starting in January 1922, Jordan advertising took a turn for the better. The ad would appear as usual, but at the bottom of the page a beautiful scenic view would appear accompanied by a remarque. These scenes featured the Grand Canyon, several western scenes, seashores, rivers, lakes and various other views. In the author's opinion, the drawings and remarques were better than the ads which were still fairly dull.

With the September 16, 1922, edition of the *Post*, Jordan's advertising suddenly perked up and ads were now aimed at women and young people. Someone, presumably Ned, had decided that women wielded great influence when it came to purchasing a new car and catered to their desires. Add the young generation and a ready made market was at hand.

Ads with titles of "Every Woman Loves This Car," "The Women Will Decide," "Any Woman Can Tell," "What Every Woman Wants," "When She Comes Home," "Off to the Land of Over Yonder," "A Million Miles from Dull Care," "The Promise of Happy Days,"

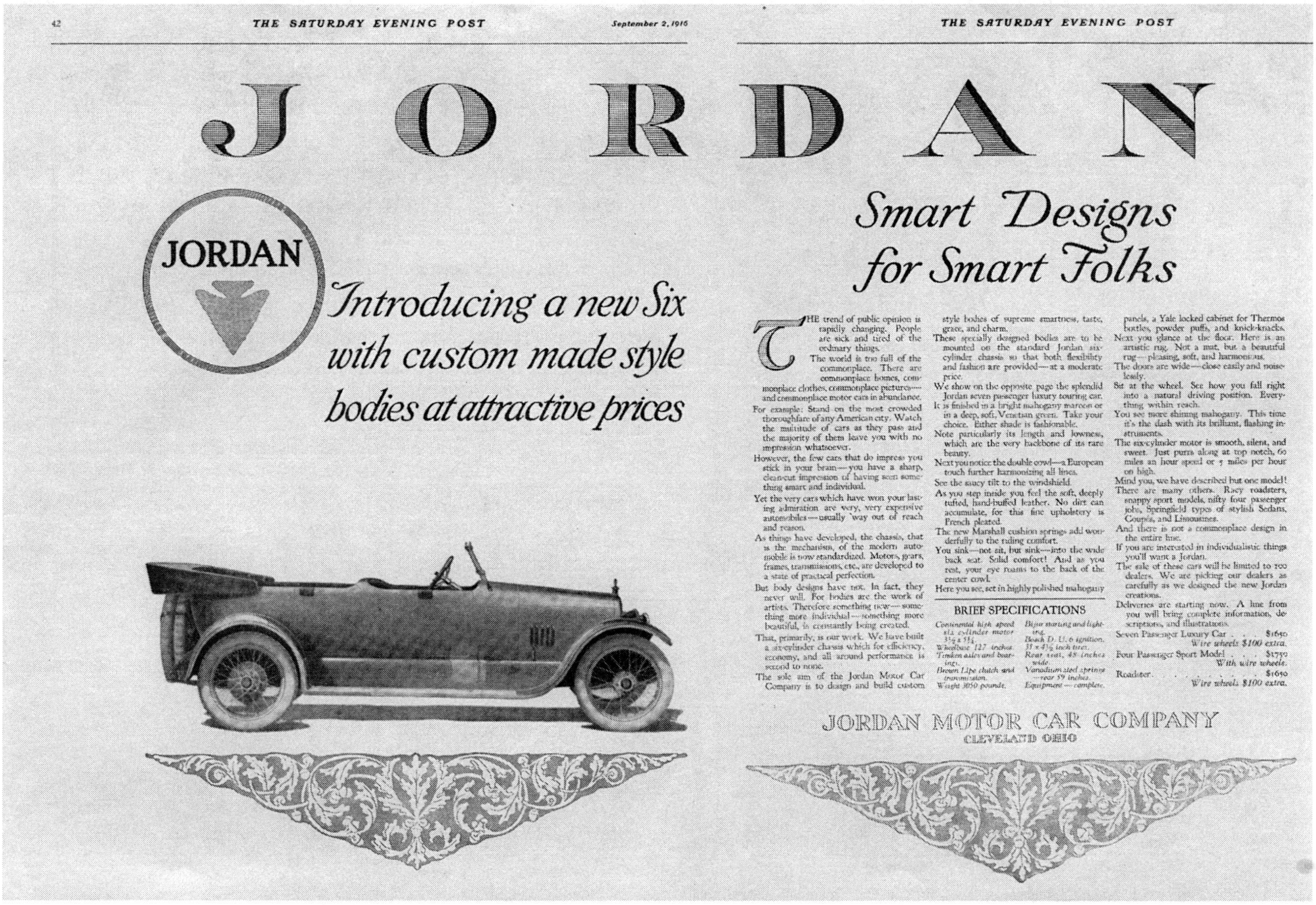

Jordan's first ad intended for the motoring public, September 1916.

"The Vagabond Days Have Come" and "It's Vacation Time in Arcady" dominated Jordan's advertising for 16 months.

Full color made its appearance once again with "The Jordan Blue Boy" in Blue Devil Blue appearing in *House and Garden* in November 1922. Several other color ads followed.

On June 23, 1923, the *Saturday Evening Post* carried an ad that would immortalize Jordan forever. "Somewhere West of Laramie" was a sensation that would be considered one of the best pieces of advertising copy ever written. From that day forth, Jordan would be synonymous with "West of Laramie." This same ad appeared in *The American Magazine* a couple of months later and a full color version, though slightly changed and with the car going in the opposite direction, appeared in two other high quality publications about the same time. This ad probably accounted for half of Jordan sales for a few years.

After "Laramie," full color was used occasionally, but it would be March 1924 before it would be featured prominently. At that time a series of ads aimed at the young and affluent began to appear. "A Golden Girl from Somewhere," "Pay Off the Grinning Caddy" and "I Think She Came from a Land of Fire" were beautiful renditions in both color and content. Add to this "After All—It's the Way You Feel" and "Your Children's Opportunity" which were carried in the *Post* and a brilliant run of advertising was evident.

Things got dull again with the introduction of the 1925 models, but the scenes and remarques reappeared at the bottom of the page and rescued them. A series of full page, full color renditions of the Model A Great Line Eights were featured in early 1925.

The 1926 Model J was treated about the same as the Model A, but some great ads by artist Fred Cole, who had done "Laramie," started appearing in February. The Playboy got the largest share but the Sedan was also featured prominently. "I Am the Playboy" was featured in a bright red in one high quality magazine

and also in blue in the *Saturday Evening Post* of April 3, 1926. *Vanity Fair, House and Garden* and the *Saturday Evening Post* were now carrying most, if not all, Jordan advertising.

Early in 1927 Ned was again called on the carpet for corrupting the morals of the nation's young people. An ad entitled "In the Middle of the Night" appeared in the January issue of *House and Garden* and one other magazine. The Society for the Suppression of Vice did not care for such advertising and wrote Ned another editorial admonishing him to exercise better supervision over his advertising department. This time he did not apologize.[2]

In December 1926, to announce production of a small car to be called the "Little Custom,"[3] Jordan did a series of ads in the *Post* and other magazines. Though full color, these were not nearly as attractive as earlier ads. The Little Custom never got off the ground as production delays held up delivery until May, by which time Jordan's financial position was so precarious that advertising virtually stopped. A couple of ads appeared after that and then it was virtually over. Not a single ad

***Left:* An early ad for Jordan's closed cars, September 1916. *Below:* Jordan Success ad, September 1917.**

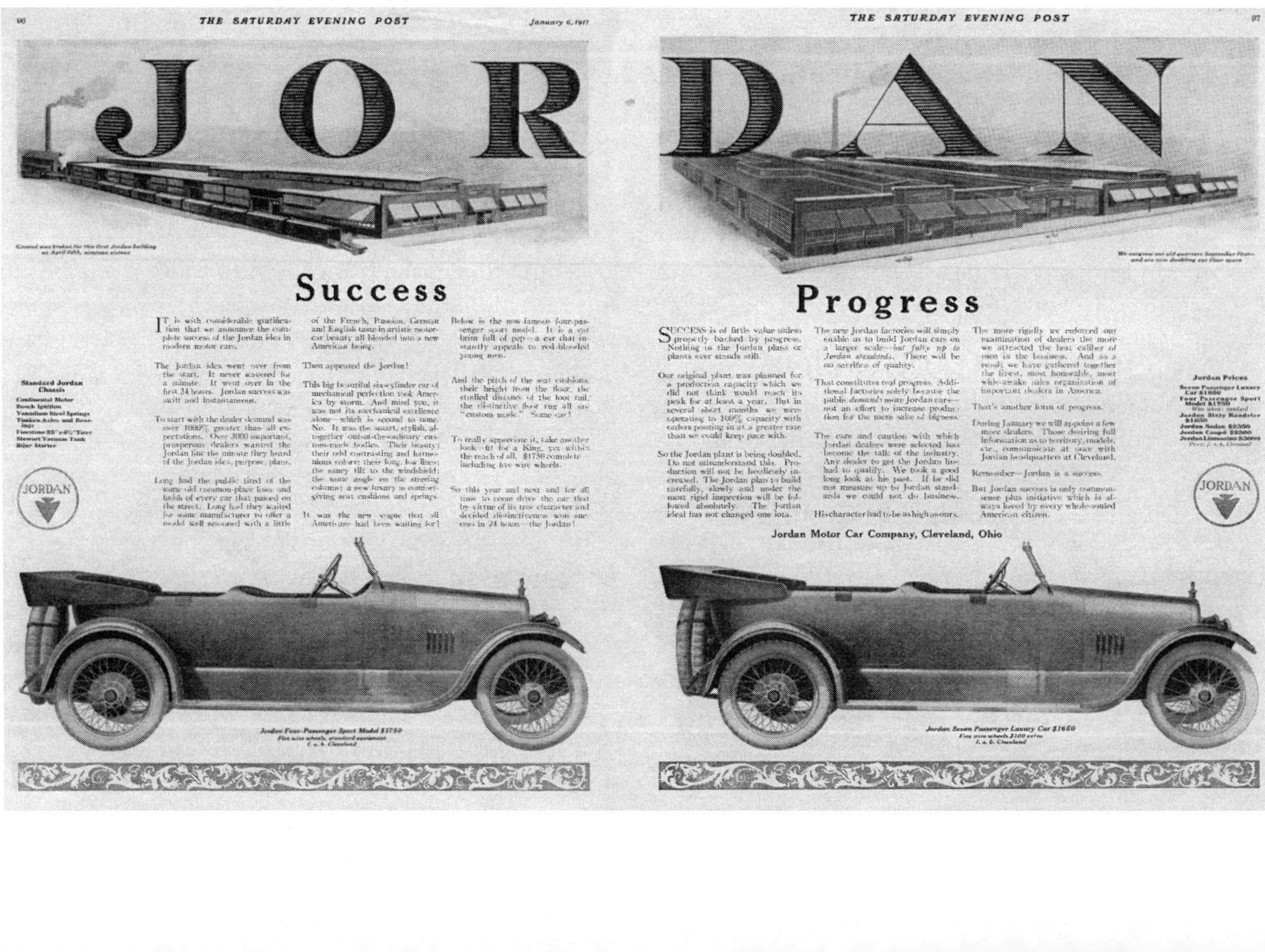

Top, left: Jordan's first color ad appeared in the *Atlantic Monthly* in February 1918. *Top right:* Sport Marine ad, December 1917. *Bottom, left:* A May 1918 ad for the Suburban Seven, the seven passenger companion to the Sport Marine. *Bottom, right:* January 1919 ad for the Jordan Brougham.

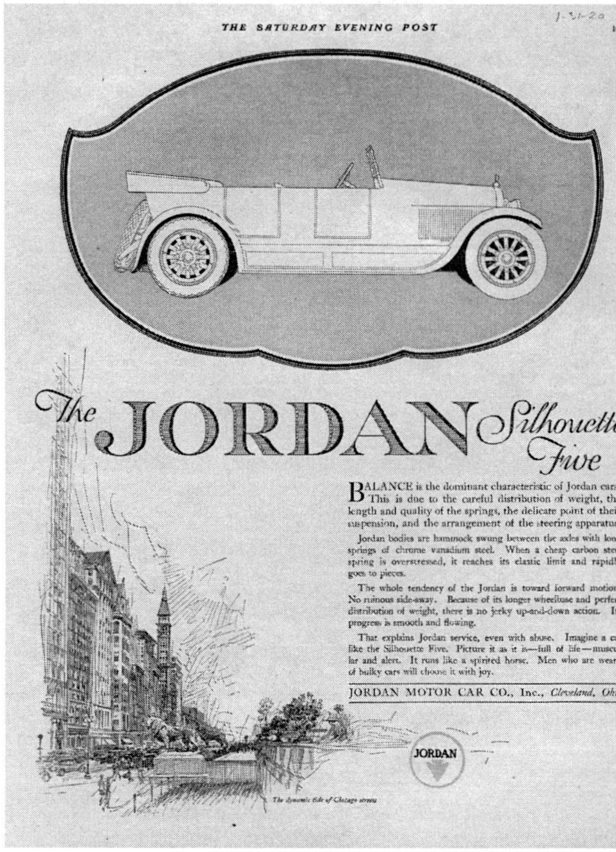

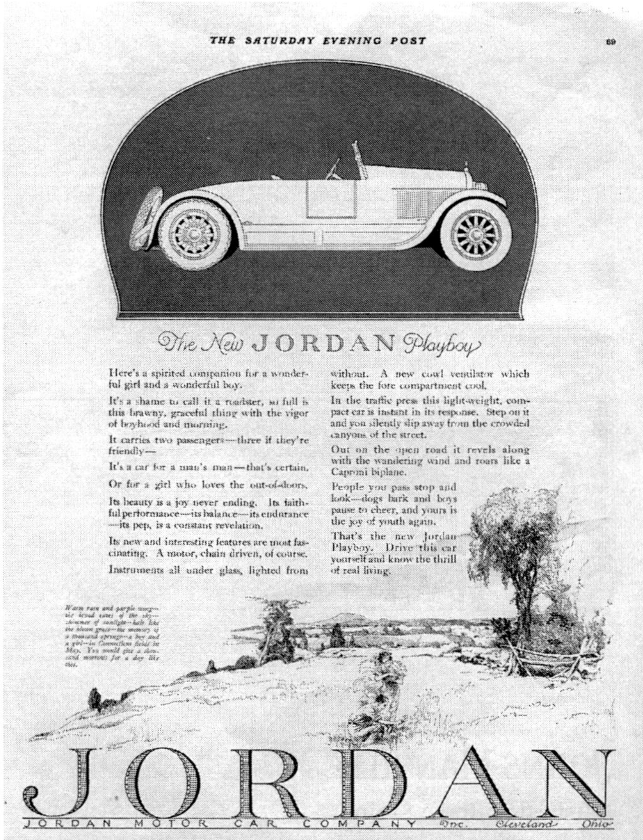

Top, left: April 1919 ad for the Silhouette. *Top, right:* September 1920 ad for the Model MX Silhouette Five Touring. *Bottom, left:* A Silhouette ad. *Bottom, right:* April 1922 ad for the new Model MX Playboy, showing an early model with split windshield.

***Left:* August 1922 ad for the early Model H Touring Sedan. *Right:* This November 1922 ad for the second style Model MX Two Door Brougham shows a prominent theme of Jordan advertising of the time.**

appeared in any magazine for the public and only a couple in trade magazines during 1928.[4]

A beautiful Jordan Playboy ad with the car a lovely shade of blue was featured in the August 1929 edition of *House and Garden* and one other publication and then it ended.

Ned took credit for Jordan advertising but it is highly unlikely that he did it all. In the beginning he did have considerable influence over everything concerning the new company, but when the dream was fully realized he was too busy traveling, speaking and selling to be burdened with the everyday responsibilities of doing it all. To be sure, he had a great influence and guided that department in the ways he liked, but by spending six to eight months a year on the road, he just did not have the time that department required.

Ned took full credit for the "Laramie" ad but the author has personally corresponded with someone who has a different version. That person, who knew Ned personally, related that Ned confessed that his advertising manager, Joe Fewsmith, had a great deal to do with it. It was Ned's idea, as were several of the other great ads, but it is the author's opinion that Ned cannot take credit for everything. When Joe Fewsmith was asked about the creation of the ad, his answer was, "It was his company and he could take the credit if he so desired."[5] It is unclear what Joe Fewsmith's real connection with Jordan was. He was an advertising genius and was listed as Jordan's advertising manager, but he also worked for other firms. Wherever he worked seemed to get the Jordan business.

A group of artists including Frank Godwin, Popini and Erickson and others did several ads. Erickson did a few before the others, his best being the first Playboy advertisement, which, in the author's opinion, is a classic.

The logo these artists used consisted of the letters R E surrounded by some artwork that made it resemble a baseball. Research has failed to uncover further evidence of the firm or anything about Erickson or Popini, but from mid–1919 until 1921 they were the favored illustrators.

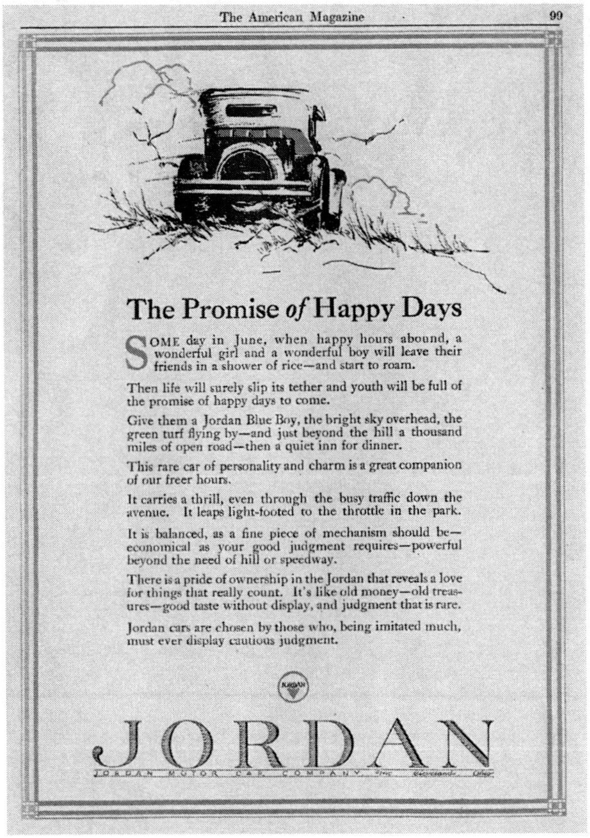

Top, left: An early Model H Blueboy is depicted in this 1922 ad. *Top, right:* The famous "Somewhere West of Laramie" ad for the 1923 Model MX Playboy. *Bottom, left:* A January 1925 ad showing the Model A Playboy. *Bottom, right:* An October 1925 ad touting the "Astounding Jordan Sedan," a 1926 Model J with all steel body.

Left: **This late advertising brochure was printed on cheap paper and contained no illustrations.** ***Above:*** **This ad for the Model Z appeared in the Philadelphia Athletic Club magazine in May 1930 (courtesy Macdonald Leach).**

Ned gave Fred Cole credit for the "Port of Missing Men" ad, but the Erickson Agency did it with Frank Godwin being the artist. Fred Cole did do the "Middle of the Night" ad which landed Ned in hot water a second time. One of the best automotive illustrators in the profession, he did the "West of Laramie" ad (both versions) and several other great ones. There were several other beautiful ads never attributed to anyone, many of which had to be done by Cole. His style appears everywhere. Only his name was missing.

Frank (Frances) Godwin (1889–1939) was the son of the city editor of the *Washington Star*. Born in Washington, D.C., he started his career as an apprentice at the *Star*. He later studied at the Art Students League and received much help from his mentor, James Montgomery Flagg. He divided his skills among many media and his work appeared in *Collier's*, *Liberty* and *Cosmopolitan*, to name a few. He did ads for Prince Albert Tobacco, Texaco and Coca-Cola in addition to his automobile illustrations for Jordan.[6]

Fred Cole (1893–1967) was born in Chicago but moved to Sioux Falls, South Dakota, at an early age. He loved the outdoors and was an avid fisherman. After high school he returned to Chicago and studied at the Art Institute. To help pay his way he ushered at Chicago's Orchestra Hall where he developed a lifelong love of classical music. He became acquainted with Joe Fewsmith and that connection brought the Jordan work. He did automobile illustrations for Packard, Lincoln, Velie, Essex, Marmon, DeSoto, Dodge, LaSalle, Chrysler, LaFayette, Willys Overland, Studebaker, Reo, Cadillac and in later years Chevrolet, including Corvette and truck ads. He also produced fine illustrations for many other manufacturers of various products.[7] In the author's opinion, Fred Cole was one of the greatest automotive artists who ever lived.

Haddon Sundblom (1899–1976) was born in June 1899, the youngest of nine children of Swedish-American parents. He was raised in Chicago and at the age of 19 decided that art would be his vocation. He was

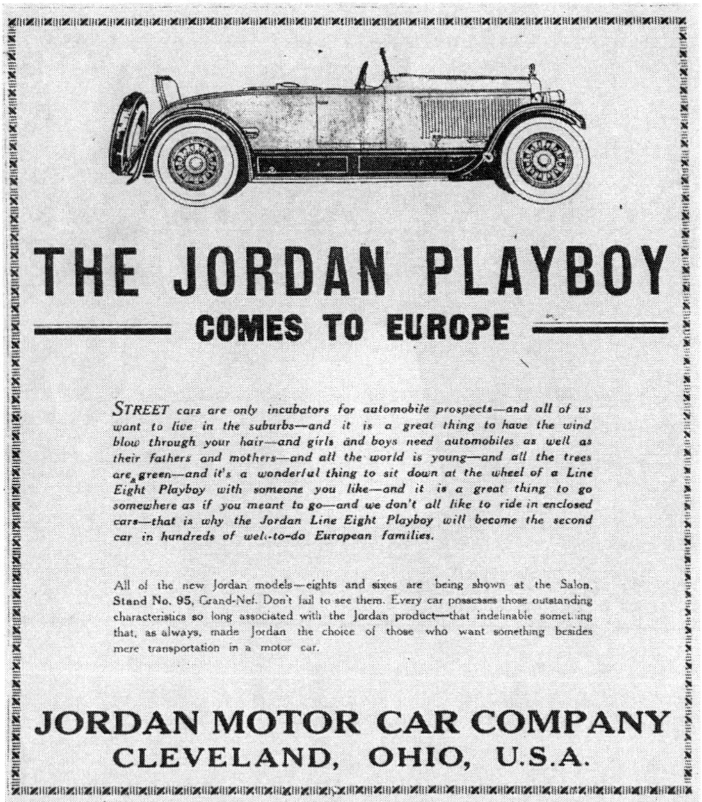

This Playboy ad appeared in the Paris edition of the *New York Herald Tribune* in October 1927.

employed as a construction worker by day and attended the Art Institute of Chicago by night for four years. He also studied at the American Academy in Chicago for three and one-half years. He founded Stevens, Sundblom, and Henry Studios in the mid–1920s and eventually had 30 artists working for that firm, which grew to occupy one entire floor in Chicago's Palmolive Building. Sundblom did "A Golden Girl from Somewhere," "Pay Off the Grinning Caddy," "I Think She Came from a Land of Fire" and probably several others for Jordan in 1924. Some of his early work was the creation of the Quaker Oats man and Aunt Jemima. He also did some work for Packard, but his lasting claim to fame came as the creator of the Coca-Cola Santa Claus from 1931 until 1966. He was credited with being one of the best illustrators to ever practice his trade. He and his wife raised four daughters and he passed away on March 10, 1976.[8]

Distributors and dealers were supplied with a steady stream of handouts during the life of the Jordan. At first they were fairly bland, but like their magazine counterparts, they soon developed into beautiful renditions which are highly prized by today's collector. Later, as the magazine advertising began to wane, the dealer handouts suffered the same fate. They were few in number and of very poor quality. Good examples from the late 1920s were few and far between.

A large black and white portfolio featuring the Little Custom Model R was delivered to dealers shortly after the Blue Boy was added to the line in May 1927. The exception to mediocrity would be the brochure announcing the Model G, which ranks as one of the better Jordan brochures ever done. Jordan also supplied a large color folio of the Model G series to dealers, but it is highly unlikely they were ever given to customers. Buyers probably would get a look at these if they expected to order a car. The Model Z, as grand as it was, had only one brochure of poor quality and with no photo or drawings whatsoever. The Line 70, Model U Sunshine Sedan suffered the same fate.

Jordan did supply its dealers and distributors with newspaper advertisements. They would print it up exactly as specified, with a space at the bottom which read, "Dealer's Name Here, in this size type, address here in this size type (Positively nothing but local dealer's name, address and phone number to be put here)." Some foreign papers occasionally carried Jordan ads.

THIRTEEN

Dealers and Distributors

Automobile empires do not usually start on a grand scale, especially if the founder is not born to great wealth. The idea for his own company started while Ned worked for Jeffery. He learned rather quickly that it is necessary to have not only good manufacturing facilities, but ways to dispose of the product you are making. Thus Ned started early courting dealers and distributors to build a good network. Even before the Jordan Company had become a reality he had made many contacts with those who would sell his automobiles. While other officers and employees tended to the problems of building a new factory, designing the car, procuring equipment and lining up supplies, Ned was busy promoting the new vehicle.

Almost all automobiles were shipped by train in those days, so the most likely distribution points would be the larger metropolitan areas which were served by the major railroads. Most dealers were supplied by a distributor who would purchase large lots of cars and then distribute them to the dealer network. If a dealer's business was within driving distance of Cleveland, he usually picked up his cars at the factory and drove them home. It is not certain but the Jordan Ohio Company may have been the distributor for all of Ohio, and the dealer may have bought through them and picked his purchase up at the factory.

Left: **Petersen Motors, Jordan distributor in Philadelphia.** ***Right:*** **Jordan service managers received clipboards like this example (courtesy Dan Jordan).**

***Top, left:* Showroom of Petersen Motors in Philadelphia. *Top, right:* Keychain from a Jordan dealer (courtesy Dan Jordan). *Bottom:* The Jordan Michigan Company, distributors in Detroit.**

Some distributors and most dealers carried more than one brand of car. There was little need to sell more than one make in a certain price range. No one wanted to compete with his own offerings. Usually a dealer would sell a brand in the upper price range, another in the middle and still another in the lower range. The larger manufacturers usually made cars in all price ranges and would not permit their dealers to sell anything but their products. General Motors had a price range for everyone and Ford dealers didn't need any other brand.

Jordan dealers were usually those who sold other independent brands.

Small dealerships were not in a financial position to stock large inventories. There were no "floor plans" in those days as compared to today. Many cars were ordered from factory literature and photographs.

Jordan announced early that their dealers would be limited to 100. What they really meant was their distributors would be limited to that number. In fact they never reached that number but did end up with 85 distributors scattered across the United States. It is safe to assume that anyone who wanted to be a dealer became one.

Jordan strived to make their selling agents successful. They supplied literature, advertised nationally in major magazines and furnished the dealer with newspaper ads. All he had to do was to put his name, address and telephone number at the bottom and run it in the local paper. Jordan was very strict about one point: Nothing but what they supplied was to be used. Hon-

Top, left: **The C.D. Rand & Co. dealership in San Francisco.** ***Top, right:*** **Showroom of C.D. Rand & Co. in San Francisco. (Both photographs: *Jordan Arrow*, courtesy Arthur Grove).** ***Middle, left:*** **A 1920 Model F Touring in front of the C.D. Rand & Co. dealership in San Francisco (courtesy Paul V. Osika).** ***Middle, right:*** **Southwest Motor Co. in Kansas City.** ***Bottom, left:*** **The Wisconsin Motor Car Company in Milwaukee.** ***Bottom, right:*** **The St. Louis Motor Car Co.**

esty was their policy and they wanted no false claims to be made about their automobile.

Another Jordan policy was to feature their dealers in factory publications as often as possible. The *Jordan Idea* and *Arrow* were used frequently for this purpose. Dealers would also be featured in trade magazine advertisements as often as possible.

***Top, left:* The Sears Automobile Company in Des Moines, Iowa. *Top, right:* The W.C. Norris Motor Sales Co. in Tulsa, Oklahoma. *Above:* Jordans on display at the Budapest auto show, circa 1927 (courtesy Brooks Brierley). *Left, middle:* A dealership in Vienna, circa 1926–1927 (courtesy Brooks Brierley). *Left, bottom:* The Chase-Morrill Co. in San Francisco (John Conde).**

Good customer service was expected from anyone who sold Jordan automobiles. A satisfied customer was one who would buy another Jordan and tell his friends about it also. The company followed up on sales and often sent the new owner a letter congratulating him on his purchase. It would be signed by Ned when possible, but many times his signature was faked.

Foreign sales were never especially meaningful for Jordan until about the latter half of 1926, having accounted for only a small percentage of sales. But Jordan's overproduction in 1926 and the debacle of the Little Custom made overseas distributors and dealers suddenly very important. August 1927 saw Jordan establishing a foreign sales branch. They began showing cars at all major European shows and establishing distributors and dealerships abroad whenever possible. Former judge John W. Stockwell went on such a mission in July 1927. He visited several European countries and did sign up some distributors. Australia and New Zealand were also targeted for the sales blitz with moderate success. Nonetheless sales continued to slump and Jordan's

A photograph taken in Berlin of (*left to right*) Jordan representative J.W. Stockwell with Edward Tauch of Deutsche Bank and Walter Spitz, Jordan's Berlin agent, in July 1927.

Posing with a Little Custom Jordan in Berlin, July 1927.

Showroom of Jordan Distributors Inc. in Houston, December 1929 (Detroit Public Library, National Automotive History Collection).

Exterior of the Jordan Ohio Company in Cleveland, August 5, 1929 (Detroit Public Library, National Automotive History Collection).

share of the foreign and domestic market was getting smaller. Rumor has it that hundreds of Little Custom Jordans sat on a Chicago pier for over a year while the company tried to peddle them overseas.

By January 1929, Jordan supposedly had representatives in 32 foreign countries and their overseas business was 115 percent better in 1928 than 1927. A 115 percent increase meant little, though, if the starting number was tiny. Jordan hoped for much better foreign sales in 1929, but they never happened and with the

JORDAN

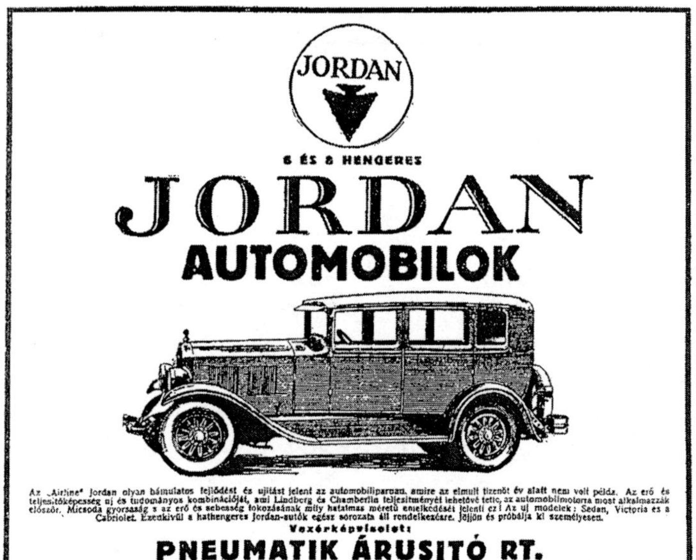
JORDAN
6 ÉS 8 HENGERES
JORDAN
AUTOMOBILOK
Az „Airline" Jordan olyan bámulatos fejlődést és ujitást jelent az automobiliparban, amire az elmult tizenöt év alatt nem volt példa. Az erő és teljesitőképesség uj és tudományos kombinációját, ami Lindberg és Chamberlin teljesitményét lehetővé tette, az automobilmotorra most alkalmazzák először. Micsoda gyorsaság s az erő és sebesség fokozásának mily hatalmas méretű emelkedését jelenti ez! Az uj modelek: Sedan, Victoria és a Cabriolet. Ezenkivül a hathengeres Jordan-autók egész sorozata áll rendelkezésre. Jöjjön és próbálja ki személyesen.
Vezérképviselet:
PNEUMATIK ÁRUSITÓ RT.
VI., Andrássy-ut 27.
Telefon: Teréz 134—78.

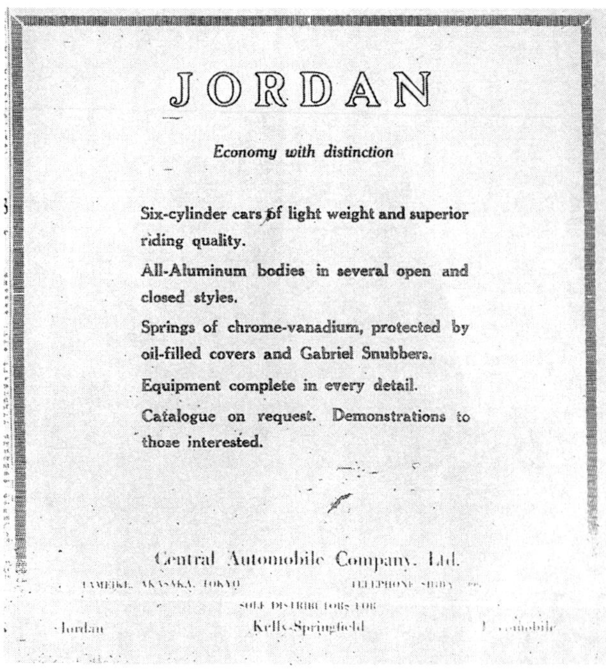
JORDAN
Economy with distinction
Six-cylinder cars of light weight and superior riding quality.
All-Aluminum bodies in several open and closed styles.
Springs of chrome-vanadium, protected by oil-filled covers and Gabriel Snubbers.
Equipment complete in every detail.
Catalogue on request. Demonstrations to those interested.
Central Automobile Company, Ltd.
Kelly-Springfield

onset of the Depression the foreign market virtually ceased.

The domestic market was shrinking every day, even before the Depression, as dealers had many more brands to choose from and started getting out. Jordan's relations with its dealers had always been good, but as sales fell and dealers started to reduce overhead by stocking fewer cars, the company started to apply pressure. Consequently, many dealers opted to get out, which served to make matters worse instead of better. With the dealer network shrinking there was but one thing to do and that was to reduce production. For a small company competing with the giants of the industry, the results of such action can be catastrophic. For Jordan, they were.

Opposite: Top, left: **Showroom of the Jordan Ohio Company showing the new models, August 5, 1929. *Top, right:* Another view inside the Jordan Ohio Company showroom. *Middle, left:* New and used car storage at the Jordan Ohio Company, August 5, 1929. *Middle, right:* New car storage area at the Jordan Ohio Company, August 5, 1929. (All four photographs: Detroit Public Library, National Automotive History Collection). *Bottom, left:* An ad from Budapest, Hungary (courtesy Brooks Brierley). *Bottom, right:* A Japanese ad from the Central Automobile Company, Ltd.**

Chapter Notes

Chapter One

1. U.S. Social Security Act, Application for Account Number, U.S. Treasury Department, Internal Revenue Service, November 24, 1936.

2. The National Archives, Veterans Records, National Archives and Records Administration, Washington, D.C.; U.S. Census, June 22, 1900, City of Merrill, 2nd Ward, Lincoln County, Wisconsin; Death certificate, Katie Eveline Jordan, University of Wisconsin, Oshkosh, Libraries and Learning Resources; Death certificate, Anne Jordan, State of Illinois, Cook County, City of Chicago, October 5, 1934.

3. The National Archives, Veterans Records, National Archives and Records Administration, Washington, D.C.

4. *Ibid.*

5. *Ibid.*

6. The National Archives, Veterans Records, National Archives and Records Administration, Washington, D.C.; Carvell, Kenneth L. "Historic Beverly in the Tygart Valley." *Wonderful West Virginia*, February 2001, pp. 20–23.

7. The National Archives, Veterans Records, National Archives and Records Administration, Washington, D.C.

8. *Ibid.*

9. U.S. Census, June 22, 1900, City of Merrill, 2nd Ward, Lincoln County, Wisconsin; Death certificate, Kate Jordan, State of Wisconsin, Department of Health, Bureau of Vital Statistics, May 27, 1912; Jordan, Ned, "With Ned Jordan," *Automotive News*, October 15, 1951, pp. 22, 52.

10. Jordan, Ned, "With Ned Jordan," *Automotive News*, October 15, 1951, pp. 22, 52; Death certificate, Anne Jordan, State of Illinois, Cook County, City of Chicago, October 5, 1934.

11. Jordan, Ned, "With Ned Jordan," *Automotive News*, July 16, 1951, p. 13, October 15, 1951, pp. 22, 52.

12. Jordan, Ned, "With Ned Jordan," *Automotive News*, October 15, 1951, pp. 22, 52.

13. *Ibid.*

14. Jordan, Ned, "With Ned Jordan," *Automotive News*, July 16, 1951, p. 13.

15. City directories, For Scott Kansas, 1871–1875; Jordan, Ned, "With Ned Jordan," *Automotive News*, June 29, 1953, p. 14, October 15, 1951, p. 22.

16. U.S. Census, 1880, State of Wisconsin, City of Fond du Lac, 1st Ward, Fond du Lac County, Wisconsin.

17. State of Wisconsin, County of Fond du Lac, Records of Deaths.

18. Birth certificate, State of Wisconsin, Lincoln County, City of Merrill.

19. Marriage license, State of Wisconsin, Lincoln County, Wisconsin State Historical Society, University of Wisconsin, Madison, Wisconsin.

20. Register of deaths, Wisconsin State Historical Society, University of Wisconsin, Madison, Wisconsin.

21. Jordan, Ned, "With Ned Jordan," *Automotive News*, July 10, 1950, p. 14, July 18, 1955, p. 35; Gilkey manuscript (unpublished), Merrill Historical Society Archives, Merrill, Wisconsin.

22. Graduation program, Merrill High School, June 9, 1899, Merrill, Wisconsin.

23. University of Wisconsin Archives, admission records, Edward Stanlaw Jordan, September 16, 1901; Jordan, Edward S., *The Inside Story of Adam and Eve*, Utica, NY: Howard Coggeshall, Inc., 1945; Jordan, Ned, "With Ned Jordan," *Automotive News*, April 18, 1955, p. 45.

24. University of Wisconsin Yearbooks (*The Badger*), 1905, 1906.

25. University of Wisconsin Archives, admissions records, Charlotte (Lottie) Eva Hannahs, August 29, 1901.

26. City directories, 1905–1914, City of Kenosha, Wisconsin, Kenosha Public Libraries, Simmons Branch.

27. University of Wisconsin Yearbooks (*The Badger*), 1905–1906; Jordan, Ned, "With Ned Jordan," *Automotive News*, April 18, 1955, p. 45.

28. Jordan, Edward S., *The Inside Story of Adam and Eve*, Utica, NY: Howard Coggeshall, Inc., 1945, pp. 56–57; Forbes, B.C., and Foster, O.D., *Automotive Giants of America*, New York: B.C. Forbes Publishing Company, 1926, pp. 155–168; Jordan, Ned, "With Ned Jordan," *Automotive News*, November 16, 1953, p. 30.

29. Jordan, Ned, "With Ned Jordan," *Automotive News*, May 8, 1950, p. 8, April 18, 1955, p. 45.

30. Marriage license, State of Wisconsin, Racine County, February 1, 1906.

31. Record of birth, The Secretary of Public Health, City of Cleveland Police Department, Cleveland, Ohio, Dr. J.J. Thomas, attending physician, August 9, 1906.

32. Jordan, Ned, "With Ned Jordan," *Automotive News*, June 29, 1953, p. 14.

33. Jordan, Ned, "With Ned Jordan," *Automotive News*, November 16, 1953, p. 30.

34. Jordan, Ned, "With Ned Jordan," *Automotive News*, April 10, 1950, p. 11; Jordan, Edward S., *The Inside Story of Adam and Eve*, Utica, NY: Howard Coggeshall, Inc., 1945, p. 74.

35. Jordan, Ned, "With Ned Jordan," *Automotive News*, April 14, 1952, pp. 50, 51, October 17, 1955, p. 22.

36. Jordan, Ned, "With Ned Jordan," *Automotive News*, April 14, 1952, p. 50; Kimes, Beverly Rae, "A Family in Kenosha: The Story of Rambler and Jeffery," *Automobile Quarterly* 16:2 (Second Quarter 1978), pp. 128–145.

37. City directories, 1907–1912, City of Kenosha, Wisconsin, Kenosha Public Libraries, Simmons Branch.

38. Jordan, Ned, "With Ned Jordan," *Automotive News*, January 7, 1952, p. 17, November 24, 1952, p. 20.

39. Records, Kenosha Lodge #47, Free and Accepted Masons, Kenosha, Wisconsin; Records, Kenosha Chapter #3, Royal Arch Masons, Kenosha, Wisconsin.

40. Records of births, State of Wisconsin, Racine County, 1908–1910.

41. Jordan, Ned, "With Ned Jordan," *Automotive News*, October 8, 1951, p. 36.

42. Obituary, *The Merrill Star Advocate*, May 29, 1912.

43. Kimes, Beverly Rae, "A Family in Kenosha: The Story of the Rambler and Jeffery," *Automobile Quarterly*, 16:2 (Second Quarter 1978), pp. 128–145.

44. Jordan, Ned, "With Ned Jordan," *Automotive News*, May 1, 1950, p. 11.

Chapter Two

1. "Jordan Out at Jeffery Selling," *Automobile Topics*, January 15, 1916, p. 962.
2. Jordan, Ned, "With Ned Jordan," *Automotive News*, October 8, 1951, p. 36.
3. *Ibid.*
4. Jordan, Ned, "With Ned Jordan," *Automotive News*, April 14, 1952, pp. 50–51.
5. Kimes, Beverly Rae, "A Family in Kenosha: The Story of the Rambler and Jeffery." *Automobile Quarterly*, 16:2 (Second Quarter 1978), pp. 128–145.
6. "Jordan to Build Car: Leaves Jeffery Company to Take Charge of Concern Now Being Formed," *Motor Age*, January 20, 1916, p. 18; "New Company Will Make Medium Price Cars: Jordan, Zens and Begg Leave Jeffery—To Start Manufacture Shortly," *The Automobile*, January 20, 1916, p. 158.
7. Jordan, Ned, "With Ned Jordan," *Automotive News*, June 11, 1951, p. 12.
8. *Ibid.*
9. "Jordan Motor Car Company Organized: Capitalization $800,000—Company Is Based on Co-operative Plan," *The Automobile*, January 27, 1916, p. 200.
10. *Ibid.*
11. "Jordan Motor Car Company Takes Detroit Office," *The Automobile*, February 10, 1916, p. 288.
12. Jordan, Ned, "With Ned Jordan," *Automotive News*, June 11, 1951, p. 12, September 4, 1950, p. 10.
13. Jordan, Ned, "With Ned Jordan," *Automotive News*, May 21, 1951, p. 13; untitled article and obituary, *The Jackson Citizen Patriot*, Jackson, Michigan, May 13, 1943.
14. Jordan, Ned, "With Ned Jordan," *Automotive News*, May 21, 1951, p. 13; Letter, Girl to Borton, April 3, 1916.
15. "Jordan Locates in Cleveland," *Motor Age*, April 6, 1916, p. 31.
16. "Jordan Organization Completed," *Motor World*, June 14, 1916, p. 43.
17. Jordan, Ned, "With Ned Jordan," *Automotive News*, November 19, 1951, p. 21; Factory photograph, circa 1916.
18. Letter, Withington to Borton, praising the new Jordan car, May 5, 1916.
19. "Stutz and Jordan Order Spartons," *Automobile Topics*, May 6, 1916, p. 1169.
20. "Jordan Organization Completed," *Motor World*, June 14, 1916, p. 43; Jordan advertisement, "The Jordan Organization," *Motor World*, August 16, 1916, pp. 69–70.
21. Jordan, Ned, "With Ned Jordan," *Automotive News*, June 11, 1951, p. 12.
22. Jordan advertisement, "A New Luxury Car for 1917—With a Choice of Custom Style Bodies," *The Automobile*, July 6, 1916, pp. 73–74.
23. "Cleveland Business Men Inspect Jordan," *Motor Age*, July 13, 1916, p. 10; "Recent Trade Developments, Jordan Plant Starts Work," *The Horseless Age*, July 15, 1916, p. 62.
24. Jordan advertisement, "A New Luxury Car for 1917—With a Choice of Custom Style Bodies," *The Automobile*, July 6, 1916, pp. 73–74; Jordan advertisement, "Distinctive and Irresistible—A New Luxury Car," *The Automobile*, July 13, 1916.
25. Jordan advertisement, "The Realization of a Great Dream," *The Automobile*, July 20, 1916, pp. 69–76.
26. "From Everywhere," *Motor World*, August 30, 1916, p. 44.
27. Jordan news release, "Blended Ideals in Jordan—New Six Possesses Many Points of Distinction, Etc.," *The Automobile*, July 20, 1916, pp. 98–99; Jordan Owners Instruction Manual, Model 60, circa 1916.
28. Jordan advertisement, "Jordan Introducing a New Six with Custom Styled Bodies at Attractive Prices," *The Saturday Evening Post*, September 2, 1916, pp. 42–43.
29. Jordan news release, "Blended Ideals in Jordan—New Six Possesses Many Points of Distinction, Etc.," *The Automobile*, July 20, 1916, pp. 98–99.
30. Jordan news release, "Jordan Reveals New Closed Bodies," *Motor World*, August 29, 1917, pp. 11–12.
31. "Springfield Body Sues Fisher—Charges Infringement of Two Design Patents, Etc.," *The Automobile*, November 23, 1916, p. 876.
32. "Jordan Builds Five Cars a Day," *The Automobile*, August 31, 1916, pp. 373–374.
33. "Jordan to Double Capacity," *The Automobile*, October 19, 1916, p. 647.
34. "Jordan's New Plant Rushed," *The Automobile*, September 28, 1916, p. 543; "The Month in the Motor Industry," *Motor*, August 16, 1916, p. 103.
35. Jordan advertisement, "Jordan Success," *The Automobile*, November 30, 1916, pp. 49–56.
36. "Six to Seven Jordans a Day," *Motor World*, September 27, 1916, p. 41; Jordan advertisement, "Jordan Success," *The Automobile*, November 30, 1916, pp. 49–56.

Chapter Three

1. "Jordan to Double Capacity," *Motor Age*, February 15, 1917, p. 14.
2. "Jordan Prices Up $145.00," *The Automobile*, March 22, 1917, p. 580.
3. "Cleveland Manufacturers Expanding," *The Automobile*, March 22, 1917, p. 603.
4. "Jordan Makes Cars Chic for Smart Spring Trade," *Motor World*, April 11, 1917, p. 55.
5. "Shaw Buys Jordan Taxi's," *Motor Age*, April 26, 1917, p. 17.
6. "Jordan Production to Date," *Motor Age*, May 17, 1917, p. 10.
7. Jordan advertisement, "This Is the Inside Story of How Jordan Made Good," *Motor Age*, May 10, 1917; Jordan brochure, "This Is the Inside Story of How Jordan Made good," circa 1917.
8. "Jordan Adds Space," *Motor Age*, May 17, 1917, p. 20.
9. "Production," *The Automobile*, June 14, 1917, p. 1119.
10. "Announces Sport Roadster," *Motor Age*, June 21, 1917, p. 17; "New Jordan Sport Roadster," *The Automobile*, June 21, 1917, p. 1155.
11. "Jordan Gives July Options," *Motor Age*, July 5, 1917, p. 14; Jordan advertisement, "Six Striking Colors for July," *Motor Age*, July 5, 1917.
12. Jordan advertisement, "Jordan $2,626,500 Worth of Jordan Cars," *Motor Age*, July 12, 1917.
13. "Jordan Elected to N.A.C.C.," *Motor Age*, July 12, 1917, p. 25.
14. "Jordan to Build Trucks," *The Automobile and Automotive Industries*, August 23, 1917, p. 342.
15. "Jordan Reveals New Closed Bodies," *Motor World*, August 29, 1917, pp. 11–12; "Jordan Dealers Meet," *Motor Age*, August 30, 1917, p. 23.
16. "Jordan Dealers Meet," *Motor Age*, August 30, 1917, p. 23; Jordan advertisement, "Jordan Custom Style Enclosed Carriages," *Motor*, September 17, 1917.
17. "Jordan Reveals New Closed Bodies," *Motor World*, August 29, 1917, pp. 11–12.
18. "Jordan Sessions Are Full of Pep," *Automobile Topics*, September 1, 1917, p. 386.
19. *Ibid.*
20. "Seven Body Styles for Jordan," *The Automobile and Automotive Industries*, August 30, 1917, p. 385; "Jordan Adds Four Body Types," *Motor Age*, August 30, 1917, pp. 40–41.
21. "New Jordan Prices," *Motor Age*, October 4, 1917, p. 13.
22. "Disteel Pressed Steel Disc Wheels Now Being Manufactured," *Automotive Industries*, December 13, 1917, p. 1059.
23. "Jordan Shipments Are Normal," *Automotive Industries (The Automobile)*, December 6, 1917, p. 1021.
24. "Jordan—Jordan Motor Car Company, Cleveland," *Motor World*, December 26, 1917, p. 70; "What the Dealer Will Find at the New York Show," *The Horseless Age*, January 1, 1918, p. 42.

Chapter Four

1. "Jordan," *Automotive Industries (The Automobile)*, January 31, 1918, p. 258.
2. "The New Suburban Seven," *Automobile Trade Journal*, April 1918, p. 151A.
3. "1,727 Jordan Cars in 1917," *Motor World*, February 13, 1918, p. 43.
4. Jordan advertisement, "Drive Your Own Car," *Motor Age*, August 1, 1918, pp. 65–66; Photograph, Jordan Brougham, *Motor Age*, August 15, 1918, p. 41.
5. Jordan advertisement, "The Aluminum Sedan," *Motor Age*, August 29, 1918, pp. 67–68.
6. "The Chicago Show," *Automobile Trade Journal*, February 1919, pp. 143–145.
7. Jordan advertisement, "The Jordan Town Sedan," *Motor World*, February 5, 1919, p. 86.
8. "Jordan Prices Drop," *Motor Age*, February 6, 1919, p. 13.
9. Jordan advertisement, "The Jordan Silhouette," *Automobile Topics*, April 19, 1919; "Silhouette and Playboy Are Jordan's New Models," *Motor World*, April 30, 1919, p. 41.
10. "Jordan Adds Silhouette and Playboy," *Motor Age*, April 17, 1919, p. 40.
11. Jordan, Ned, "With Ned Jordan," *Automotive News*, May 28, 1951, p. 10; Jordan, Edward S., *The Inside Story of Adam and Eve*, Utica, NY: Howard Coggeshall, Inc., 1945, pp. 14–16.
12. Untitled article and obituary, *Cleveland*

Plain Dealer, July 2, 1994; Letter, Rudolph Garfield, March 12, 2002.
13. Jordan advertisement, "The Jordan Silhouette," *Motor Age*, April 17, 1919.
14. Jordan advertising brochure, "The New Silhouette," circa 1919; Jordan advertisement, "The New Silhouette," *Motor Age*, April 17, 1919.
15. Jordan, Ned, "With Ned Jordan," *Automotive News*, September 6, 1954, p. 30.
16. "Jordan Seizes on Silhouette Idea," *Automobile Topics*, April 19, 1919, pp. 1324, 1360.
17. "Jordan Starts Building for Larger Production," *Automobile Topics*, May 17, 1919, p. 153.
18. Jordan advertisement, "Sixty Striking Stories of Satisfaction," *Motor Age*, May 22, 1919.
19. Advertisement, Guide Motor Lamp Manufacturing Company, *Automobile Trade Journal*, June 1919, p. 138.
20. Baumgardt, Kenneth, "Somewhere West of Laramie," unpublished manuscript, Glenville, Pa.; *The Chronicle* (Financial News), August 16, 1919, p. 683 (courtesy Ken Baumgardt).
21. *Ibid.*
22. "Jordan Motor Car Company Having Trouble Getting Parts," *Motor World*, July 2, 1919, p. 44.
23. Jordan advertisement, "Jordan Policy," *The Saturday Evening Post*, September 6, 1919, p. 71.
24. *Jordan Idea* (Jordan company publication), circa 1919.
25. "American Automotive Men Go to Europe," *Motor Age*, November 13, 1919, p. 15.
26. "A Pair of the New Jordan Bodies," *Motor World*, October 29, 1919, p. 33.
27. "New Jordan Silhouette Models," *Motor Age*, November 27, 1919, p. 33.
28. "Jordan M," *Motor Age*, January 29, 1920, p. 52; Jordan Owners Instruction Manual, Model M, circa 1920.
29. *Ibid.*
30. "Manufacturers Notes," *Motor Record*, December 1919, p. 42.
31. Jordan advertising brochure, *Economy with Distinction*, circa 1920.
32. Advertising brochure, "A Better Car for You," *The General Top Company*, Cleveland, Ohio, circa 1919–1920.
33. Letter (from daughter of W.B. Riley) to the author.

Chapter Five

1. "General Car Prices Advance Is Seen by Automotive Men," *Motor Age*, April 8, 1920, p. 31.
2. "High Pressure Grease Lubrication," *Motor*, June 20, p. 71.
3. "These Cars Have Reduced in Price," *Motor Age*, October 7, 1920, p. 8.
4. Jordan advertisement, "The Port of Missing Men," *The Saturday Evening Post*, November 6, 1920, p. 69; Jordan advertisement, *The Literary Digest*, November 13, 1920, pp. 94–95; Jordan advertisement, *The Country Gentleman*, November 20, 1920, p. 21.
5. Jordan advertisement, "The Jordan Silhouette Five," *The Saturday Evening Post*, November 8, 1919, p. 66; Jordan advertisement, "The Jordan Silhouette Brougham," *The Literary Digest*, November 29, 1919, p. 45.
6. Jordan advertisement, "The Jordan Silhouette Brougham," *The Country Gentleman*, August 28, 1920, p. 2.
7. *The New York Times*, January 9, 1921, p. 2.
8. "New Models at the Show," *Automobile Trade Journal*, January 1921, p. 37.
9. *The New York Times*, January 9, 1921, p. 2; Photograph, *Motor World*, January 12, 1921, p. 21.
10. Jordan Parts Manual, Model MX, circa 1922.
11. "Jordan Makes Cut in Price," *Motor Age*, May 5, 1921, p. 22.
12. *Ibid.*
13. "Marmon and Jordan Set New Schedules," *Automobile Topics*, May 7, 1921, p. 1117.
14. "June Shipments Beat April or May," *Automotive Industries—The Automobile*, July 14, 1921, p. 93.
15. "New Jordan Has Exclusive Design on Unit Parts," *Motor World*, October 5, 1921, pp. 28–31; "Jordan of Entirely New Design," *Motor Age*, October 6, 1921, pp. 12–14; "Important Changes Feature the New Jordan Model," *Automotive Industries—The Automobile*, October 6, 1921, pp. 654–657.
16. "New Jordan Is a Bid for Leadership," *Automobile Topics*, October 8, 1921, pp. 634–636.
17. "Jordan Production Held Up," *Automobile Topics*, January 21, 1922, p. 898.
18. "Jordan Goes Strong at Chicago," *Automobile Topics*, February 18, 1922, p. 19.
19. "Jordan Production Takes Jump," *Automobile Topics*, March 4, 1922, p. 187.
20. "Miscellaneous Headlamps and Method of Lens Removal," *Motor Age*, March 2, 1922, pp. 20–21.
21. "Jordan Cut Restores Pre-War Price Level," *Automotive Industries—The Automobile*, March 30, 1922, p. 739.
22. "Reduction of $300 to $400 on Jordan Cars Announced," *Motor Age*, March 30, 1922, p. 27.
23. "Jordan Selling 300 Cars a Day," *Automotive Industries*, April 29, 1922, p. 944.
24. "Jordan Production Now at 12,000 Cars Yearly," *Automobile Topics*, July 15, 1922, p. 769.
25. "Manufacturers Notes," *Motor Record*, August 1922, p. 21.
26. "Chassis Units Employed in 1923 Cars," *Motor*, January 1923, p. 192; "Why the Buyer Is Interested in Hydraulic Frames," *Automobile Trade Journal*, December 1919, p. 163.
27. "Jordan Builds New Sport Model Called Blue Boy," *Automotive Industries*, August 31, 1922, p. 446.
28. "Some Novel Features Sketched at the Show," *Motor World*, January 17, 1923, p. 17.
29. "Jordan Blue Boy, a New Four Passenger," *Motor Age*, September 7, 1922, p. 17.
30. "Changes in Design of Jordan Sedan and Brougham," *Motor Age*, October 5, 1922, p. 14.
31. *Ibid.*
32. "Big Jordan Increase," *Motor Age*, October 26, 1922, p. 40.
33. "Jordan Dealers Order 4,350 Automobiles," *The Accessory and Garage Jorunal*, December 25, 1922, p. 75.
34. "Annual Statistical Review of the Automobile Industry," National Automobile Chamber of Commerce, 366 Madison Avenue, New York, N.Y., report of the Jordan Motor Car Company, Inc., for 1922 (Detroit Public Library, National Automotive History Collection).
35. "Jordan Is Started on 80 Cars a Day Schedule for New Year," *Motor Age*, January 18, 1923, p. 39.

Chapter Six

1. "An Education at the Show," *Motor Age*, February 1, 1923, p. 20; Excerpt from 1923 New York Automobile Show Directory.
2. "Jordan Moving Cars at Rate of 62 Daily," *Motor World*, March 28, 1923, p. 41.
3. Jordan, Ned, "With Ned Jordan," *Automotive News*, August 7, 1950, p. 13.
4. "Jordan Adds Four Door Brougham," *Automobile Topics*, April 21, 1923, p. 930; "Jordan Joins Four-Door Ranks with Brougham," *Automobile Topics*, May 5, 1923, p. 1149.
5. "Jordan's New Resale Policy Is Drastic," *Automobile Topics*, April 28, 1923, p. 1015, 1022; "Jordan Inaugurates Nation Wide Resale Plan," *Automobile Topics*, May 5, 1923, pp. 1135–1136, 1142.
6. "Jordan Reduces Prices," *Motor Age*, May 31, 1923, p. 30.
7. "Jordan Lowers Prices; Adds Two New Models," *Automobile Topics*, June 2, 1923, p. 215.
8. Jordan advertisement, "The New Jordan Sedan," *The Saturday Evening Post*, December 8, 1923, p. 85.
9. "Price Cut Helps Jordan Sales," *Automobile Topics*, June 9, 1923, p. 318.
10. "Spreading the Flat Rate Gospel to Owners," *Motor World*, June 13, 1923, p. 30.
11. Jordan advertisement, "Somewhere West of Laramie," *The Saturday Evening Post*, June 23, 1923, p. 129; Jordan, Edward S., *The Inside Story of Adam and Eve*, Utica, NY: Howard Coggeshall, Inc., 1945, pp. 80–81.
12. "Jordan Makes New Record," *Automobile Topics*, July 21, 1923, p. 943.
13. Delco advertisement, "When Ned Jordan's Boy Drove Across the Country," *The Library Digest*, April 12, 1924, p. 79; "When Ned Jordan's Boy Drove Across the Country," *Automotive Industries*, April 24, 1924, p. 74.
14. *Jordan Idea* (Jordan company publication), circa 1923.
15. Jordan advertisement, "Here Is Distinction with Economy," *The Saturday Evening Post*, January 5, 1924, p. 57.
16. Jordan Parts Manual, Model MX and H, circa 1923.
17. Letter, the Jordan Ohio Company, Cleveland, Ohio, to Hay Motor Company, Canton, Ohio, September 10, 1923.
18. "Jordan and Judson Fly on Fishing Expedition," *Automobile Topics*, September 15, 1923, p. 416.
19. "Jordan Declares Dividend," *Automobile Topics*, September 15, 1923, p. 420.
20. "Nine Manufacturers Display Variety of New Body Types," *Motor Age*, October 4, 1923, p. 33; "Jordan Presents New Two-Door Model," *Automobile Topics*, October 13, 1923, p. 847.

21. "Jordan Recapitalization Gets Stockholders O.K.," *Automobile Topics*, December 29, 1923, p. 625; "Jordan Stockholders May Let Jordan Car Be Their Santa," *Motor Age*, December 20, 1923, p. 32.
22. "Jordan Recapitalization Gets Stockholders O.K.," *Automobile Topics*, December 29, 1923, p. 625.
23. "Jordan Tells What He Knows About Engineers at S.A.E.," *Motor Age*, December 20, 1923, p. 33.
24. "Four Wheel Brakes and Balloon Tires Available on Jordan," *Motor Age*, January 10, 1924, p. 18.
25. "Jordan Makes Four Wheel Brakes Standard," *Motor World*, January 31, 1924, p. 12.
26. "Jordan Shares Underwritten," *Automobile Topics*, February 16, 1924, p. 22.; "Jordan Issue Oversubscribed," *Automobile Topics*, February 23, 1924, p. 120.
27. "Jordan Motor Stock Offering Over Subscribed," *Automobile Trade Journal*, March 1924, p. 61.
28. "Jordan Production in 1923 was 9,000," *Automobile Topics*, February 9, 1924, p. 1416; "Annual Statistical Review of the Automobile Industry," National Automobile Chamber of Commerce, 366 Madison Avenue, New York, N.Y., report of the Jordan Motor Car Company, Inc., for 1923 (Detroit Public Library, National Automotive History Collection).
29. "Seek to List Jordan on Exchange," *Automobile Topics*, March 29, 1924, p. 638.
30. "Jordan Shows Early Profits This Year," *Automobile Topics*, April 5, 1924, p. 747.
31. "Howatt Associated with Studebaker," *Automobile Topics*, April 19, 1924, p. 958.
32. "Jordan Wins $1,000 Prize," *Automobile Topics*, June 21, 1924, p. 526.
33. "Jordan Announces Line Eight," *Motor Age*, June 26, 1924, p. 40.
34. "Distinctive Body Lines Featured," *Automobile Topics*, August 16, 1924, pp. 40–42.
35. "First of Great Jordan Line Eights Displayed by Dealers," *Motor Age*, August 14, 1924, p. 41.
36. "Line Eight Sales Start Strong," *Automobile Topics*, July 12, 1924, p. 821.
37. "Jordan Eight Output Up," *Automobile Topics*, August 16, 1924, p. 19; "Distinctive Body Lines Feature Jordan Eight," *Automobile Topics*, August 16, 1924, pp. 40–42.
38. "Prices Readjusted on Jordan Used Cars," *Automobile Topics*, September 6, 1924, p. 315.
39. "Jordan Hits the Trail," *Automobile Topics*, November 29, 1924, p. 208.
40. "Jordan Offers Friendly Three," *Automobile Topics*, December 20, 1924, p. 478.
41. Jordan, Ned, "With Ned Jordan," *Automotive News*, July 23, 1951, p. 14.

Chapter Seven

1. "Group of Silver Anniversary Bodies," *Automotive Industries*, January 8, 1925, p. 57; "Jordan Adds a Sedan," *Motor Age*, January 8, 1925, p. 16; "Jewett, Lincoln, and Jordan Stock and Special Bodies," *Automobile Trade Journal*, February 1926, p. 27.
2. "Jordan Earnings in 1924 Were $858,469," *Automobile Topics*, February 14, 1925, p. 19; "Annual Statistical Review of the Automobile Industry," National Automobile Chamber of Commerce, 366 Madison Avenue, New York, N.Y., report of the Jordan Motor Car Company, Inc., for 1924 (Detroit Public Library, Automotive History Collection).
3. "Jordan Directors Reelected," *Automobile Topics*, March 21, 1925, p. 484.
4. "Jordan Gets More Factory Space," *Automobile Topics*, May 23, 1925, p. 129.
5. "New York Sees Jordan Car on Tour," *Automobile Topics*, May 23, 1925, p. 125; *Jordan Idea* (Jordan company publication), circa 1923.
6. "Bradley Tours West," *Automobile Topics*, June 6, 1925, p. 316.
7. "Jordan Exhibits Citroen," *Automobile Topics*, June 27, 1925, p. 605.
8. "Jordan Makes Reduction of $300 on All Eights," *Automobile Topics*, August 15, 1925, p. 19.
9. "Jordan Hails Trend to All Steel Bodies," *Automobile Topics*, September 12, 1925, pp. 394, 398.
10. "Jordan Announces a Smaller Low-Priced Eight," *Automobile Trade Journal*, October 1925, pp. 53–55; "Jordan Line Eight Introduced to an Expectant Trade," *Automobile Topics*, September 19, 1925, pp. 518–520, 526.
11. Stillman, K.W., "All Steel Bodies Now Possible with Moderate Productions," *Automotive Industries*, November 5, 1925, p. 778.
12. "Jordan Shipments Soar," *Automobile Topics*, December 5, 1925, p. 309; "Writes His Own," *Time Magazine*, November 23, 1925, pp. 36–37.
13. "Jordan Adopts Glassmobile," *Automobile Topics*, December 12, 1925, p. 403; "Jordan Declares Regular," *Automobile Topics*, December 12, 1925, p. 406.
14. "Jordan Running at Capacity," *Automobile Topics*, December 19, 1925, p. 509.
15. "New Body and Chassis Features," *Automotive Industries*, January 7, 1926, p. 22.
16. "Jordan Has Red Playboy," *Motor Age*, January 14, 1926, pp. 18–19.
17. "Automobile Business Is in Pioneer Days," *Automobile Topics*, January 16, 1926, p. 978.
18. "Jordan to Speak at Breakfast," *Automobile Topics*, March 6, 1926, p. 288.
19. "Jordan Reports Net Profits of $790,475," *Automotive Industries*, March 18, 1926, p. 509; "Annual Statistical Review of the Automobile Industry," National Automobile Chamber of Commerce, 366 Madison Avenue, New York, N.Y., report of the Jordan Motor Car Company, Inc., for 1925 (Detroit Public Library, Automotive History Collection).
20. "Jordan Increases Prices," *Automobile Topics*, March 20, 1926, p. 512.
21. "Jordan Cuts Prices," *Motor Age*, April 8, 1926, p. 32.
22. Newspaper articles, unknown sources and dates; Personal papers of Ned Jordan (author's collection).
23. Jordan company photographs; Personal papers of Ned Jordan; *The Spizerinctum*—A Publication of the Lord Motor Company, Los Angeles; *Jordan Idea* (Jordan factory publication), circa 1926 (all in author's collection).
24. Graduation program, Choate School, Brookline, Massachusetts, June 11, 1926.
25. Records of admissions 1927, University of Arizona Archives, Tucson, Arizona.
26. "Two New Bodies on Jordan Large Eight," *Automotive Industries*, June 24, 1926, p. 1114.
27. "New Jordan Types," *Motor Age*, July 1, 1926, p. 37; "Sedan and Victoria Are Jordan's Latest," *Automobile Topics*, August 7, 1926, p. 1213.
28. "Associated Ad Men Hear Jordan's Views," *Automotive Industries*, June 24, 1926, p. 1113.
29. "Camera Snaps Industry's Activities," *Automobile Topics*, August 21, 1926, p. 129.
30. "Jordan Passes Dividend in Planning Development," *Automobile Topics*, September 11, 1926, p. 418.
31. "Jordan Adds Two Models," *Motor Age*, September 23, 1926, p. 37.
32. "5,000 at Big Auditorium to See New Jordan Line," *Motor Age*, September 23, 1926, p. 38.
33. Records, U.S. Patent and Trademark Office, Washington, D.C.
34. *Jordan Idea* (Jordan company publication), circa 1926; Advertisement, *The Evening Tribune*, San Diego, California, Saturday, December 18, 1926.
35. Jordan advertising brochures, "The Jordan Line Eight Seven Passenger Sedan," circa 1926.

Chapter Eight

1. Jordan advertising insert, "The First Truly Fine American Small Car by Jordan," *Motor Age*, January 6, 1927, pp. 121–128.
2. "Jordan, Falcon, Peerless and Other New Models Introduced," *Automotive Industries*, January 15, 1927, p. 51; "Jordan," *Automobile Trade Journal*, February 1927, pp. 26, 50–52.
3. "Financial Position of Jordan Much Improved," *Automobile Topics*, March 12, 1927, pp. 408, 417; "Annual Statistical Review of the Automobile Industry," National Automobile Chamber of Commerce, 366 Madison Avenue, New York, N.Y., Report of the Jordan Motor Car Company, Inc., for 1926 (Detroit Public Library, National Automotive History Collection).
4. "New Models Are Shown by Golden Gate Dealers," *Motor Age*, May 19, 1927, p. 31.
5. "Jordan Announces Chassis Details of Custom Model," *Motor Age*, June 9, 1927, pp. 35–37; "Jordan Now in Active Production on 'Custom' Model," *Automotive Industries*, June 11, 1927, pp. 902–904.
6. "Jordan Bruised in Car Mishap," *Motor Age*, April 28, 1927, p. 31.
7. "Jordan Lays Down Several Rules for Selling Cars in Address at Houston, Texas," *Motor Age*, May 19, 1927, p. 35.
8. "Blue Boy Is the Latest Little Jordan Custom," *Automobile Topics*, June 25, 1927, p. 585.
9. "Jordan Announces Two New Series 'AA' Models," *Automotive Industries*, July 16, 1927, p. 101; "Jordan Adds Two," *Motor Age*, July 21, 1927, p. 22.
10. "Jordan Is Tickled by Slogan Contest," *Motor Age*, June 23, 1927, p. 15.
11. "No Jordan Merger Planned," *Automobile Topics*, July 23, 1927, p. 950.
12. "Airplane Type Engine Developed by

Jordan," *Automotive Industries*, August 20, 1927, p. 283; "Jordan Car to Have New Power Plant," *Motor Age*, August 25, 1927, p. 14.

13. "European Progress Noted by Jordan," *Motor Age*, August 25, 1927, p. 13.

14. "Air Line 8 Is Jordan's Fastest," *Motor Age*, September 15, 1927, p. 19; "The New Air Line Eight Is a Larger Jordan," *Automobile Topics*, October 1, 1927, pp. 708–709.

15. "Jordan Brings Out Air Line 8," *Automobile Trade Journal*, October 1927, p. 66.

16. "Three Paragraphs—And a Tag Line," *Motor Age*, October 20, 1927, p. 9.

17. "Jordan Adopts Air-Line Head to Model J," *Automobile Topics*, November 12, 1927, p. 21.

18. "Price Announcements and Changes," *Motor Age*, January 12, 1928, p. 18.

19. Jordan company letter, January 30, 1928.

20. "Jordan Passes Dividend," *Motor Age*, February 7, 1928, p. 10.

21. Jordan advertising brochure, "The New Jordan Air Line Eight with Special Equipment," circa 1928.

22. Newspaper article, unknown source, March 8, 1928.

23. "Begg Joins Budd," *Motor Age*, April 5, 1928, p. 20.

24. "Paul Zens, Jordan Vice President, Elected Director of Northern Finance," attributed to *Automobile Topics*, July 14, 1928, p. 830.

25. "Zens Heads Cleveland Office," attributed to *Automobile Topics*, August 13, 1929, p. 1074.

26. Grayson, Stan, "The All Steel World of Edward Budd," *Automobile Quarterly* 16:4 (4th Quarter 1978), p. 359.

27. "Jordan Orders Continue Gain," *Motor Age*, April 19, 1928, p. 14.

28. "Jordan's Cross Country Six Replaces Little Custom," *Motor Age*, April 26, 1928, pp. 29, 32.

29. *Ibid.*

30. "Pierce and Jordan Combine Is Studied," *Automobile Topics*, June 2, 1928, p. 285.

31. Ralston, Mark, *Pierce Arrow*, San Diego, California: A.S. Barnes & Company Inc., 1980, p. 147.

32. "Jordan Adds New Series Air Line 8," *Motor Age*, June 14, 1928, p. 16.

33. Jordan company flyer, "Drive Away Day," June 25, 1928.

34. "Jordan Offers New Model," *Motor Age*, August 30, 1928, p. 9; Jordan advertising brochure, "The New Series Jordan Air Line Eight Landau Brougham," circa 1928; Jordan factory photographs.

35. "Jordan Motor Car Offers Stock," unknown newspaper, September 19, 1928.

36. Newspaper article, unknown source, October 17, 1928.

37. Jordan, Ned, "With Ned Jordan," *Automotive News*, June 12, 1950, p. 11.

38. "Jordan Stock Subscribed," *Automotive Industries*, January 5, 1929, p. 37.

Chapter Nine

1. "New Jordan and Peerless Straight Eight Appear at Show," *Automotive Industries*, January 12, 1929, pp. 50–51.

2. Jordan advertising brochure, "The New Jordan Eight," circa 1929.

3. Blanchard, Harold F., "The New York Show," *Motor*, February 1929, pp. 30–31, 102; "Jordan—Improved 6 and 8 with Longer Wheelbase and Handsome Bodies," *Motor*, February 1929, pp. 53, 178.

4. Jordan advertising brochure, "The Jordan Six," circa 1929.

5. "A Six and an Eight," *Automobile Trade Journal and Motor Age*, February 1929, p. 59; "New Jordan and Peerless Straight Eight Appear at Show," *Automotive Industries*, January 12, 1929, pp. 50–51.

6. "Jordan Planning Output of 60 Daily in February," *Automotive Industries*, January 19, 1929, p. 112.

7. "Jordan Appoints Buckner," *Automotive Industries*, February 23, 1929, p. 352.

8. "Reichel Made Sales Manager," *Automotive Industries*, December 28, 1929, p. 956.

9. *New York Times*, April 5, 1929.

10. Newspaper article, unknown source, April 20, 1929.

11. Letter from Allied Motor Industries to Ned Jordan, March 12, 1929 (author's collection).

12. "Jordan Emphasizes Advertising Need," *Automotive Industries*, May 18, 1929, p. 785.

13. Bulletin to St. Louis Automobile Dealers, June 11, 1929; Telegram by Jordan Official to Company Headquarters, June 18, 1929.

14. "Jordan Announces Three Car Models at Prices from $1,795 to $2,795," *Automotive Industries*, July 6, 1929, p. 18; Jordan advertising brochure, "Jordan Great Line Ninety," circa 1929.

15. "Jordan Announces Three Car Models at Prices from $1,795 to $2,795," *Automotive Industries*, July 6, 1929, p. 18; Jordan advertising brochure, "Jordan Standard Line Eight," circa 1929.

16. "Jordan Adds Small Eight," *Automobile Trade Journal and Motor Age*, August 1929, pp. 62–63, 78; Letter from Jordan Company to a Customer (author's collection).

17. "General News," *Autobody*, October 1929, p. 145.

18. "January New Car Sales Figures," *Automobile Topics*, March 15, 1930, p. 470.

Chapter Ten

1. "Jordan Prices Reduced," *Automotive Industries*, January 11, 1930, p. 69.

2. "Jordan News Item," Sweeny & James Advertising, January 1930, "To be released during the New York Automobile Show January 4–11, 1930" (Philadelphia Public Library, Automobile Reference Collection).

3. Denham, Athel F., and Toboldt, W.K., "Jordan and Elcar Announce 1930 Series at New York," *Automotive Industries*, January 11, 1930, pp. 44–46.

4. "Jordan—Two New Lines Characterized by Unusual Body Lines Are Added," *Automobile Trade Journal and Motor Age*, February 1930, pp. 53, 88; "Specifications—Report to National Automobile Chamber of Commerce" (NACC), January 1930 (Detroit Public Library, National Automotive History Collection).

5. "Line 70 Sunshine Sedan" (photograph), *Automobile Topics*, March 8, 1930, p. 359; Jordan factory photographs.

6. Jordan letter to J.L. Elbert, March 7, 1930 (collection of Charles Boles).

7. "Reflections of the National Automobile Shows," *Autobody*, February 1930, pp. 31–33.

8. "Jordan—Two New Lines Characterized by Unusual Body Lines Are Added," *Automobile Trade Journal and Motor Age*, February 1930, pp. 53, 88; "A New Type Arrives," *Automobile Topics*, January 11, 1930, p. 955.

9. Jordan factory photographs (author's collection).

10. "Reflections of the National Automobile Show," *Autobody*, February 1930, pp. 31–33.

11. Jordan factory photographs (author's collection).

12. "A New Type Arrives," *Automobile Topics*, January 11, 1930, p. 955.

13. Jordan advertising brochure (Model Z), "Judgment and Good Taste in the Selection of a Fine Motor Car," Distributed by Jordan Distributors Inc. Chicago, Illinois (author's collection).

14. City directories, Cleveland, Ohio, 1929, 1930, 1931; Ohio Secretary of State Files (research done by John and Peggy Willi, Cleveland, Ohio).

15. Newspaper article, unknown source (author's collection).

16. *Ibid.*

17. Records, Washoe County, Nevada, 2nd Judicial District Court, March 1930.

18. State of California, Department of Health Services, death certificate of Minnie Jordan Miller.

19. "Jordan Reports Loss of $652,408 for 1929," *Automobile Topics*, April 26, 1930, p. 959; "Jordan Motors Get Reorganization Offer," *Automobile Topics*, October 11, 1930, p. 757.

20. "Jordan Plan Assured," *Automotive Industries*, December 20, 1930, p. 917.

21. "Jordan Reports Loss," *Automotive Industries*, December 6, 1930, p. 843.

22. "Receiver for Jordan," *Automobile Trade Journal*, June 1931, p. 50; "Jordan Receivership to Administer Company," *Automobile Topics*, May 16, 1931, p. 89.

23. "Receivers to Make 262 Cars," *Automobile Topics*, August 1, 1931, p. 903; Letter from Felz Motor Sales to a Prospective Customer (collection of Charles Boles).

24. "Plan a Revival of Old Jordan Motors," *Automobile Topics*, November 19, 1932, p. 104; Letters, documents, parts books of Jordan Automobile Parts and Services Company (author's collection).

25. Letters, brochures and postcards written to Hollon Rawnsley from Jordan Automobile Parts and Service Copmany (author's collection).

26. *Motor*, November 1932, p. 99.

27. Newspaper article, unknown source, September 30, 1932 (author's collection).

28. *Ibid.*

29. "What the Industry Is Talking About," *Motor*, December 1932, p. 96.

Chapter Eleven

1. Jordan, Ned, "With Ned Jordan," *Automotive News*, June 25, 1951, p. 13, May 9, 1955, p. 34.

2. Jordan, Ned, "With Ned Jordan," *Automotive News*, June 25, 1951, p. 13, July 18, 1955, p. 35, June 17, 1957, p. 59.
3. Jordan, Ned, "With Ned Jordan," *Automotive News*, June 25, 1951, p. 13.
4. *Ibid.*
5. Jordan, Ned, "With Ned Jordan," *Automotive News*, June 25, 1951, p. 13, September 6, 1954, p. 30.
6. Jordan, Ned, "With Ned Jordan," *Automotive News*, June 25, 1951, p. 13.
7. "E.S. Jordan Returns to Advertising Business," *Automobile Topics*, April 9, 1932, p. 588.
8. "E.S. Jordan Joins Studebaker Sales," *Automotive Industries*, December 16, 1934, p. 723; "E.S. Jordan Joins Studebaker Sales Corp.," *Automobile Topics*, December 22, 1934, p. 318.
9. State of California, Department of Health Services, Office of Vital Records, death certificate, June 22, 1930; State of Illinois, Department of Health, Division of Vital Statistics, death certificate, October 5, 1934; Untitled article, *Merrill Star* (Merrilll, Wisconsin), October 9, 1934.
10. State of New York, certificate and record of marriage, July 17, 1935.
11. Personal conversation, Kate Jordan Wallace, 2002.
12. *Ibid.*
13. City of New York, Department of Health, Vital Records Division, birth certificate.
14. Jordan, Edward S., *The Inside Story of Adam and Eve*. Utica, New York: Howard Coggeshall, Inc., 1945.
15. State of Connecticut, Litchfield County, Superior Court, January 10, 1947 (Court Records, Volume 43, pp. 457–458).
16. Jordan, Ned, "With Ned Jordan," *Automotive News*, April 9, 1951, p. 13; Personal conversation, Kate Jordan Wallace, 2002.
17. Jordan, Ned, "With Ned Jordan," *Automotive News*, March 20, 1950, p. 2, March 27, 1950, p. 2.
18. Jordan, Ned, "With Ned Jordan," *Automotive News*, September 21, 1953, p. 22, August 8, 1955, p. 31, June 17, 1957, p. 59, July 1, 1957, p. 16; American Nurses Association, Washington, D.C., press release, February 25, 1952.
19. Jordan, Ned, "With Ned Jordan," *Automotive News*, September 21, 1953, p. 22.
20. "15th Annual Meeting," *Antique Automobile* 15:2 (June 1951), p. 83.
21. Untitled article, *Cleveland Plain Dealer*, January 24, 1952; Untitled article, unknown source, (author's collection).
22. Jordan, Ned, "With Ned Jordan," *Automotive News*, April 14, 1952, pp. 50–51.
23. Jordan, Ned, "With Ned Jordan," *Automotive News*, January 30, 1956, p. 61. City of New York, Department of Health, certificate of death, December 30, 1958; Conversation with Kate Jordan Wallace, 2002.
24. Conversation with Kate Jordan Wallace, 2002.
25. Obituary, *Lakeville Journal*, Lakeville, Connecticut; State of Rhode Island and Providence Plantations, Department of Health, certification of death, June 4, 1981.
26. State of Connecticut, Death Index 1942–2001; Social Security Records, U.S. Treasury Department, Internal Revenue Service, Washington, D.C.

Chapter Twelve

1. Jordan, Edward S., *The Inside Story of Adam and Eve*, Utica, New York: Howard Coggeshall, Inc., 1945.
2. Letter from the New York Society for the Suppression of Vice, April 12, 1927 (author's collection).
3. Advertising insert, "Everyone Has Wondered Why Someone Did Not Build a Truly Fine Quality Small Car," attributed to *Motor Age*, December 23, 1926.
4. The author's opinion, based on 35 years of collecting.
5. Mrs. Joseph Fewsmith, Jr., letter to the author.
6. Reed, Walt, *The Illustrator in America 1860–2000*, New York, N.Y.: The Society of Illustrators, 2000.
7. Griffiths, Gwilym G., "Packard's Artists: The Mastery of Fred Cole," *The Packard Cormorant* #35 (Summer 1984), pp. 10–17.
8. *The Refresher*, Dec. 1953, pp. 15–16, May 1964.

APPENDIX I

Partial List of Distributors and Dealers

The A&T Garage	Milwaukee, Wisconsin
Charles Aronson	Merrill, Wisconsin
The Alliance Motor Car Co.	Alliance, Ohio
Atlantic City Jordan Sales Co.	Atlantic City, New Jersey
Austin Cars Ltd.	Brisbane, Australia
Avenue Motor Sales	Chicago, Illinois
B.M.P. Motors, Inc.	Englewood, New Jersey
Babbitt-Polson	Arizona
Charles E. Backus Co.	Jamestown, New York
G.W. Baker	Middletown, New York
Baker-Fisk-Hugill	Detroit, Michigan
Barger-Mitchell Co.	Toledo, Ohio
Joseph Bayer Jordan Sales	Long Island City, New York
George R. Bentel	San Francisco, California
Bishop Motor Car Co.	Cincinnati & Dayton, Ohio
Carlinville Motor Sales Co.	Carlinville, Illinois
Central Auto Co.	Virginia, Minnesota
Central Automobile Company Ltd.	Tokyo, Japan
Chapman-Marvin Co.	Jacksonville, Florida
Chase-Morrill Co.	San Francisco, California
Chicago Motor Car Co.	Chicago, Illinois
Comfort Motor Sales	Quebec, Canada
Cornell Motors Inc.	Chicago, Illinois
Cressy-Jordan Motor Co.	South Bend, Indiana
Crockett Automobile Co.	San Antonio, Texas
John G. Dale Agency	New York, New York
Charles R. Dann	New Rochelle, New York
Davies-Overland Co.	San Diego, California
Julius Debits	Chicago, Illinois
De Groff–Jordan Co.	Delavan, Wisconsin
Diversey Motor Sales	Chicago, Illinois
J.B. Duffey & Sons	Fostoria, Ohio
B.K. Elias	Painesville, Ohio
Elm City Jordan Co.	New Haven, Connecticut
Embry-Weir Motors Co. Inc.	Louisville, Kentucky
Emdee Motor Car Co.	Lafayette, Indiana
Englewood Jordan Co.	Englewood, New Jersey
L.S. Ferris	Bridgeport, Connecticut
Gardinell Motors Co.	S. Orange, New Jersey
Gardinell Motors Co.	Montclair, New Jersey
Gardinell Motors Co.	Newark, New Jersey
Frank B. Galyon Co.	Knoxville, Tennessee
Gingras Auto & Supply Co.	Cocoa, Florida
Gran Brothers Motor Sales Co.	Chicago, Illinois
E.H. Habersham	Baltimore, Maryland
Haggart Motor Sales	Brooklyn, New York
Harris-Levey Motor Sales Co.	Santa Rosa, California
L.F. Hart	W. Palm Beach, Florida
Ralph E. Hay Motor Co.	Canton, Ohio
Hinchcliffe-Patterson Motor Car Co.	Boston, Massachusetts
Horn Jordan Co.	Hempstead, Long Island, New York
Hudson County Jordan Sales	West New York
Jefferson Motors Inc.	Perth Amboy, New Jersey
The Jordan Columbus Co.	Columbus, Ohio
Jordan Distributors Inc. of Illinois	Chicago, Illinois
The Jordan Michigan Co.	Detroit, Michigan
Jordan Morristown	Morristown, New Jersey
Jordan Motor Sales Co.	Erie, Pennsylvania
Jordan Motor Sales Inc.	Providence, Rhode Island
Robert L. Jordan Motors	Chicago, Illinois
Jordan Newbury Co.	Asbury Park, New Jersey
Jordan–North Philadelphia Sales Co.	Philadelphia, Pennsylvania
Jordan Ohio Co.	Cleveland, Ohio
Jordan Sales & Service	Washington, DC
Jordan Sales Co.	Bronx, New York
Jordan Springfield Co.	Springfield, Massachusetts
Jordan Waterbury Co.	Waterbury, Connecticut
Jordan Worcester Company	Worcester, Massachusetts
Jor-Land Motors, Inc.	Chicago, Illinois
William P. Knipper	Rochester, New York
Lloyd Koon Auto Sales	Chicago, Illinois
Lenox Garage, Inc.	Concord, New Hampshire
Levreau & Taylor Motor Co.	Long Beach, California
Lord Motors	San Diego, California
Lord Motor Car Co.	Los Angeles, California
Lohely Motor Sales Co.	Chicago, Illinois
M.J. Lynch Motor Sales	Chicago, Illinois

Joseph A. Mackle Ltd.	London, England
Martin Mahon & Sons	Huntington, Long Island, New York
Maple City Motor Co.	Monmouth, Illinois
McCormack Bros. Motor Car Co.	Birmingham, Alabama
Robert McCurdy	Pittsburgh, Pennsylvania
The McFarlan-Jordan Co.	Hartford, Connecticut
Earl A. McGinnis	Los Angeles, California
Middlesex Jordan Co.	Perth Amboy, New Jersey
Midwest Auto Sales & Service	Chicago, Illinois
Galbraith Miller	Milwaukee, Wisconsin
Miller-Bay Motor Co.	Denver, Colorado
Mitchell Motor & Service Co.	Seattle, Washington
Mitchell-Lewis & Staver Co.	Portland, Oregon, and Spokane, Washington
Moore Motors Co.	Greenville, South Carolina
Motor Suppliers Co.	Chicago, Illinois
Mungen & Bechtold	Herkimer, New York
H.W. Neuman Co.	Davenport, Iowa
New Brighton Garage Co.	New Brighton, New York
W.C. Norris Motor Sales Co.	Tulsa, Oklahoma
North Side Motors Co.	Chicago, Illinois
North Shore Jordan Co.	Chicago, Illinois
Northwestern Automobile Co.	Minneapolis, Minnesota
J.F. O'Connor Sales Co.	Syracuse, New York
Hugh O'Donnell & Co, Inc.	Detroit, Michigan
C.J. O'Hara	South Norwalk, Connecticut
Oradell Garage & Machine Co.	Oradell, New Jersey
Orange County Garage Co.	Santa Ana, California
Osmond-Jordan Co.	Milwaukee, Wisconsin
Carl Page	New York, New York
Pantel Motor Car Co.	St. Paul, Minnesota
C.G. Patmon & Co.	Stockton, California
Petersen Motors Inc.	Philadelphia, Pennsylvania
Petersen Motors–Baltimore	Baltimore, Maryland
Peterson Keyes Co.	Indianapolis, Indiana
Peterson Motor Car Co.	Omaha, Nebraska
W.G. Phillip	Mt. Vernon, New York
Plank Brothers, Inc.	Pasadena, California
Pneumatic Arusito Rt	Budapest, Hungary
Port Washington Jordan Co.	Port Washington, New York
Warren Post Garage	Pearl River, New York
C.D. Rand & Co.	San Francisco, California
Frank A. Reeve Co.	Montclair, New Jersey
Reilly & Gilliar	Great Neck, New York
Ralph Rice Motors	New Rochelle, New York
Harvey Ringler Motor Sales Inc.	Philadelphia, Pennsylvania
St. Louis Motor Car Co.	St. Louis, Missouri
Milton Sandman	Brooklyn, New York
Max Schmitt	Paterson, New Jersey
Sherman Schneider	Elizabeth, New Jersey
F.G. Schwartz	Poughkeepsie, New York
Seager-Clark & Co.	Los Angeles, California
Sears Automobile Co.	Des Moines, Iowa
M.M. Shelly	Modesto, California
Sherwood Automobile Corp.	Brooklyn, New York
H.S. Shurts	Decatur, Illinois
Walter E. Sloman Motors Inc.	Chicago, Illinois
C. Arthur Smith	Oyster Bay, Long Island,
New York	
South Side Motor Car Co.	Chicago, Illinois
South Motor Car Co.	Kansas City, Missouri & Kansas
Southwest Motor Co.	Kansas City, Kansas
Charles E. Stutz Sales Co.	Indianapolis, Indiana
Trio Motor Sales	Chicago, Illinois
Herbert B. Tyler	Valparaiso, Indiana
Union Motor Car Co.	Memphis, Tennessee
Vaast Brothers Garage	S. Norwalk, Connecticut
C.E. Vail	Mansfield, Ohio
Van Matan Motors Inc.	Jamaica, New York
Van Kleech Motor Co.	Pittsburgh, Pennsylvania
A. Vincent Sons Co.	Chicago, Illinois
J.E. Walter Co.	Anaheim, California
Lee Waterfield	East Orange, New Jersey
Webel Automobile Corp.	Albany, New York
Weir Motor Sales Co.	Buffalo, New York
White Plains Motor Co.	Canton, Ohio
Wisconsin Motor Car Co.	Milwaukee, Wisconsin
Wolff & Johnson	Yonkers, New York

APPENDIX II

Chassis Specifications

These specifications have been drawn from many sources. Every attempt has been made to insure their authenticity. However, they should be used with caution. Jordan itself sometimes made mistakes, and other sources are notorious for publishing the wrong information.

Many models used more than one type of carburetor, generator, starter, or other components during the model year. Weights are a source of frustration. I have used information supplied by Jordan where possible.

For specifications not supplied by the factory, I have made use of many sources. I have found as many as three different weights for some models and some cars are listed in the wrong year, make, etc.

The author would be happy to assist any Jordan owner in any way possible to make the correct decisions concerning a Jordan automobile. Write to me in care of the publisher.

Model 60

Engine Continent 7 N 6 cylinder
Bore and Stroke 3½ × 5¼
Carburetor Stromberg LB2
Ignition Bosch DU6 Magneto
Generator Bijur L-61 & M-832 or 1090
Starter Bijur ED-160 & M-979
Fuel Supply Stewart vacuum tank
Spark Plugs AC "Titan"
Radiator Fedders
Frame Parish & Bingham
Clutch Brown-Lipe multiple disc
Transmission Brown-Lipe
Front Axle Timken
Rear Axle Timken Detroit
Steering Gemmer
Brakes 2 wheel external contracting, mechanical
Emergency Brake Internal expanding
Springs F = 37"; R = 59"; semi elliptic, Mather
Wheels Hayes Wire, Houk Wire, wood
Tires 35 × 4½ Firestone
Wheelbase 127 inch
Body Walker-Wells
Weight Touring = 3,050

Model 60C

Engine Continent 10 N 6 cylinder
Bore and Stroke 3½ × 5¼
Carburetor Stromberg
Ignition Delco Distributor 5175
Generator Bijur L-61 & M 1080 or 1195
Starter Bijur ED-160 & M-979A
Fuel Supply Stewart vacuum tank
Spark Plugs AC
Radiator Fedders
Frame Parish & Bingham
Clutch Brown-Lipe multiple disc
Transmission Brown-Lipe
Front Axle Timken
Rear Axle Timken Detroit
Steering Gemmer
Brakes 2 wheel external contracting, mechanical
Emergency Brake Internal expanding
Springs F = 37"; R = 59"; semi elliptic, Mather
Wheels Hayes Wire, wood
Tires 32 × 4½ (Sport Marine = 32 × 4) Goodyear; Suburban 7 = 33 × 4½), Firestone
Wheelbase 127 inch
Body Walker-Wells
Weight Suburban 7 = 3100

Model 60, Series F & Model F, Series F

Engine Continent 9 N 6 cylinder
Bore and Stroke 3½ × 5¼
Carburetor Stromberg LB2
Ignition Delco Distributor 5175 + 5215
Generator Early: Bijur L-61 + M1080 + 1195; Late: Delco 180
Starter Early: Bijur ED160 & M979A; Late: Delco 179
Fuel Supply Stewart vacuum tank
Spark Plugs Champion "Titan"
Radiator Fedders, Sparton
Frame Hydraulic Pressed Steel Co.

Clutch Early: Borg & Beck; Late: Timken
Transmission Detroit Gear
Front Axle Timken
Rear Axle Timken Detroit
Steering Gemmer
Brakes 2 wheel external contracting, mechanical
Emergency Brake Internal expanding
Springs F = 37"; R = 59⅜; semi elliptic, Mather
Wheels Hayes Wire, Disteel Disc, wood (Firestone Rims Type E)
Tires 32 × 4½ Goodyear (Firestone optional)
Wheelbase 127 inch
Body American, Ohio, Walker-Wells
Weight Four Passenger Touring = 3,150; Seven Passenger Touring = 3,240; Seven Passenger Sedan = 3,750

Model M

Engine Continental 7 R 6 cylinder
Bore and Stroke 3¼ × 4½
Carburetor Stromberg LSZA
Ignition Delco Distributor 5207
Generator Delco 165
Starter Delco 164
Fuel Supply Stewart vacuum tank
Spark Plugs Champion "Toledo"
Radiator Sparton
Frame Hydraulic Pressed Steel Co.
Clutch Detroit
Transmission Detroit Gear
Front Axle Timken
Rear Axle Timken Detroit
Steering Gemmer
Brakes 2 wheel external contracting, mechanical
Emergency Brake Internal expanding
Springs F = 36⅞; R = 55½"; semi elliptic, Perfection
Wheels Hayes Wire, Disteel Disc, wood
Tires 32 × 4
Wheelbase 120 inch
Body American, Ohio
Weight Touring car = 2900; Playboy = 2850; Brougham = 3100; Landaulet = 3100; Sedan = 3200

Model MX

Engine Continental 6S 6 cylinder
Bore and Stroke 3 5/16 × 4¾
Carburetor Stromberg LS2 +02
Ignition Delco Distributor 5264
Generator Delco 234 + 256
Starter Delco 181 + 208
Fuel Supply Stewart vacuum tank
Spark Plugs Champion "Toledo"
Radiator Sparton, Cleveland
Frame Hydraulic Pressed Steel Co.
Clutch Detroit
Transmission Detroit Gear
Front Axle Timken
Rear Axle Timken Detroit
Steering Gemmer
Brakes 2 wheel external contracting, Mechanical
Emergency Brake Internal expanding
Springs F = 36⅞"; R = 55¾"; semi elliptic, Perfection
Wheels Hayes Wire, Wire Wheel Corp., Disteel Disc, Budd Disc, wood. Rim: Motor Wheel Corp., Firestone Type E
Tires 32 × 4
Wheelbase 120 inch
Body American, Bryant, Ohio, Walker
Weight 5 Passenger Touring = 2,825; Sedan = 3,242; Playboy = 2,790; Brougham = 3,160; Landaulet = 3,160; Blueboy = 3,000

Model H

Engine Continental 6S 6 cylinder
Bore and Stroke 3 5/16 × 4¾
Carburetor Stromberg LS2 + 02
Ignition Delco Distributor 5264
Generator Delco 234 + 256
Starter Delco 181 + 208
Fuel Supply Stewart vacuum tank
Spark Plugs Champion "Toledo"
Radiator Sparton, Cleveland
Frame Hydraulic Pressed Steel Co., Parish & Bingham
Clutch Detroit
Transmission Detroit Gear
Front Axle Timken
Rear Axle Timken
Steering Gemmer
Brakes 2 wheel external contracting, mechanical
Emergency Brake Internal expanding
Springs F = 36⅞"; R = 55¾"; semi elliptic, Perfection
Wheels Hayes Wire, Wire Wheel Corp., Disteel Disc, Budd Disc, wood. Rim: Motor Wheel Corp., Firestone Type E
Tires 32 × 4½
Wheelbase 124½ inch
Body Bryant
Weight Blueboy = 3,125; 7 Passenger Sedan = 3,585

Model K

Engine Continental 6S 6 cylinder
Bore and Stroke 3 5/16 × 4¾
Carburetor Stromberg 02
Ignition Delco Distributor 5264
Generator Delco 256
Starter Delco 208
Fuel Supply Stewart vacuum tank
Spark Plugs Champion "Toledo"
Radiator Sparton, Cleveland
Frame Parish & Bingham
Clutch Detroit
Transmission Detroit Gear
Front Axle Timken
Rear Axle Timken Detroit
Steering Gemmer
Brakes 1st Type: External contracting 2 wheel mechanical
2nd Type: External contracting 4 wheel hydraulic, Lockheed
Emergency Brake 2 wheel mechanical = Internal Expanding; 4 wheel hydraulic = External Contracting-Transmission
Springs F = 37⅞"; R = 55¾; semi elliptic, Perfection
Wheels Wire Wheel Corp., Tuarc Disc, wood. Rims = Jaxon, Firestone
Tires 32 × 4½ (2 wheel brakes), 32 × 6 (4 wheel brakes)
Wheelbase 120 inch
Body American, Bryant, Ohio, Walker
Weight Five Passenger Touring = 3,135; Playboy = 3,075; Victoria = 3,304; 4 Door Brougham = 3,430

Model L

Engine Continental 6S 6 cylinder
Bore and Stroke 3 5/16 × 4¾

Carburetor Stromberg 02
Ignition Delco Distributor 5264
Generator Delco 256
Starter Delco 208
Fuel Supply Stewart vacuum tank
Spark Plugs Champion "Toledo"
Radiator Sparton, Cleveland
Frame Hydraulic Pressed Steel Co., Parish & Bingham
Clutch Detroit
Transmission Detroit Gear
Front Axle Timken
Rear Axle Timken Detroit
Steering Gemmer
Brakes 1st Type: External contracting 2 wheel mechanical. 2nd Type: External contracting 4 wheel hydraulic, Lockheed
Emergency Brake 2 wheel mechanical = Internal Expanding; 4 wheel hydraulic = External Contracting-Transmission
Springs F = 37"; R = 55¾"; semi elliptic, Perfection
Wheels Wire wheel Corp., Tuarc Disc, wood. Rims: Jaxon, Firestone
Tires 32 × 4½ (2 wheel brakes), 32 × 6 (4 wheel brakes)
Wheelbase 124½ inch
Body Bryant
Weight Blue Boy = 3,210; 5 Passenger Sedan = 3,490; 7 Passenger Sedan = 3,600

Model A & AA

Engine Continental 9K 8 cylinder
Bore and Stroke 3 × 4¾
Carburetor Stromberg OX2
Ignition American Bosch Distributor 8202
Generator American Bosch 1261
Starter American Bosch 937
Fuel Supply Stewart vacuum tank
Spark Plugs Champion
Radiator Cleveland, Fedders
Frame Parish & Bingham
Clutch Detroit
Transmission Detroit Gear
Front Axle Early: Timken; Late: Eaton
Rear Axle Early: Timken; Late: Eaton
Steering Gemmer
Brakes 4 wheel hydraulic contracting, Lockheed
Emergency Brake External contracting, transmission
Springs F = 37"; R = 55¾"; semi elliptic, Mather
Wheels Tuarc Disc, wood
Tires 32 × 6.20 (Firestone 20 inch rims)
Wheelbase 125½" & 132"
Body A Bodies: Sedan = Bryant; Brougham = Ohio; Touring = Ohio; Playboy = Ohio; Victoria = Bryant; 7 Passenger Sedan = Ohio (?); Friendly three = Bryant. AA Bodies: Custom Sedan = Bryant; Custom Victoria = Bryant; Touring = Ohio; Sport Coupe (?)
Weight A: Five Passenger Touring = 3,340; Brougham = 3,635; Five Passenger Sedan = 3,525; Playboy = 3,035; Seven Passenger Sedan = 3,785. AA: Custom Sedan = 3,525; Sport Coupe = 3,340; Custom Victoria = 3,625 Friendly Three ?; Seven Passenger Touring ?

Model J, Early J1

Engine Continental 8S 8 cylinder
Bore and Stroke 2⅞ × 4¾
Carburetor Stromberg OX2
Ignition American Bosch Distributor 8202, 8218
Generator American Bosch 1261, 1277
Starter American Bosch 937, 965
Fuel Supply Stewart vacuum tank
Spark Plugs Champion
Radiator Cleveland, Fedders
Frame Parish & Bingham
Clutch Long
Transmission Warner Gear
Front Axle Timken
Rear Axle Timken Detroit
Steering Gemmer
Brakes 4 wheel hydraulic contracting, Lockheed
Emergency Brake External contracting, transmission
Springs F = 37"; R = 55¾; semi elliptic, Mather
Wheels Disc, wood (Firestone rims)
Tires 30 × 6
Wheelbase 116 inch & 132 inch
Body Victoria = Ohio; 5 Passenger Sedan = Budd; 7 Passenger Sedan = Budd (?); Playboy = Budd
Weight Five Passenger Sedan = 3,200; Playboy = 3,035; Victoria = 3,290

Model J1 (Late)

Engine Continental 8S 8 cylinder
Bore and Stroke 2⅞ × 4¾
Carburetor Stromberg OX2
Ignition Autolite Distributor 1B-4004-A
Generator Autolite GAB-4002
Starter Autolite MUA-4003
Fuel Supply Stewart vacuum tank
Spark Plugs Champion #4
Radiator Cleveland, Fedders
Frame Parish & Bingham
Clutch Long
Transmission Warner Gear
Front Axle Timken
Rear Axle Timken Detroit
Steering Gemmer
Brakes 4 wheel hydraulic contracting, Lockheed
Emergency Brake External contracting, transmission
Springs F = 37"; R = 55¾; semi elliptic, Mather
Wheels Disc, wood (Firestone rims)
Tires 30 × 6
Wheelbase 116 inch
Body Sedan = Budd; Playboy = Budd; Custom Victoria = Ohio; Sport Coupe = Ohio
Weight Five Passenger Custom Sedan = 3,200; Sport Coupe = 3,070; Custom Victoria = 3,200; Playboy = 2,915

Model R
Little Custom

Engine Continental 12E 6 cylinder
Bore and Stroke 3¼ × 4
Carburetor Stromberg OX-2
Ignition Autolite IGA4013
Generator Autolite GYA4207
Starter Autolite MN4124
Fuel Supply Stewart vacuum tank
Spark Plugs Champion
Radiator Fedders
Frame Parish & Bingham, Midland
Clutch Long
Transmission Warner Gear
Front Axle Columbia

Rear Axle Columbia (worm drive); gear furnished by Cleveland Worm & Gear Co.
Steering Gemmer
Brakes 4 wheel hydraulic contracting, Lockheed
Emergency Brake External contracting, transmission
Springs F = 36"; R = 55¼"; semi elliptic, Mather
Wheels Wire, disc, wood (Firestone & Goodyear rims)
Tires 28 × 5.25
Wheelbase 107 inch
Body Blueboy = Ohio; Sport Salon = Ohio; Sedan = Murray; Tomboy = Murray
Weight Tomboy = 2,650; Sport Salon = 2,775; Sedan = 2,775; Blueboy = 2,800

Model JE (Early & Mid-Year) Air Line Eight

Engine Continental 14S 8 cylinder
Bore and Stroke 3 × 4¾
Carburetor Stromberg 00–2
Ignition Autolite 1GU4001
Generator Autolite GAG4105
Starter Autolite MUA4003
Fuel Supply Stewart vacuum tank
Spark Plugs Champion
Radiator Fedders
Frame Midland
Clutch Long
Transmission Warner Gear
Front Axle Timken
Rear Axle Timken Detroit
Steering Gemmer
Brakes 4 wheel hydraulic contracting, Lockheed
Emergency Brake External contracting, transmission
Springs F = 38"; R = 57"; semi elliptic, Mather
Wheels Wood, wire (midyear), 18 inch (Motor Wheel rims)
Tires 30 × 6
Wheelbase 116 inch
Body Murray
Weight Five Passenger Sedan = 3,300; Victoria = 3,275; Coupe = 3,185

Model RE Cross Country Six

Engine Continental 14E 6 cylinder
Bore and Stroke 3⅜ × 4
Carburetor Stromberg TXV2
Ignition Autolite GA4013
Generator Autolite GYA4207
Starter Autolite MN4124
Fuel Supply Stewart vacuum tank
Spark Plugs Champion
Radiator Fedders
Frame Midland
Clutch Long
Transmission Warner Gear
Front Axle Columbia
Rear Axle Columbia (worm drive); gear furnished by Cleveland Worm & Gear Co.
Steering Gemmer
Brakes 4 wheel hydraulic contracting, Lockheed
Emergency Brake External contracting, transmission
Springs F = 36"; R = 55¼"; semi elliptic, Mather
Wheels Wire, disc, wood (Rims: Firestone, Goodyear)
Tires 28 × 5.25
Wheelbase 107 inch
Body Sport Four = Ohio; Sedan = Murray; Tomboy = Murray
Weight Tomboy = 2,650; Sport 4 = 2,775; Sedan = 2,775

Model JE (Late) Air Line Eight

Engine Continental 15S 8 cylinder
Bore and Stroke 3 × 4¾
Carburetor Stromberg 002
Ignition Autolite IGU4001
Generator Autolite GAG4105
Starter Autolite MUA4003
Fuel Supply Stewart vacuum tank
Spark Plugs Champion
Radiator Fedders
Frame Midland
Clutch Long
Transmission Warner Gear
Front Axle Timken
Rear Axle Timken Detroit
Steering Gemmer
Brakes 4 wheel hydraulic contracting, Lockheed
Emergency Brake External contracting, transmission
Springs F = 38"; R = 57"; semi elliptic, Mather
Wheels Wire, wood (18 inch Motor Wheel rims)
Tires 30 × 6
Wheelbase 116 inch
Body Murray
Weight Five Passenger Sedan = 3,300; Victoria = 3,275; Coupe = 3,185; Landau Sedan = 3,300

Model JJ

Note: Very little information for the Model JJ exists.
Engine Continental 14S 8 cylinder
Bore and Stroke 3 × 4¾
Carburetor Stromberg 002
Ignition, Generator, and Starter were probably same as Early Model JE
Starter American Bosch 965
Fuel Supply Stewart vacuum tank
Spark Plugs Champion
Radiator Cleveland, Fedders
Frame Parish & Bingham
Clutch Long
Transmission Warner Gear
Front Axle Timken
Rear Axle Timken Detroit
Steering Gemmer
Brakes 4 wheel hydraulic contracting, Lockheed
Emergency Brake External contracting, transmission
Springs F = 37"; R = 55¾"; semi elliptic, Mather
Wheels Disc, wood (Firestone rims)
Tires 30 × 6
Wheelbase 116 inch
Body Sedan = Budd (?); Coupe = Ohio (?)
Weight Five Passenger Sedan = 3,200; Sport Coupe = 3,070

Model G Great Line Ninety

Engine Continental 15S 8 cylinder
Bore and Stroke 3 × 4¾
Carburetor Stromberg UU2
Ignition Autolite Distributor 1GJ4001-A
Generator Autolite GAG-4109
Starter Autolite MUA-4007

Fuel Supply Motor driven fuel pump (Stewart Warner)
Spark Plugs Champion, AC
Radiator Jamestown Metal Equipment Co.
Frame Midland
Clutch Long 9AB
Transmission Warner Gear T 69
Front Axle Columbia
Rear Axle Columbia
Steering Gemmer (Marles Type)
Brakes 4 wheel hydraulic expanding, Wagner
Emergency Brake External contracting, transmission
Springs F = 37"; R = 55¾"; semi elliptic, Mather
Wheels Wire, wood (Rims: Kelsey Hayes)
Tires 30 × 6.00
Wheelbase 125"; 131" (Seven Passenger Touring, Limousine, 7 Passenger Sedan)
Body Murray ?
Weight Sedan = 3,850; Speedboy = 3,600; Playboy = 3,525; Coupe = 3,600; Sport Sedan = 3,600; Collapsible Coupe = 3,540; Seven Passenger Touring = 3,725; Seven Passenger Sedan = 3,900; Seven Passenger Limousine = 3,900

Model E

Engine Continental 18C 6 cylinder
Bore and Stroke 3⅜ × 4⅝
Carburetor Stromberg UX2
Ignition Autolite Distributor 1GB 4006-A
Generator Autolite GAG-4114
Starter Autolite MAD-4104
Fuel Supply Engine driven fuel pump
Spark Plugs Champion
Radiator Fedders, Jamestown Metal Equipment co.
Frame Midland
Clutch Long 9ABM
Transmission Warner Gear T64K
Front Axle Columbia
Rear Axle Columbia
Steering Gemmer
Brakes 4 wheel hydraulic expanding, Lockheed
Emergency Brake External contracting, transmission
Springs F = 37"; R = 52"; semi elliptic, Mather
Wheels Wire, wood
Tires 550 × 18 (28 × 5.50)
Wheelbase 116
Body Murray ?
Weight 3,500

Model T Standard Line 80

Engine Continental 17S 8 cylinder
Bore and Stroke 2⅞ × 4¾
Carburetor Stromberg U2
Ignition Autolite Distributor 1GH-4005A
Generator Autolite GAL4126
Starter Autolite MUA4007
Fuel Supply Engine driven fuel pump
Spark Plugs Champion
Radiator Jamestown Metal Equipment Co.
Frame Midland
Clutch Long 9AB
Transmission Warner Gear T2C
Front Axle Columbia
Rear Axle Columbia
Steering Gemmer (Marles type)
Brakes 4 wheel hydraulic expanding, Wagner
Emergency Brake External Contracting, transmission
Springs F = 37"; R = 55¾"; semi elliptic, Mather
Wheels Wire, wood (18 inch Motor Wheel Corp.); Rims = Firestone
Tires 28 × 5.50
Wheelbase 120 inch
Body Murray ?
Weight Sedan = 3,590; Coupe = 3,440

Model U Line 70 Sunshine Sedan

Engine Continental 17S 8 cylinder
Bore and Stroke 2⅞ × 4¾
Carburetor Tillotson
Ignition Autolite Distributor IGH-4005A
Generator Autolite GAL4126
Starter Autolite MUA4007
Fuel Supply Engine driven fuel pump
Spark Plugs Champion
Radiator Jamestown Metal Equipment Co.
Frame Midland
Clutch Long
Transmission Warner Gear
Front Axle Columbia
Rear Axle Columbia
Steering Ross
Brakes 4 wheel expanding, cable controlled, mechanical, Bendix
Emergency Brake Internal expanding, rear wheels
Springs F = 37"; R = 55¾"; semi elliptic, Mather
Wheels Wire, wood (Motor Wheel Corp.); Rims = Firestone
Tires 28 × 5.50
Wheelbase 120 inch
Body ? Probably Facto
Weight ?

Model Z Sportsman & Speedway Ace

Engine Continental 12K 8 cylinder
Bore and Stroke 3⅜ × 4½
Carburetor Schebler
Ignition Auto-Lite LGJ-EO 1164 Distributor
Generator Auto-Lite GAG-4108
Starter Auto-Lite ML 4146
Fuel Supply Engine driven fuel pump (A-C)
Spark Plugs Champion
Radiator Jamestown Metal Equipment Co.
Frame Midland
Clutch Borg-Beck 11-Q
Transmission Warner Gear (4 Speed) T4B
Front Axle Columbia
Rear Axle Columbia
Steering Gemmer 215 (Marles type)
Brakes 4 wheel hydraulic expanding, Wagner
Emergency Brake External contracting, transmission
Springs F = 37"; R = 55¾"; semi elliptic, Mather
Wheels Wire (Motor Wheel Corp.); Firestone rims
Tires 18 × 7.00
Wheelbase 145 inch
Body Facto Auto body Company, Cleveland, Ohio
Weight Sportsman Sedan = 4,575; Ace Roadster = 4,340

Appendix III

Engine Specifications

Specifications are taken from original Jordan documents and various other sources.

Model	*Engine*	*Cyl*	*Bore & Stroke*	*C.I.D.*	*SAE-NACC-H.P.*	*Brake H.P.*
60	7N	6	3½ × 5¼	303.30	29.40	50 @ 1,900 rpm
60C	10N	6	3½ × 5¼	303.30	29.40	56 @ 2,300 rpm
60F	9N	6	3½ × 5¼	303.30	29.40	56 @ 2,300 rpm
F	9N	6	3½ × 5¼	303.30	29.40	56 @ 2,300 rpm
M	7R	6	3¼ × 4½	224.00	25.35	56 @ 2,750 rpm
MX	6S	6	3⁵⁄₁₆ × 4¾	245.60	26.33	56 @ 2,400 rpm
H	6S	6	3⁵⁄₁₆ × 4¾	245.60	26.33	56 @ 2,400 rpm
K	6S	6	3⁵⁄₁₆ × 4¾	245.60	26.33	56 @ 2,400 rpm
L	6S	6	3⁵⁄₁₆ × 4¾	245.60	26.33	56 @ 2,400 rpm
A	9K	8	3 × 4¾	268.60	28.80	74 @ 3,000 rpm
AA	9K	8	3 × 4¾	268.60	28.80	74 @ 3,000 rpm
J	8S	8	2⅞ × 4¾	246.60	26.40	64 @ 3,000 rpm
J1	8S	8	2⅞ × 4¾	246.60	26.40	64 @ 3,000 rpm
JJ	14S	8	3 × 4¾	268.60	28.90	80 @ 3,200 rpm
R	12E	6	3¼ × 4	199.00	25.35	62 @ 3,000 rpm
RE	14E	6	3⅜ × 4	215.00	27.34	61 @ 3,000 rpm
JE	14S	8	3 × 4¾	268.60	28.90	80 @ 3,200 rpm
JE Late	15S	8	3 × 4¾	268.60	28.90	85 @ 3,200 rpm
E	18C	6	3⅜ × 4⅝	248.30	27.40	70 @ 3,000 rpm
G	15S	8	3 × 4¾	268.60	28.90	85 @ 3,200 rpm
GL 90	15S	8	3 × 4¾	268.60	28.90	85 @ 3,200 rpm
T	17S	8	2⅞ × 4¾	246.70	26.45	80 @ 3,000 rpm
U	17S	8	2⅞ × 4¾	246.70	26.45	80 @ 3,000 rpm
Z	12K	8	3⅜ × 4½	322.00	36.45	114 @ 3,200 rpm

Appendix IV

Serial Numbers

The following are from an official Jordan bulletin issued to distributors and dealers in March 1927.

Year	Model	Serial Number
1916	60	152–600
1917	60	601–2,157
1918	60-C	3,001–5,049
1919	60-C	5,050–5,298
1919	F	5,401–7,250
1919	M	10,001–10,700
1920	F	7,251–8,300
1920	M	10,701–13,500
1921	F	8,301–8,785
1921	M	13,501–15,491
1922	F	8,786–9,249
1922	MX	20,001–25,000
1923	MX	25,001–31,700
1923	H	35,001–38,000
1924	MX	31,701–33,320
1924	H	38,001–38,341
1924	K	50,001–51,400
1924	L	40,001–41,800
1925	K	51,401–52,649
1925	L	41,801–42,310
1925	A	60,001–64,200
1926	A & AA	64,201–66,825
		AA starts at #66,418
1926	J	70,001–79,920
1927	AA	DL682L
1927	J & J1	DY992S
1927	R	DE000S

The following are from Jordan instruction books.

Model MX	20,001–
Model MX-H	MX = 20,001–
	H = 35,001–
Model MX-H (2nd Edition)	MX = 20,001
	H = 35,001
Model K-L	K = 50,001
	L = 40,001
Model A	60,001
Model J	70,001
Model J (2nd Edition)	70,001
Model R Series (Fedco #)	DE000S and SD000S
Model RE	DE255S
Model JE	ST500S
Model E	95,000 Up
Model G	130,001 and Up
Model G—Great Line Ninety	131,153 and Up
Model T	96,001 and Up

The following serial numbers come from Jordan specifications sent to the National Automobile Chamber of Commerce (NACC).

Model U	Starting at 170,000
Model Z	Starting at 200,001

The following serial numbers come from sources other than Jordan. They should not be used as an absolute guide. In all probability they are inaccurate to some degree.

Model AA	1927	DL682L and Up
Model J & J1	1927	DY992S and Up
Model AA	1928	DL740D to DL772D
Model J1	1928	DN425D to DN583A
Model R	1927–1928	DE000S to DE255D
Model JE	1928	ST500S to ST650E
Model JJ	1928	DN583Y to DN658R
Model RE	1929	DE255S to DE431K
Model JE	1929	ST651D to ST728D
Model JE	1929	127,281 to 130,000

JE Models have both Fedco and regular Data Plates

Model G	1929 (30)	130,001 to 131,152
Model E	1929	95,001 to 95,999
Model G Great Line 90	1930	131,153, to 131,799
Model T	1930	96,000 to 96,399
Model Z	1930	200,001 and Up
		200,014 last Serial Number known

Model T	1931	96,400 to 96,568
Model G		
Great Line 90	1931	131,800 to 132,000
Model T	1932	96,569 to End
Model G		
Great Line 90	1932	132,001 to End

Fedco Numbering Code

Dan Jordan, a Jordan Register member residing in California, owns several Jordan automobiles and a large collection of memorabilia.

Being intrigued by the Fedco system, he and some friends set out to break the code. After many attempts they arrived at the following:

S	T	A	R	K	L	Y	N	E	D	FEDCO # System
1	2	3	4	5	6	7	8	9	0	Actual

Translated, you may be able to find your car's actual serial number.

The following number,

D	N	3	8	4	K
0	8	3	8	4	5

translates to Model J1 serial #83845.

APPENDIX V

Wiring Diagrams

These wiring diagrams have been taken from the Jordan instruction manual for each model.

Model 60 Series F and Model F are separate diagrams
Model 60 Series F is the Bijur System.
Model F is the Delco System.

There are no known diagrams for the Model U Sunshine Sedan or the Model Z.

The Model RE Sedan and the late Series JE would have cowl lights. The wiring diagrams for these two models do not show this.

Diagrams exist for all models (except U & Z) in several publications.

Wiring Diagram 1: Model 60

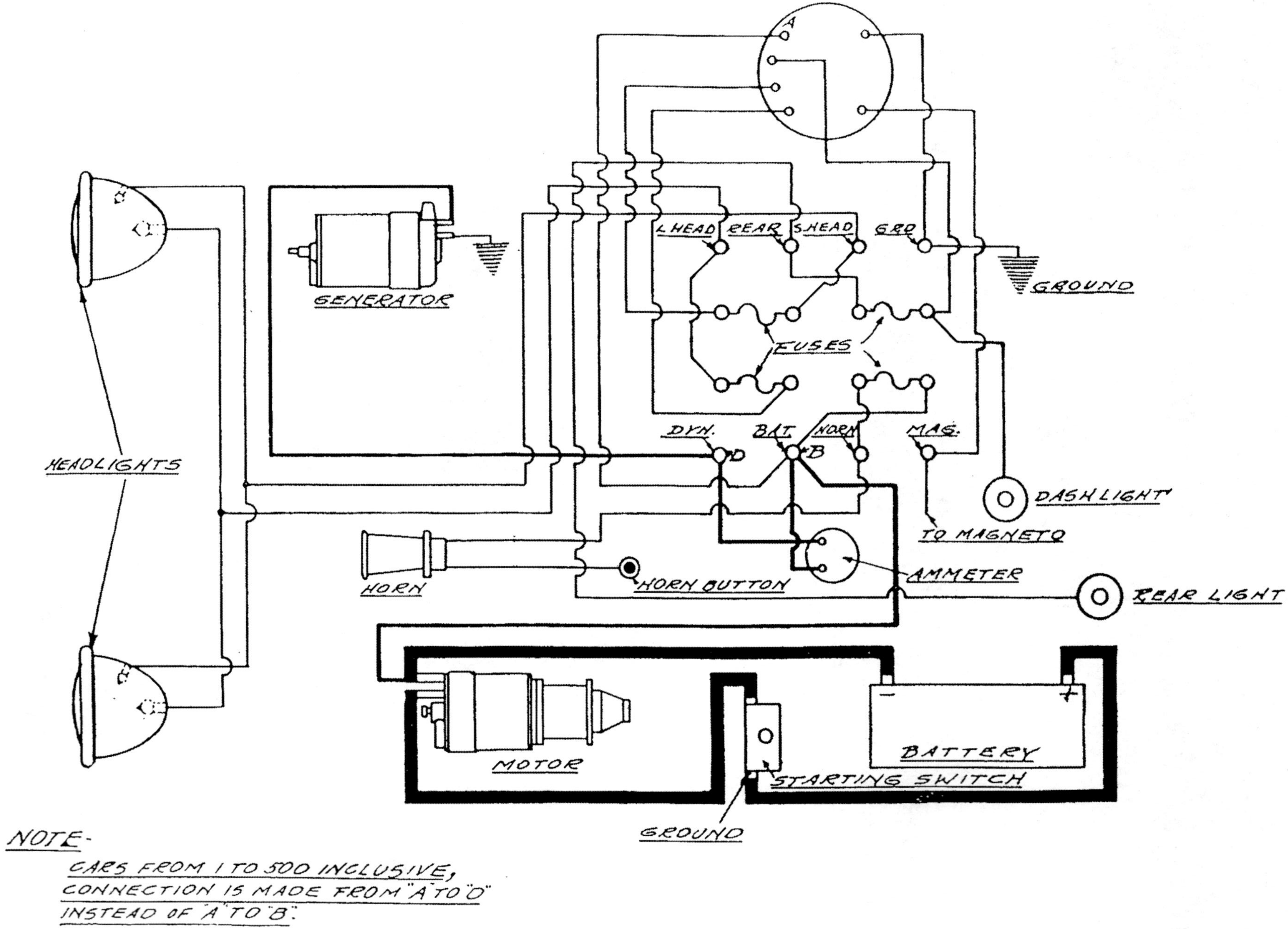

Wiring Diagram 2: Model 60 Series C

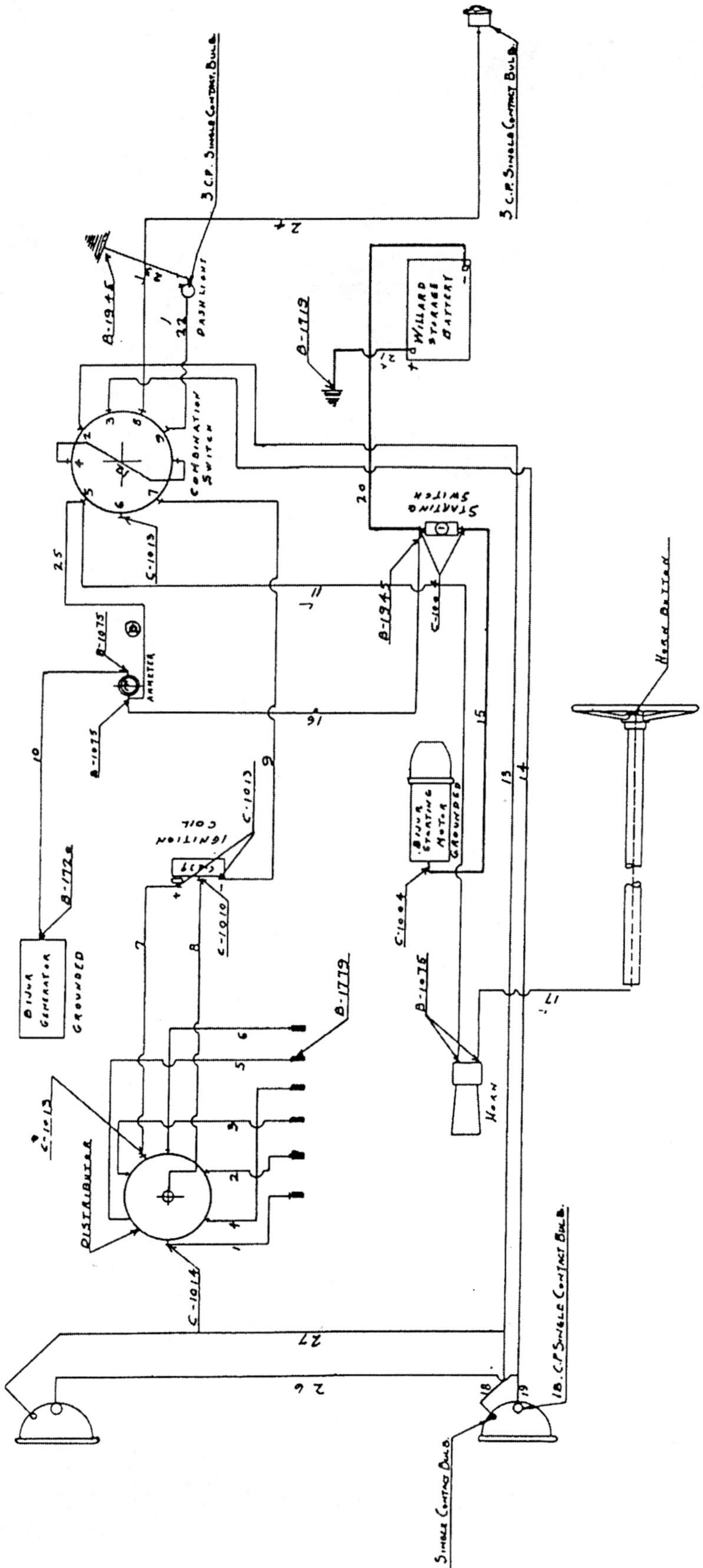

Wiring Diagram 3: Model 60 Series F

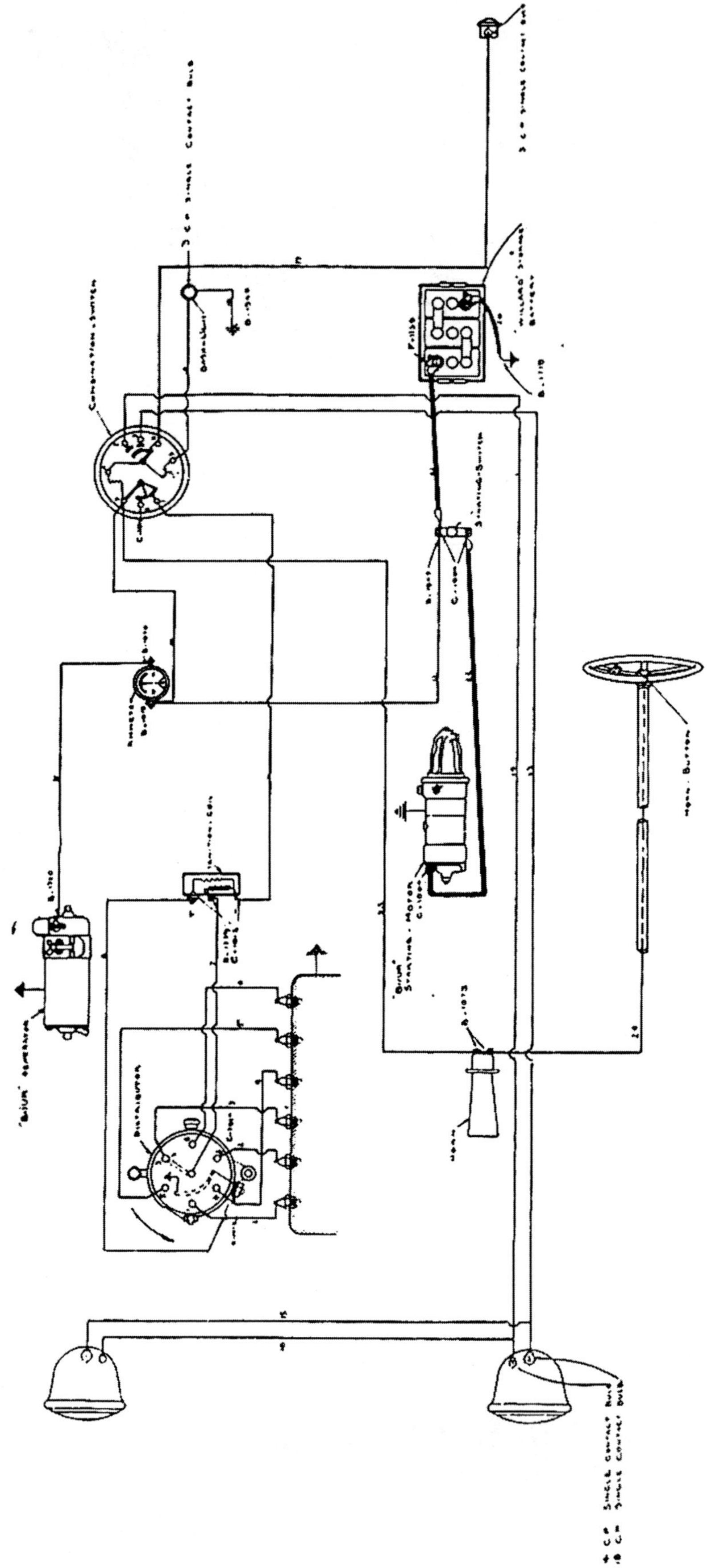

Wiring Diagram 4: Model F Series F

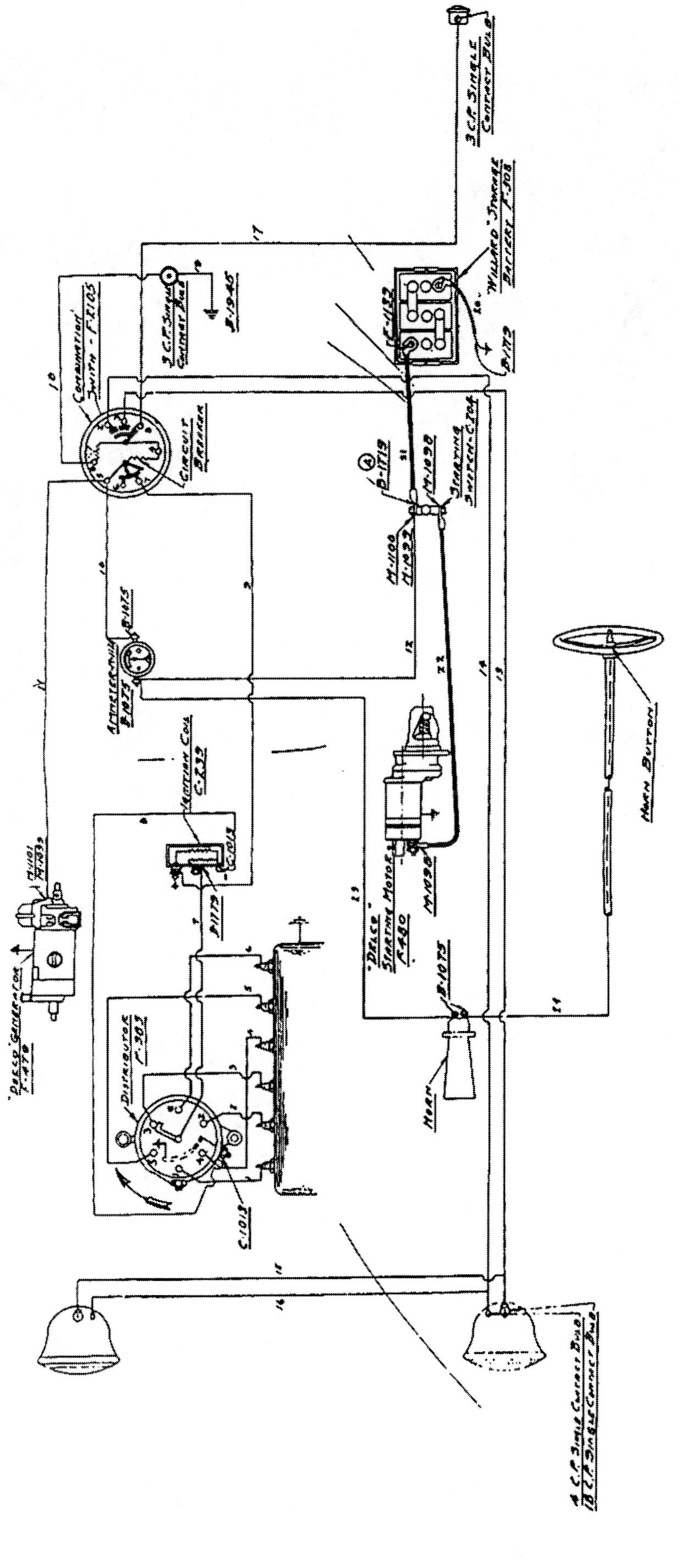

Wiring Diagram 5: Model M

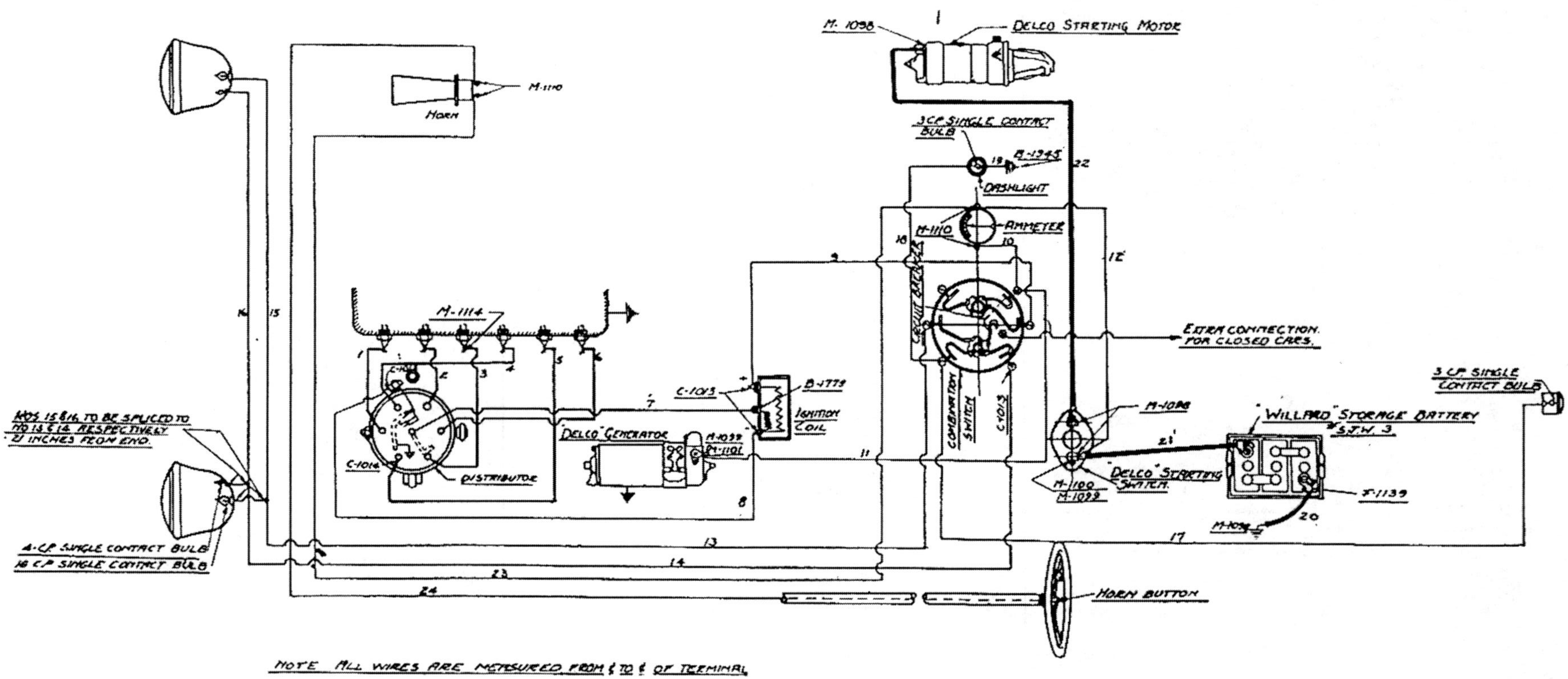

Wiring Diagram 6: Model MX-H

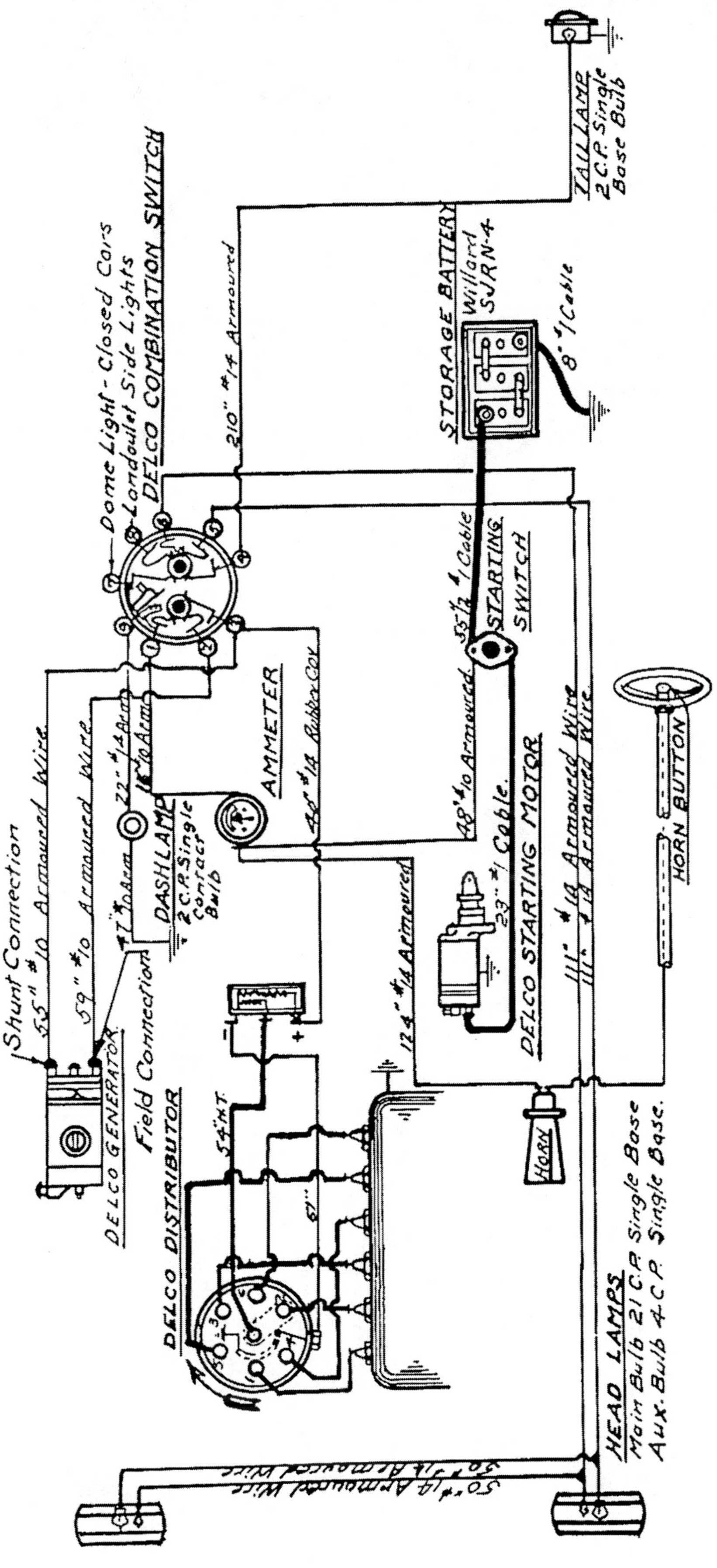

Wiring Diagram 7: Model K & L

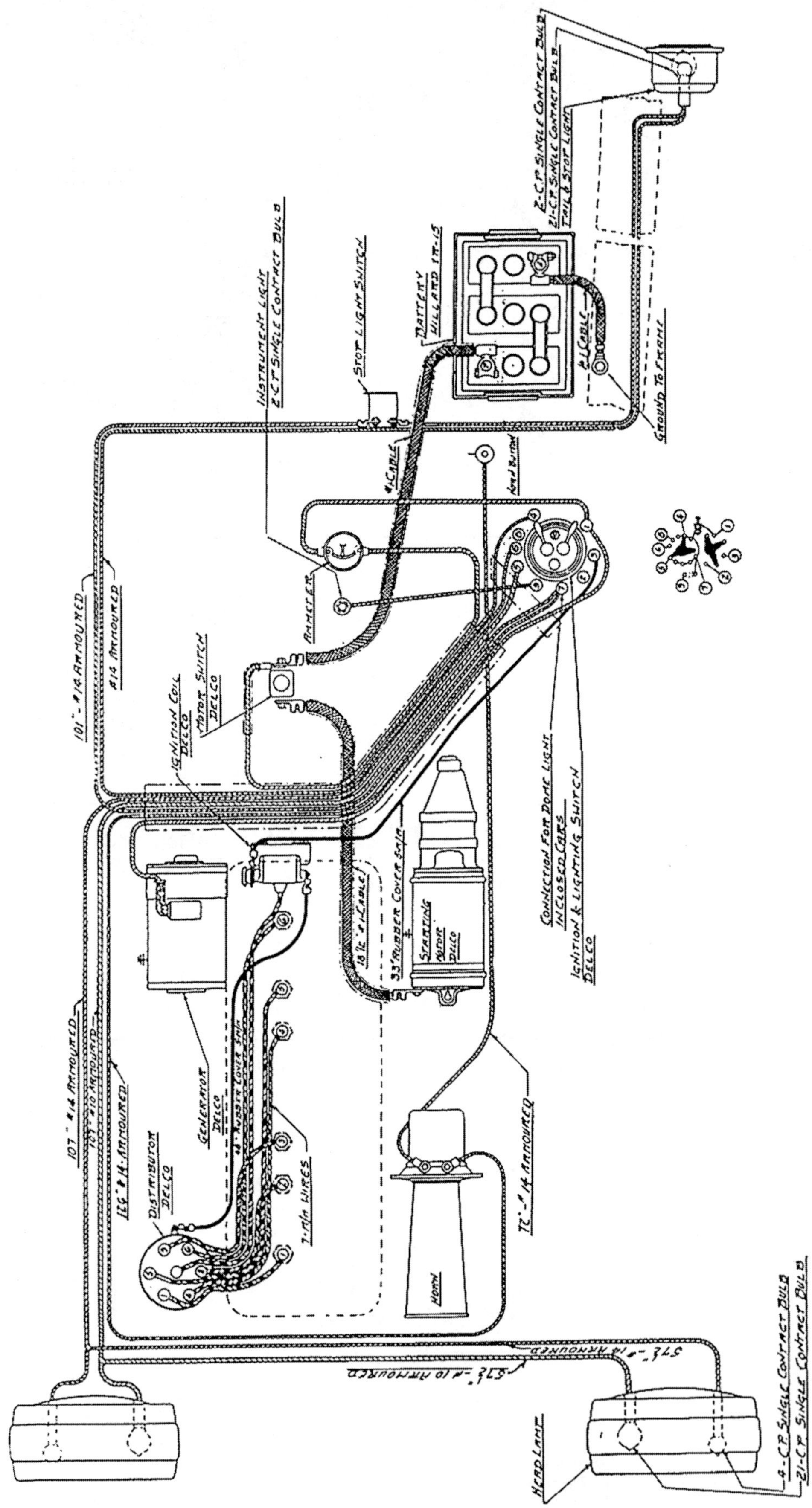

Wiring Diagram 8: Models A, AA

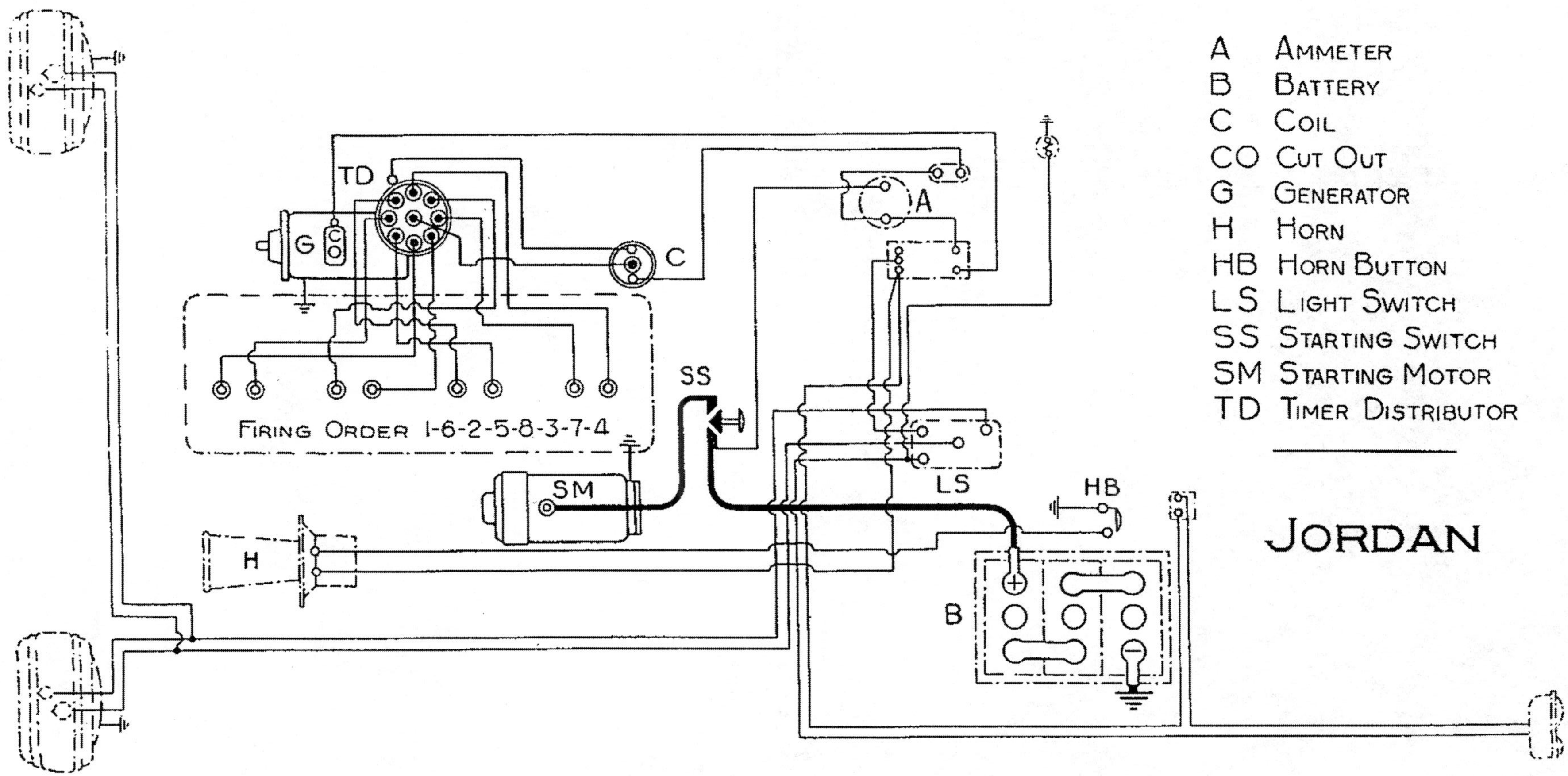

Wiring Diagram 9: Models J, J1, Possibly JJ

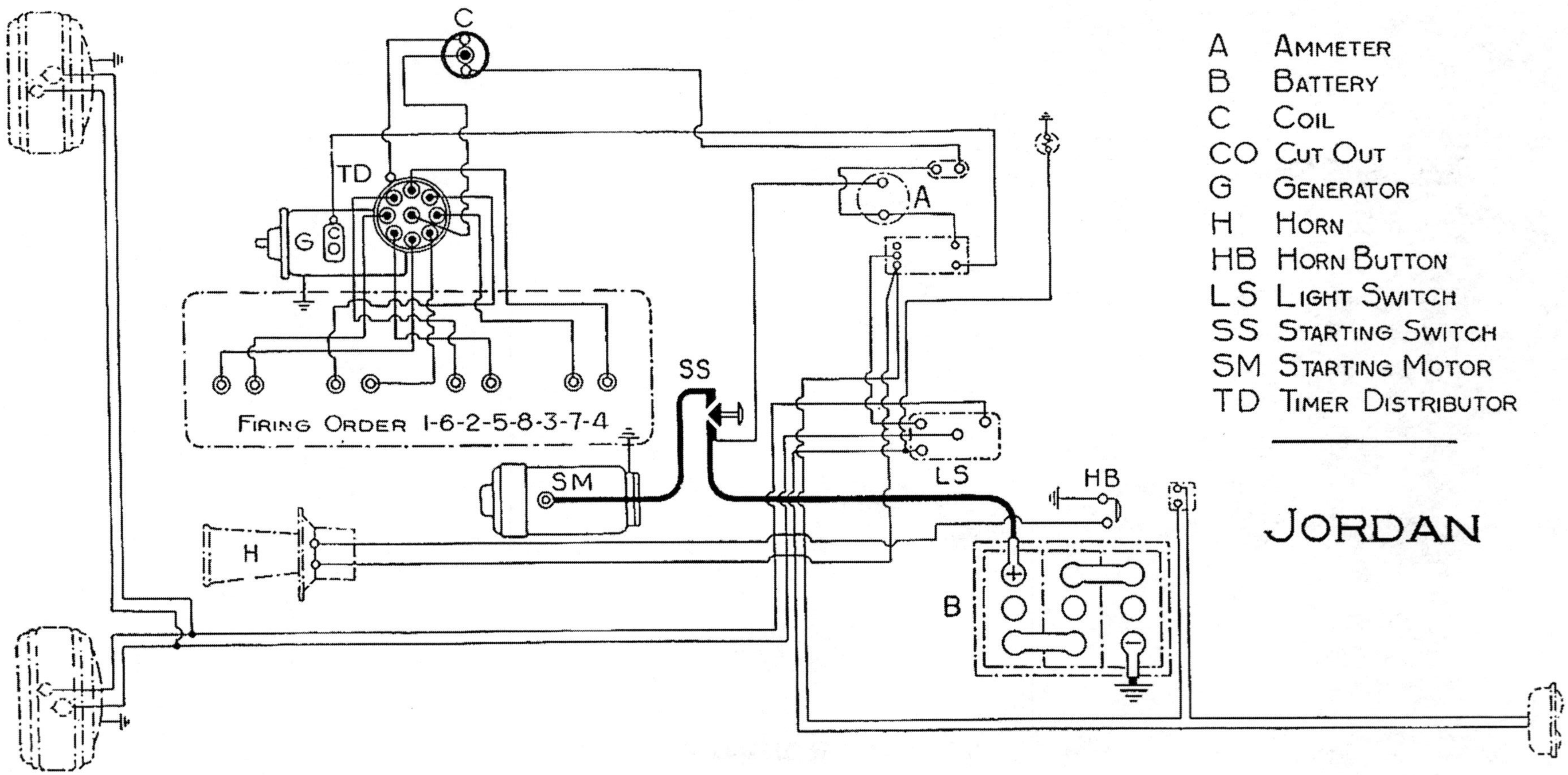

Wiring Diagram 10: Models R, RE

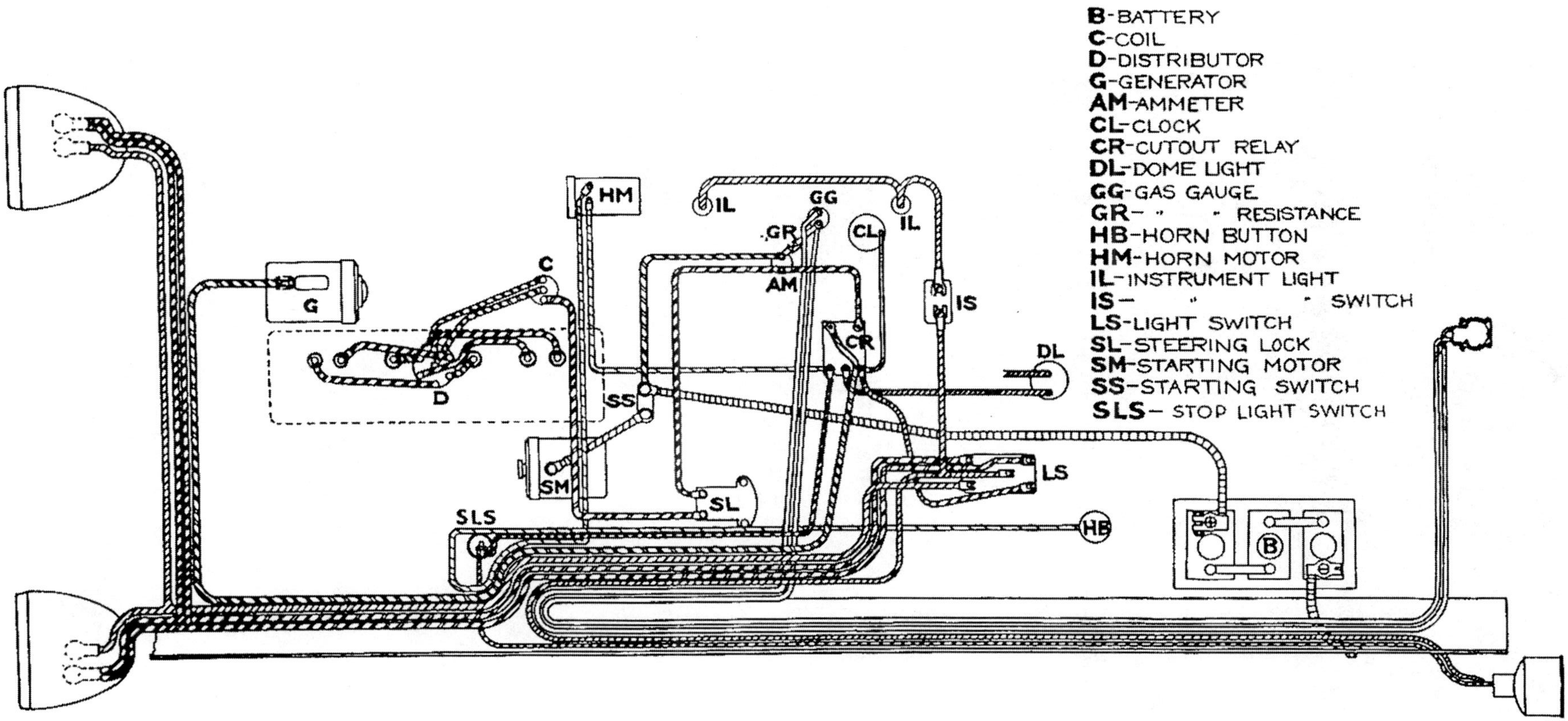

The RE Sedan had cowl lights. These would connect to the lighting switch where the former parking lights (in headlights) connected.

Wiring Diagram 11: Model JE

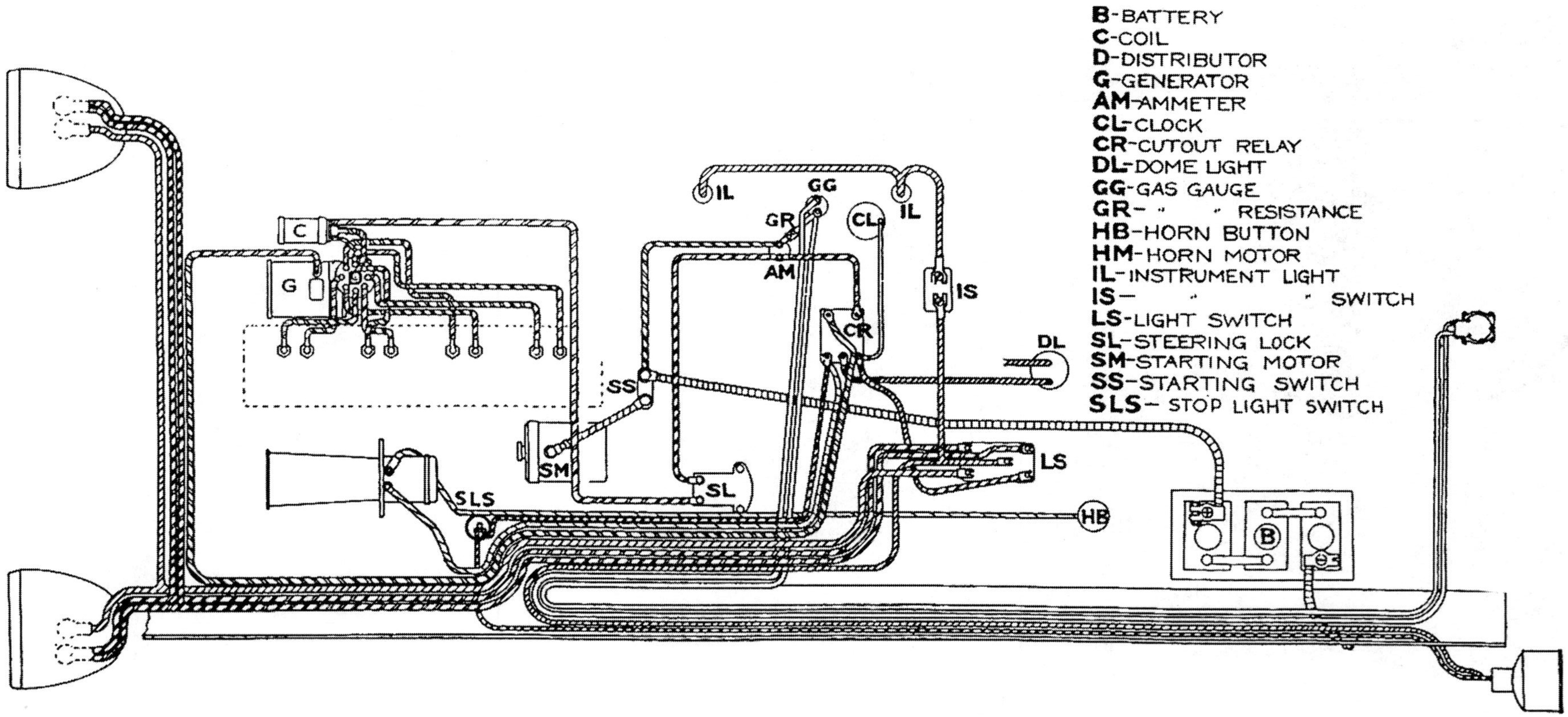

Late Series JE (15-S Engine) had cowl lights. These would connect to the lighting switch where the former parking lights (in headlights) connected.

Wiring Diagram 12: Model E

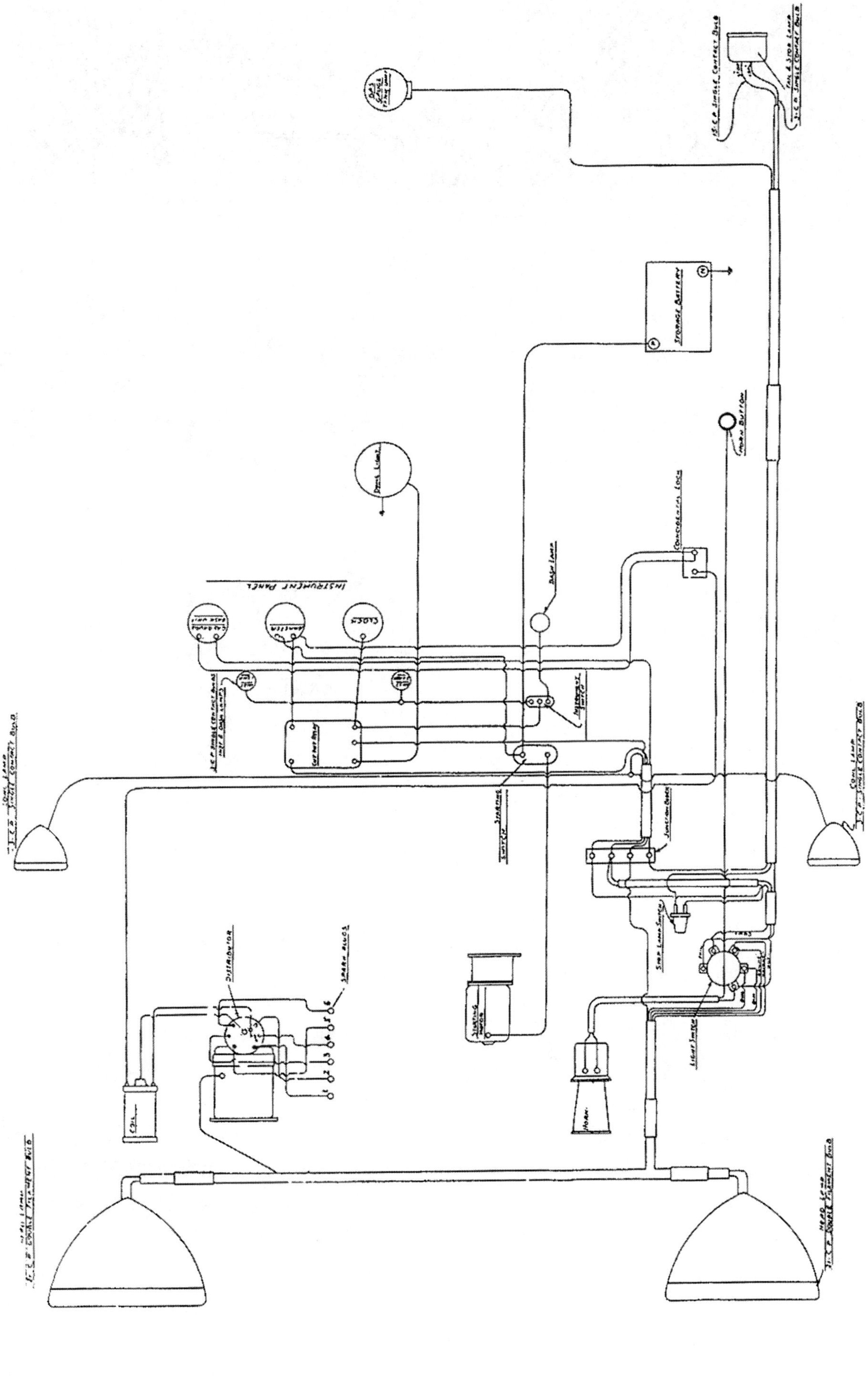

Wiring Diagram 13: Model T Standard Line 80

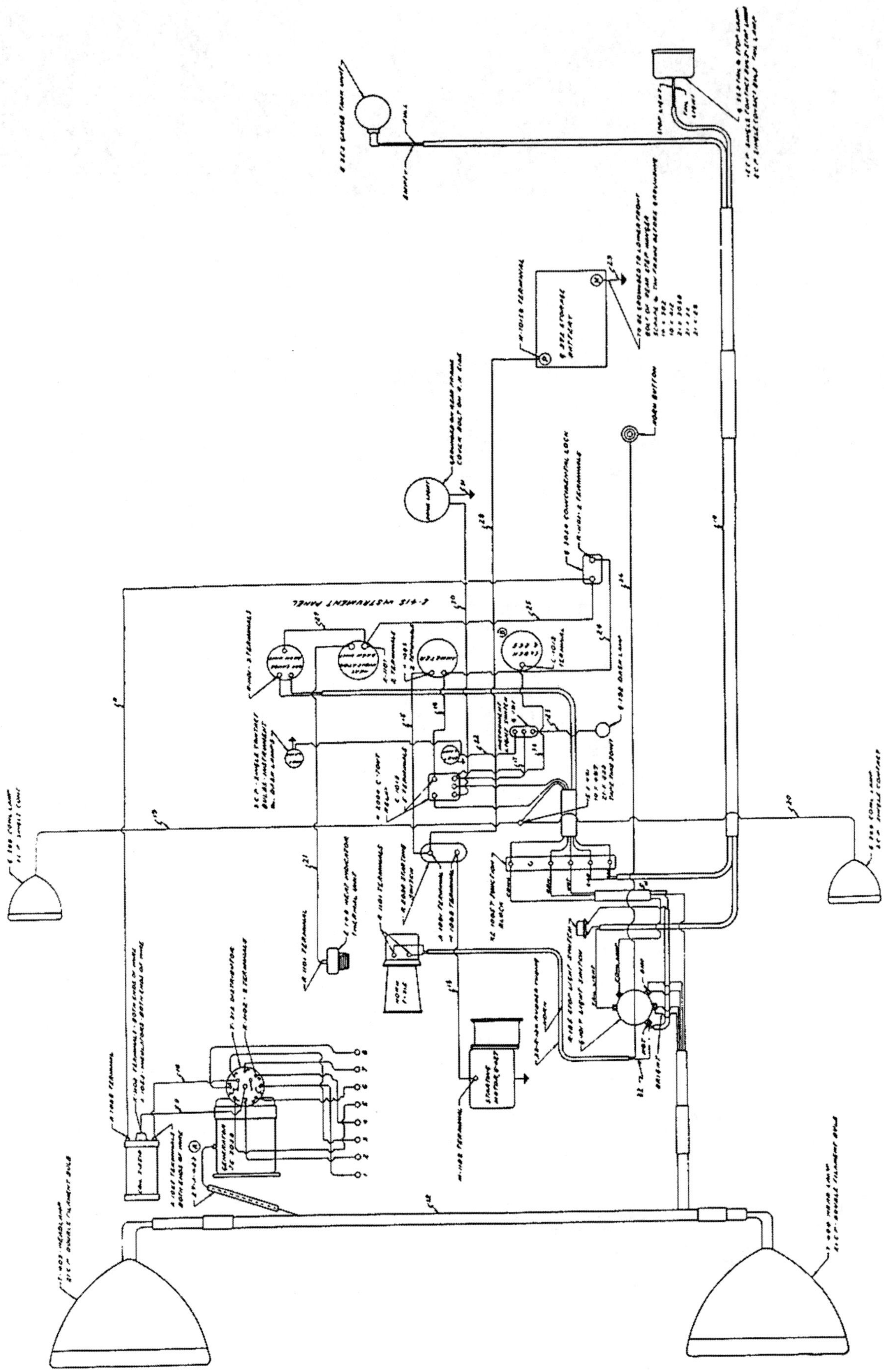

Wiring Diagram 14: Model G (1929 January to June)

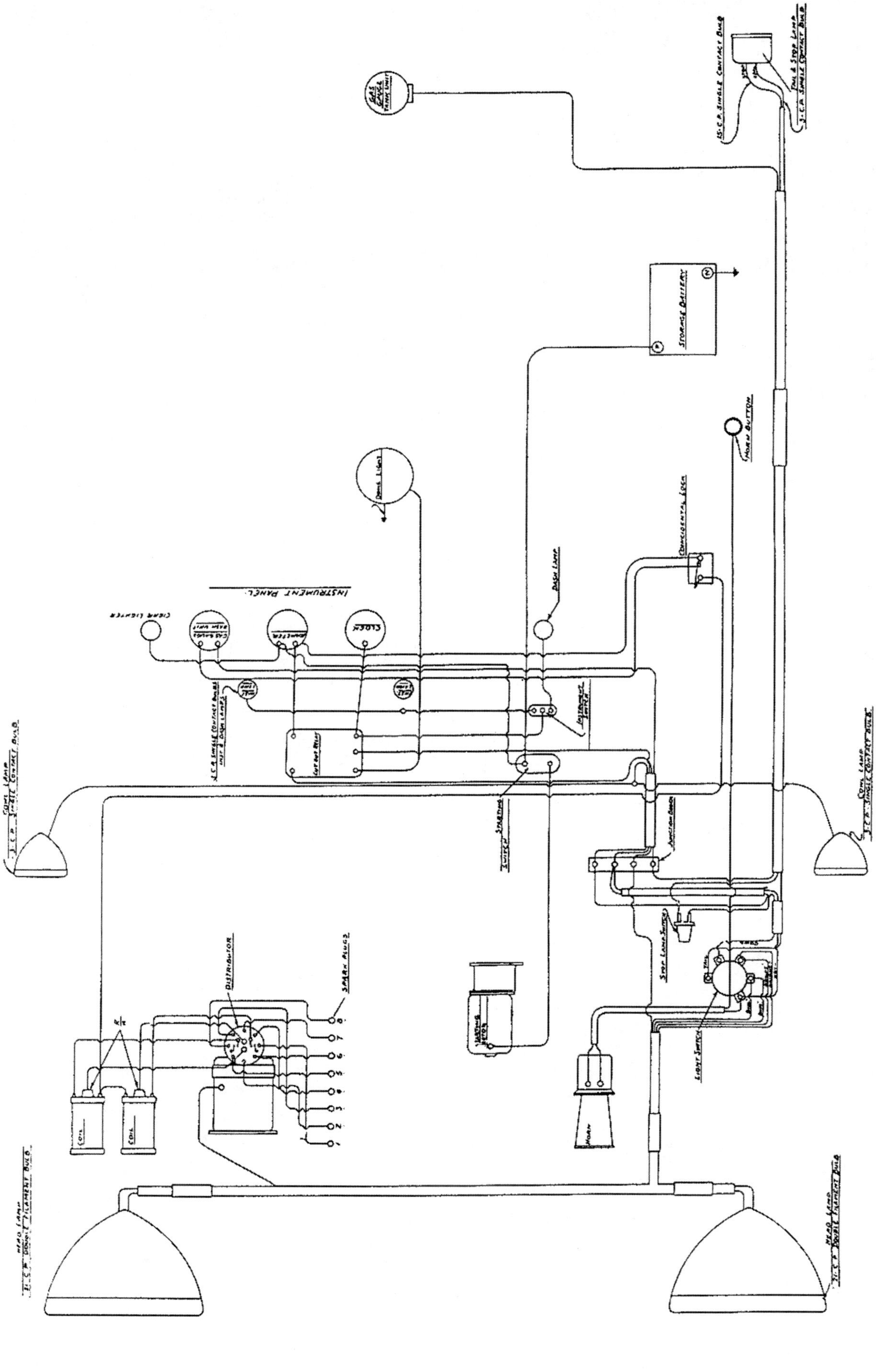

Wiring Diagram 15: Model G Great Line 90 (June 1930 to 1932)

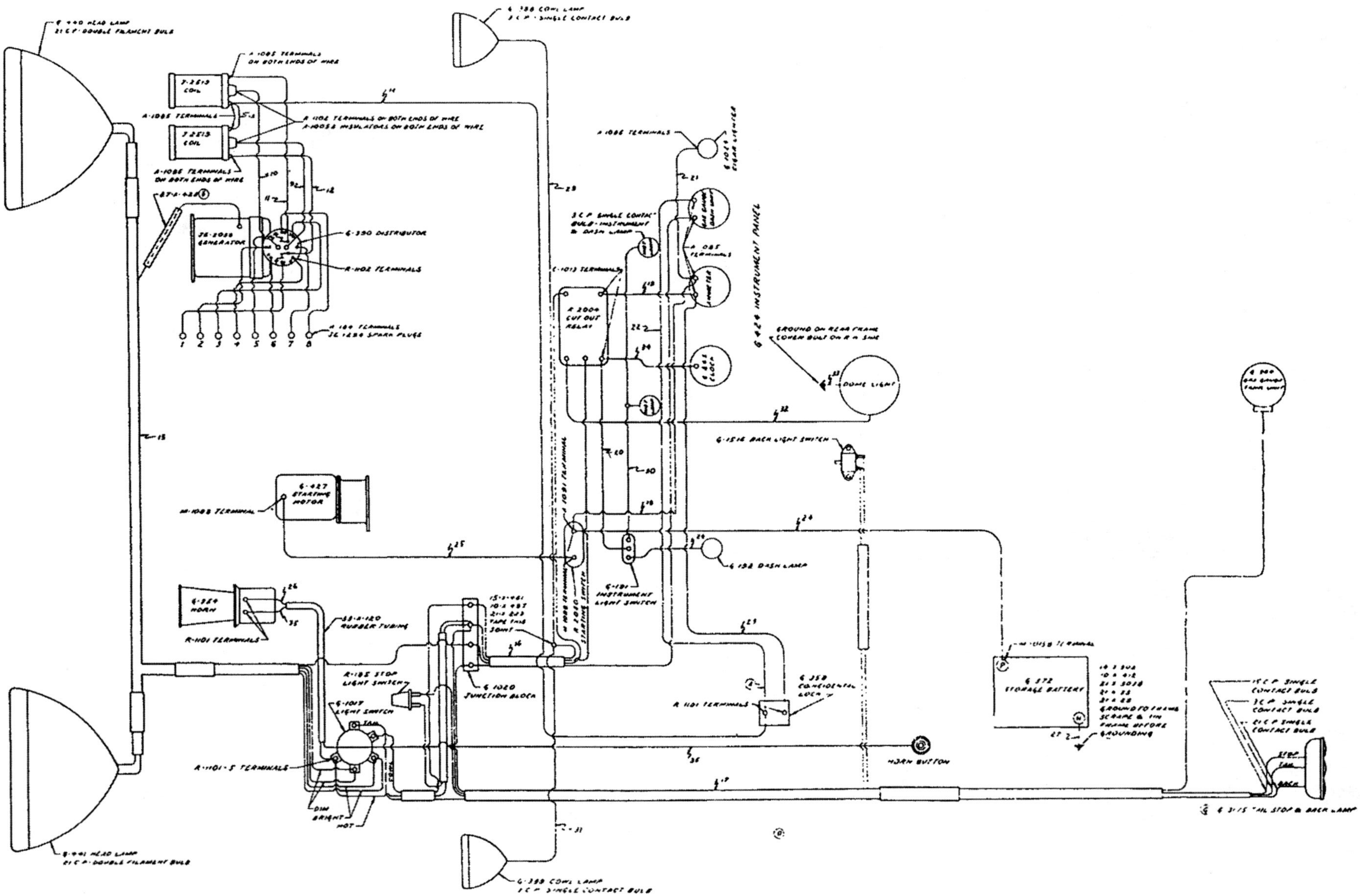

Bibliography

Books

Forbes, B.C., and Foster, O.D. *Automotive Giants of America: Men Who Are Making Our Motor Industry*. New York: B.C. Forbes Publishing Company, 1926, pp. 155–168.

Jordan, Edward S. *The Inside Story of Adam and Eve*. Utica, New York: Howard Coggeshall, 1945.

Pridemore, Jay, and Hurd, Jim. *The American Bicycle*. Osceola, Wisconsin: Motorbooks International, 1995, pp. 35–36, 108.

Ralston, Marc. *Pierce Arrow*. San Diego, California: A.S. Barnes, 1980, p. 147.

Reed, Walt. *The Illustrator in America 1860–2000*. New York: The Society of Illustrators, 2000.

Stubenrauch, Bob. *Runabouts and Roadsters*. New York: Dodd, Mead & Company, 1973, pp. 142–149.

Wager, Richard. *Golden Wheels: The Story of the Automobiles Made in Cleveland and Northeastern Ohio 1892–1932*. Cleveland, Ohio: Western Reserve Historical Society and The Cleveland Automobile Club, 1975, pp. 145–156.

Automotive Periodicals

Antique Automobile (Antique Automobile Club of America, Hershey, Pennsylvania)

"15th Annual Meeting." 15:2 (June 1951), p. 83.

Forgione, Lewis. "Somewhere West of Laramie." 33:5 (Sept./Oct. 1969), pp. 19–30.

Howley, Tim. When the Jordans Rolled." 30:2 (March/April 1966), pp. 4–20.

Lackey, James H. "Somewhere West of Laramie—The Rest of the Story." 60:5 (Sept./Oct. 1996), pp. 51–55.

Loose, Anson. "Speedboy." 65:1 (Jan./Feb.2001), pp. 30–33.

Automobile Quarterly (Automobile Quarterly Inc., Kutztown, Pennsylvania)

Grayson, Stan. "The All Steel World of Edward Budd." 16:4 (Fourth Quarter 1978), pp. 352–367.

Howley, Tim. "Ned Jordan—The Spell He Wove." 13:2 (Second Quarter 1975), pp. 160–167.

Kimes, Beverly Rae. "A Family in Kenosha: The Story of the Rambler and the Jeffery." 16:2 (Second Quarter 1978), pp. 128–145.

Langworth, Richard M. "Ned Jordan—The Cars He Built." 13:2 (Second Quarter 1975), pp. 168–181.

The Bulb Horn (The Veteran Motor Car Club of America, Glendale, Arizona)

MacIlvain, Walter O. "Who's Who in Automobilia." XX:2 (Spring 1959), pp. 5–10.

Cars & Parts (Amos Press, Sidney, Ohio)

"Forecasting Leadership." 13:1 (Oct. 1968), pp. 42–53.

Brown, Arch. "Meet the Playboy—The Most Remembered Jordan of All" (Jan. 1983), pp. 6–8.

_____. "The Magic Touch of Ned Jordan—The 1927 Jordan Line Eight Victoria" (Oct. 1989), pp. 34–37.

_____. "The Magic Touch of Ned Jordan—The Playboy and the Tomboy" (Nov. 1989), pp. 32–33, 36, 38, 40.

Shipley, Dean. "A Hint of Old Loves—1923 Jordan Playboy" (May 1996), pp. 28–30, 32–33, 36.

Zahm, Karl S. "Jordan—A Charming Something" (Aug. 1982), pp. 26–27.

_____. "Jordan—Flashy Cars and Flashy Prose" (Sept. 1982), pp. 26–82.

_____. "Jordan—The Final Years" (Oct. 1982), pp. 50–53.

Car Collector and Car Classics (Classic Publishing Inc., Norcross, Georgia)

Langworth, Richard M. "The Jordan Story from *The Inside Story of Adam and Eve*" (Dec. 1980), pp. 24–28.

_____. "Salon: 1928 Jordan Air Line Playboy" (Dec. 1980), pp. 29, 46–49.

The Classic Car (The Classic Car Club of America, Des Plaines, Illinois)

Zahm, Karl S. "The Remarkable History of Two Assembled Cars" (XXXVI:1), pp. 22–27.

Old Cars Weekly (Krause Publications, Inc., Iola, Wisconsin)

Howley, Tim. "Somewhere West of Laramie." June 30, 1988, pp. 6–7, and Feb. 9, 1995, p. 18.

The Packard Cormorant (The Packard Club Inc., Oakland, California; published at Contoocook, New Hampshire)
Griffiths, Gwilym G. "Packard's Artists: The Mastery of Fred Cole." #35 (Summer 1984), pp. 10–17.

Special Interest Autos (Special Interests Publications, Bennington, Vermont)
Gross, Ken. "It Roars Like a Caproni Biplane." #31 (Nov./Dec. 1975), pp. 18–19.
_____. "Never Carry a Package by the String." #31 (Nov./Dec. 1975), pp. 20–22, 52.
Howley, Tim. "The Last Cars from Somewhere West of Laramie." #127 (Jan./Feb. 1992), pp. 44–49.
Taylor, Rich. "Somewhere West of Laramie." #31 (Nov./Dec. 1975), pp. 12–17.

Other Periodicals

The American Magazine (Crowell Publishing Co., Springfield, Ohio), Aug. 1923.
The Atlantic Monthly (The Atlantic Monthly Co., Boston, Massachusetts), Feb. 19, 1918.
The Country Gentleman (Curtis Publishing Co., Philadelphia, Pennsylvania), August 28, 1920, p. 2; November 20, 1920, p. 21.
House and Garden (Condé Nast Publications, Inc., Greenwich, Connecticut, and New York), Nov. 1922, Jan. 1927, Aug. 1929.
The Literary Digest (Funk & Wagnalls Co., New York), Dec. 29, 1917, p. 49; Nov. 13, 1919, p. 45; Nov. 29, 1920, pp. 94–95, Apr. 12, 1924, p. 79.
Time Magazine (Time, Inc., Chicago, Illinois), November 23, 1925, pp. 36–37.
The Refresher (The Coca-Cola Company, Atlanta, Georgia), Dec. 1953, pp. 15–16; May 1964.
The Saturday Evening Post (Curtis Publishing Co., Philadelphia, Pennsylvania), Sept. 2, 1916, pp. 42–43; Nov. 18, 1916, p. 59; Sept. 6, 1919, p. 71; Nov. 8, 1919, p. 66; Nov. 6, 1920, p. 69; Sept. 16, 1922, p. 65; June 23, 1923, p. 129; Dec. 8, 1923, p. 85; Jan. 5, 1924, p. 57; Apr. 3, 1926, p. 104.
Vanity Fair (Condé Nast Publications, Inc., Greenwich, Connecticut, and New York), Aug. 1919.
Wonderful West Virginia (State of West Virginia Division of Natural Resources, Charleston, West Virginia), Feb. 2001, pp. 20–23.

Automotive Trade Journals

The Accessory and Garage Journal (Automobile Publishing Co., Pawtucket, Rhode Island), Dec. 25, 1922, p. 75.
Autobody (Autobody Publishing Co., New York), Oct. 1929, p. 145, Feb. 1930, pp. 31–33.
The Automobile (The Class Journal Co., New York) Jan. 20, 1916, p. 158; Jan. 27, 1916, p. 200; Feb. 10, 1916, p. 288; July 6, 1916, pp. 73–74; July 13, 1916 (Adv. 2 pgs.); July 20, 1916, pp. 69–76, 98–99; Aug. 31, 1916, pp. 373–374; Sept. 28, 1916, p. 543; Oct. 19, 1916, p. 647; Nov. 23, 1916, p. 876; Nov. 30, 1916, pp. 49–56; Mar. 22, 1917, pp. 580, 603; June 14, 1917, p. 1119; June 21, 1917, p. 1155.
The Automobile and Automotive Industries (The Class Journal Co., New York), Aug. 23, 1917, p. 342; Aug. 30, 1917, p. 385.
Automobile Topics (Motor Trades Publishing Co., New York), Jan. 15, 1916, p. 962; May 6, 1916, p. 1169; Sept. 1, 1917, p. 386; Apr. 19, 1919, p. 1324; Apr. 19, 1919 (Adv. 8 pgs.); May 17, 1919, p. 153; May 7, 1921, p. 1117; Oct. 8, 1921, pp. 634–636; Jan. 21, 1922, p. 898; Feb. 18, 1922, p. 19; Mar. 4, 1922, p. 187; July 15, 1922, p. 769; Apr. 21, 1923, p. 930; Apr. 28, 1923, pp. 1015, 1022; May 5, 1923, pp. 1135–1136, 1142, 1149; June 2, 1923, p. 215; June 9, 1923, p. 318; July 21, 1923, p. 943; Sept. 15, 1923, pp. 416, 420; Oct. 13, 1923, p. 847; Dec. 29, 1923, p. 625; Feb. 9, 1924, p. 1416; Feb. 16, 1924, p. 22; Feb. 23, 1924, p. 120; Mar. 29, 1924, p. 638; Apr, 5, 1924, p. 747; Apr. 19, 1924, p. 958; June 21, 1924, p. 526; July 12, 1924, p. 821; Aug. 16, 1924, pp. 19, 40–42; Sept. 6, 1924, p. 315; Nov. 29, 1924, p. 208; Dec. 20, 1924, p. 478; Feb. 14, 1925, p. 19; Mar. 21, 1925, p. 484; May 23, 1925, pp. 125, 129; June 6, 1925, p. 316; June 27, 1925, p. 605; Aug. 15, 1925, p. 19; Sept. 12, 1925, pp. 394, 398; Sept. 19, 1925, pp. 518–520, 526; Dec. 5, 1925, p. 309; Dec. 12, 1925, pp. 403, 406; Dec. 19, 1925, p. 509; Jan. 16, 1926, p. 978; Mar. 6, 1926, p. 288; Mar. 20, 1926, p. 512; Aug. 7, 1926, p. 1213; Aug. 21, 1926, p. 129; Sept. 11, 1926, p. 418; March 12, 1927, pp. 408, 417; June 25, 1927, p. 585; July 27, 1927, p. 950; Oct. 1, 1927, pp. 708–709; Nov. 12, 1927, p. 21; June 2, 1928, p. 285; Jan. 12, 1929, pp. 1032–1034; Apr. 26, 1930; Aug. 13, 1929, p. 1074; Jan. 11, 1930, p. 955; Mar. 8, 1930, p. 359 (photograph); Mar. 15, 1930, p. 470; Apr. 26, 1930, p. 959; May 16, 1931, p. 89; Aug. 1, 1931, p. 903; Apr. 9, 1932, p. 588; Nov. 19, 1932, p. 104; Dec. 22, 1934, p. 318.
Automobile Trade Journal (Chilton Co., Philadelphia, Pennsylvania), Apr. 1918, p. 151a; Feb. 1919, pp. 143–145; June 1919, p. 138; Dec. 1919, p. 163; Jan. 1921, p. 37; Mar. 1924, p. 61; Feb. 1926, p. 27; Feb. 1927, pp. 26, 50–52; Oct. 1927, p. 66; June 1931, p. 50.
Automobile Trade Journal & Motor Age (Chilton Co., Philadelphia, Pennsylvania), Aug. 29, 1929, pp. 62–63, 78; Feb. 1930, pp. 53, 88.
Automotive Industries (Chilton Co., Philadelphia, Pennsylvania), Dec. 13, 1917, p. 1059; Aug. 31, 1922, p. 446; Apr. 24, 1924, p. 74; Jan. 8, 1925, p. 57; Nov. 5, 1925, p. 778; Jan. 7, 1926, p. 22; Mar. 18, 1926, p. 509; June 24, 1926, pp. 1113, 1114; Jan. 15, 1927, p. 51; June 11, 1927, pp. 902–904; July 16, 1927, p. 101; Aug. 20, 1927, p. 283; Jan. 5, 1919, p. 37; Jan. 12, 1929, pp. 50–51; Jan. 19, 1929, p. 112; Feb. 23, 1929, p. 352; May 18, 1929, p.785; July 6, 1929, p. 18; Dec. 8, 1929, p. 956; Jan. 11, 1930, pp. 40–46, 69; Dec. 6, 1930, p. 843; Dec. 20, 1930, p. 917; Dec. 16, 1934, p. 723.
Automotive Industries—The Automobile (Chilton Co., Philadelphia, Pennsylvania), Dec. 6, 1917, p. 1021; Jan. 31, 1918, p. 258; July 14, 1921, p. 93; Oct. 6, 1921, pp. 654–657; Mar. 30, 1922, p. 739.

Automotive News (Slocum Publishing Co., Detroit, Michigan), Mar. 20, 1950, p. 2; Mar. 27, 1950, p. 2; Apr. 10, 1950, p. 11; May 1, 1950, p. 11; May 8, 1950, p. 8; June 12, 1950, p. 11; July 10, 1950, p. 14; Aug. 7, 1950, p. 13; Sept. 4, 1950, p. 10; June 11, 1951, p. 12; Mar. 12, 1951, pp. 14, 15; Apr. 9, 1951, p. 13; May 21, 1951, p. 13; May 28, 1951, p. 10; June 11, 1951, p. 12; June 25, 1951, p. 13; July 16, 1951, p. 13; July 23, 1951, p. 14; Oct. 8, 1951, p. 36; Oct. 15, 1951, pp. 22, 52; Nov. 19, 1951, p. 21; Jan. 7, 1952, p. 17; Apr. 14, 1952, pp. 50–51; Nov. 24, 1952, p. 20; June 29, 1953, p. 14; Sept. 21, 1953, p. 22; Nov. 16, 1953, p. 30; Sept. 6, 1954, p. 30; Apr. 18, 1955, p. 45; May 9, 1955, p. 34; July 18, 1955, p. 35; Aug. 8, 1955, p. 31; Oct. 17, 1955, p. 22; Jan. 30, 1956, p. 61; June 17, 1957, p. 59; July 1, 1957, p. 16.

The Horseless Age (Horseless Age Co., New York), July 15, 1916, p. 62; Jan. 1, 1918, p. 42.

Motor (International Magazine Co., New York), Aug. 16, 1916, p. 103; Feb. 1929, pp. 30–31, 53, 102, 178; Nov. 1932, p. 99; Dec. 1932, p. 96.

Motor Age (The Class Journal Co. through May 1925; Chilton Class Journal Co. June 1925 forward), Jan. 20, 1916, p. 18; Apr. 16, 1916, p. 31; July 6, 1916; July 13, 1916, p. 10; Nov. 30, 1916 (Adv. 8 pgs.), Feb. 15, 1917, p. 14; Apr. 26, 1917, p. 17; May 10, 1917 (Adv. 4 pgs.); May 17, 1917, pp. 10, 20; June 21, 1917, p. 17; July 5, 1917, p. 14 & Adv. 2 pgs.; July 12, 1917, p. 25 & Adv. 2 pgs.; Aug. 30, 1917, pp. 23, 40–41; Oct. 4, 1917, p. 13; Aug. 1, 1918, pp. 65–66; Aug. 15, 1918, p. 41; Aug. 29, 1918, pp. 67–68; Feb. 6, 1919, p. 13; Apr. 17, 1919, p. 40 & Adv. 8 Pgs; May 22, 1919 (Adv. 8 pgs.); Nov. 13, 1919, p. 15; Nov. 27, 1919, p. 33; Jan. 29, 1920, p. 52; Apr. 8, 1920, p. 31; Sept. 30, 1920, p. 26; Oct. 7, 1920, p. 8; May 5, 1921, p. 22; Oct. 6, 1921, pp. 12–14; Mar. 2, 1922, pp. 20–21; Mar. 30, 1922, p. 27; Sept. 7, 1922, p. 17; Oct. 5, 1922, p. 14; Oct. 26, 1922, p. 40; Jan. 18, 1923, p. 39; Feb. 1, 1923, p. 20; May 31, 1923, p. 30; Oct. 4, 1923, p. 33; Dec. 20, 1923, pp. 32, 33; Jan. 10, 1924, p. 18; June 26, 1924, p. 40; Aug. 14, 1924, p. 41; Jan. 8, 1925, p. 16; Jan. 14, 1926, pp. 18–19; Apr, 8, 1926, p. 32; July 1, 1926, p. 37; Sept. 23, 1926, p. 38; Jan. 6, 1927, pp. 35, 121–128; Apr. 28, 1927, p. 31; May 19, 1927, pp. 31, 35; Sept. 15, 1927, p. 19; June 9, 1927, pp. 35–37; June 23, 1927, p. 15; July 21, 1927, p. 22; Aug. 25, 1927, pp. 13, 14; Sept. 15, 1927, p. 19; Oct. 20, 1927, p. 9; Jan. 12, 1928, p. 18; Feb. 7, 1928, p. 10; Apr, 5, 1928, p. 20; Apr. 19, 1928, p. 14; Apr. 26, 1928, pp. 29, 32; June 14, 1928, p. 16; Aug. 30, 1928, p. 9.

Motor Record (Ferguson Publishing Co., New York), Dec. 1919, p. 42.

Motor World (The Class Journal Co., New York), June 14, 1916, p. 43; Aug. 16, 1916, pp. 69–70; Aug. 30, 1916, p. 44; Sept. 27, 1916, p. 41; Apr. 11, 1917, p. 55; Aug. 29, 1917, p. 11–12; Dec. 26, 1917, p. 70; Feb. 13, 1918, p. 43; Feb. 5, 1919, p. 86; Apr. 30, 1919, p. 41; July 2, 1919, p. 44; Oct. 29, 1919, p. 33; Jan. 12, 1921, p. 21; Oct. 5, 1921, pp. 28–30; Jan. 17, 1923, p. 17; Mar. 28, 1923, p. 41; June 13, 1923, p. 30; Jan. 31, 1924, p. 12.

Historical Societies

Connecticut Historical Society, Hartford, Connecticut.
Kansas State Historical Society, Topeka, Kansas.
Merrill Historical Society, Merrill, Wisconsin.
Nebraska Historical Society, Lincoln, Nebraska.
Nevada Historical Society, Reno, Nevada.
Utah Historical Society, Salt Lake City, Utah.
Wisconsin Historical Society, Madison, Wisconsin.

Libraries

Antique Automobile Club of America Library and Research Center, Hershey, Pennsylvania.
Cabell County Public Library, Huntington, West Virginia.
Detroit Public Library, National Automotive History Collection, Detroit, Michigan.
Forrest Polk Library, University of Wisconsin at Oshkosh, Oshkosh, Wisconsin.
Free Library of Philadelphia, Automobile Reference Collection, Philadelphia, Pennsylvania.
Jackson District Library, Jackson, Michigan.
Johnson Public Library, Darlington, Wisconsin.
Kenosha Public Library, Simmons Branch, Kenosha, Wisconsin.
San Francisco Public Library, San Francisco, California.
Scoville Memorial Library, Lakeville, Connecticut.
South Kingstown Library, South Kingstown, Rhode Island.
Western Reserve Historical Society Library, Cleveland, Ohio.

Newspapers

The Cleveland Plain Dealer, Cleveland, Ohio.
The Jackson Citizen Patriot, Jackson, Michigan.
The Lakeville Journal, Lakeville, Connecticut.
The Los Angeles Times, Los Angeles, California.
The Merrill Star Advocate, Merrill, Wisconsin.
The New York Times, New York, New York.
The San Diego Evening Tribune, San Diego, California.

Index

Page numbers in ***bold italics*** represent photographs and illustrations.

Advertisements ***18***, ***34***, ***52***, ***53***, ***55***, ***57***, 123–132
Allied Motor Industries Inc. 94
American Automobile Association 37
American Body Company 35, 37
American Fork & Hoe Company 15
American Nurses Association (ANA) 119
Angell, Ed 87
Antique Automobile Club of America (AACA) 119
Apex Electrical Manufacturing Company 114
Aranson, Charles 51
Art Institute of Chicago 132
Art Students League 131
artists and illustrators 129, 131, 132
Automobile Shows 22, 31, 33, 45, 58, 51, ***63***, ***67***, ***76***, ***77***, 83, 90, ***91***, 103
Automotive News 119

Baker, Charles 29, ***30***
Barger, L.E. ***24***
Begg, Russell 10, ***11***, 15, 37, 51, 72, 85
Bentley, Janie Jordan 120, 121
Bentley, Olan 121
Berndt, Blanche Edith Jordan 118
Bert S. Coler Hospital 120
body manufacturers: American 35, 37; Bryant 37, 46; Budd 66, 68; Facto 111; Murray 82, 85, 102; Ohio 37, 46; Walker 46; Walker-Wells 17
Borton, Eleanor 34, ***35***
Borton, Fred S. 35
Borton, T. Ernest ***13***, 15, 35, 36, 51, 88
Borton & Borton 35, 88
Bradley, Alva 12, 68
Bradley, Charles L. 12, 37, 51, 68
Briggs Manufacturing Company 63
Brotherhood of Locomotive Engineers 113
Bryant Body Company 37, 46
Bryn Mar College 121
Buckner, Harry R. 93, 115
Budd Body Company 66, 68
Burchard-Roberts-Wales ***15***
Burns Detective Agency 71

Camp Dennison, Ohio 3
Camp Russell, Charleston, WV 3
Central Union Trust Company 64
Chandler Motor Car Company 111
Charity Hospital 68, 86, 87
Citizens National bank 19
Citroen (Displayed by Jordan) 64
Cleveland Advertising Club 117
Cleveland Museum of Art 94
Cleveland Stock Exchange 46
Coburn, William Chester 111
Coggeshall, Howard 118
Cole, Fred 131
Common Pleas Court, Cleveland 113
Company C, 34th Regiment, Ohio Volunteer Infantry 3
Comstock, Anthony 40
Continental Motors Company 13, ***19***; chassis specifications 149–153; engine specifications 154
Coulton, George 12
Crockett Company 72
Crowell, Benedict 12

Dale, John G. Agency 16
Davidson, James L. 15, ***24***
Dayton Journal 7
Dayton News 7
dealers and distributors 133–139
Delaware Registration Trust Company 37
Dempsey (judge) 113
Disteel Wheels 35
Downing, Carlie 117
Drive Away Day ***89***
Edward G. Budd Manufacturing Company 66, 68
Edward S Jordan Company 40
Electric Auto Lite Company 113
engines: manufactured by Continental ***19***, ***43***, ***61***, ***66***, ***81***, ***84***; specifications 154
England, A.F. 85, 115
Erickson 129,131

Facto Auto Body Company 111
Fedco Numbering System 70, 71, ***72***
Felz Motor Sales Inc. 114
Fewsmith, Joseph 129
Fisher, Joseph G. 88
Flagg, James Montgomery 131
Folk, George B. 111
Fort Scott Kansas 4
France, George 87
Frost, E. ***24***
Fye, J.L. 74

Garfield, Borton 35
Garfield, Eleanor Borton 35
Garfield, James A. 35
Garfield, Rudolph 35
Garfield, Rudolph H. 35
General Top Company 39
Glentworth, C.A. 102
Globe Securities Company ***112***
Godwin, Frances (Frank) 129, 131
Gormully, Philip 8
Gormully & Jeffery 8
Gosnick, Frank A. 111
Graham, Jane 117, 119
Graham, Jane Jordan 117
Graham, Robert 117
Graham, Robert (Pete) 122
Gravell, Jacob (Cleveland chief of police) 86
Great Lakes Aircraft Corporation 94

Great Lakes biplane **94**
Griffin, Frank 4
Griffin, Jenny 4
Griffin, John 4
Griffin, Kate M. 4
Griffin, Mary 4
Griffin, Nancy Kinney 4
Griffin, Ned 4
Guardian Trust Company 88
Guenther, Morgan P. 111

Hannahs, Amelia 6
Hannahs, Charlotte Eva "Lottie" 6, 7, **8**
Hannahs, Fred C. 6
Hannahs, Manufacturing Company 6
Hardt, Harry **80**
Harris, John B. (Judge) 114
Hopkins, William R. (Cleveland city manager) 86
House, J. Arthur 88
Hupp Motor Car Corporation 111
hydraulic brakes 57, 58
Hydraulic Pressed Steel Company 37

The Inside Story of Adam and Eve 118

Jeffery, Charles T. 8, 9, 10
Jeffery, Harold 8
Jeffery, Kate 10
Jeffery, Thomas Buckland 8, 10
Jenkins, Albert G. (C.S.A. general) 3
Jordan, Anne (Anna) 4, 118
Jordan, Apolina Anderson Wilson M.D. 118, 122
Jordan, Blanche Edith 4
Jordan, Charlotte Eva Hannahs "Lottie" 55, 94, 111, 112
Jordan, Edward Stanlaw "Ned" 3, **5**, 6, 7, 8, 10, **11**, 12, 13, **17**, **24**, **25**, **26**, 28, 30, 34, 35, **37**, 40, **44**, 51, 53, **55**, 56, **65**, 66, 68, **69**, **70**, 72, 86, 94, 111, 112. 115, 116, 117, **118**, **119**, **120**, 126, 129, 133
Jordan, Ella May 4
Jordan, Jane 9, 70
Jordan, Joan 9, 94
Jordan, John 3, 4
Jordan, John Stanlaw "Jack" 7, 54, 111, 122
Jordan, Kate M. Griffin 4, 9
Jordan, Kate Wilson **118**, **119**, **120**
Jordan, Katie Eveline 4
Jordan, Minnie Estelle 4
Jordan Automobile Parts & Service Company 114, **115**
Jordan Building Company 19
Jordan Financial Statements 58, 78, 96
Jordan Motors 115
Jordan Motors Corporation, Inc. 113
Jordan price lists **30**, **60**, **61**, **64**, **69**, **72**, **82**, **84**, **98**
Joseph Wildanger Company 93
Judson, Ross **45**, 55

Keller, Henry G. 94
Kenosha Lodge # 47 F & AM 9
Kramer, Samuel E. (judge) 115

Lage & Company 58
Landis Engineering & Manufacturing Company **114**
Little, Joseph C. "Back" 12, 115
Loose, Anson "Skip" 120
Lord, Harry 69, **70**
Lord Motors 69, **70**
Loyal Order of the Red Arrow **26**
Lusitania (Ocean Liner) 9

Marine Trust Company 88
Mark of Service **52**
Marlatt, William 111
McArdle, John 85, 97, 111, 113, 115
McArthur, Charles H. 118
McArthur Advertising Company 118
McArthur, Warren 118
McCaw, Joan Jordan 111,122
McCaw, Kathryn 122
McCaw, Sandy 122
McCaw, William 122
McGean, R.L. 79
McGraw, Harrison B. 88
McKinley, William, President U.S. 3, 4, 7
Merrill Advocate 5
Merrill High School 5
Metal Parts Manufacturing Company 38
Miller, Herbert Charles 4, 9
Miller, Minnie Estell Jordan 4, 117
Miller, Otto 37
Milwaukee Journal 7
Model A (Great Line Eight): Brougham **59**; Five Passenger Sedan **59**; Five Passenger Touring 59, **61**; Friendly Three **62**; Playboy **59**; Seven Passenger Sedan 63; Seven Passenger Sedan with Partition 63, **64**; Victoria **59**
Model AA (Great Line Eight): Custom Sedan 70, **72**; Custom Victoria 70, **72**; Playboy 79, 83; Seven Passenger Sedan **74**, 75; Sport Coupe 79
Model E: Coupe **92**; Sedan **92**
Model G: Coupe 90, **91**; Playboy 90, **91**; Sedan **90**; Speedboy **91**
Model G (Great Line Ninety): Convertible Coupe 98, **99**; Five Passenger Sedan 98; Playboy 101; Seven Passenger Limousine **100**; Seven Passenger Sedan 98, **100**; Seven Passenger Touring 98, **100**; Speedboy 98, **100**; Sport Sedan 98, **100**; Standard Coupe 98, **100**
Model H: Blueboy (Blue Boy) 46, **48**, **49**, **54**, **55**; Seven passenger Sedan 52, **53**; Touring Sedan 47; Touring Sedan (2nd version) **55**
Model J (Line Eight): Playboy 65; Sedan **66**; Victoria **67**, 68
Model JE (Air Line Eight; 1st version): Five Passenger Sedan **82**, **84**; Four Passenger Playboy Coupe (collapsible top) 82, **83**; Four Passenger Playboy Coupe (permanent top) 82, **83**; Victoria 82, **83**, **84**
Model JE (Air Line Eight; 2nd version): Five Passenger Sedan 83, **85**; Victoria 83
Model JE (Air Line Eight; 3rd version): Five Passenger Sedan **87**; Four Passenger Playboy Coupe (collapsible top) **87**; Landau Brougham **88**; Victoria 87, **88**
Model J1 (Line Eight): Custom Sedan 72; Custom Victoria 72; Seven Passenger Sedan **74**, **75**; Sport Coupe 72, 74
Model K: Brougham **57**; Victoria (2-wheel brakes) **56**; Victoria (4-wheel hydraulic brakes) **57**
Model L: Blueboy **58**; Touring Sedan **58**
Model M (Silhouette): Brougham **37**; Enclosed Special **38**; Five Passenger Touring **38**; Landaulet Coupe 41, **42**; Playboy **38**
Model MX: Brougham 44, **46**; Brougham (2nd version) 47, **50**; Brougham (4-door version) **52**; Five Passenger Sedan 44, **46**; Five Passenger Sedan (2nd version) 47, **50**; Five Passenger Touring (Silhouette 5) **44**; Landaulet Coupe 44, **45**; Playboy 44, **45**; Playboy (2nd version) 46, **47**; Victoria 53
Model R (Little Custom): Blueboy **80**, **81**, 83; Playboy **76**, **77**; Sedan **77**, **80**; Sport Salon **77**, **80**; Tomboy **79**
Model RE (Cross Country Six): Sedan **85**, 86; Sport Four **86**; Tomboy **85**, 86
Model 60: Coupe **20**, 21; Four Passenger Sport Touring 16, **18**, **19**; Limousine **20**, 21; Roadster 16, **18**; Sedan **20**, 21; Seven Passenger Luxury Car (Touring) 16, **18**
Model 60 (2nd version): Coupe **22**; Limousine **22**; Roadster **22**, **25**; Sedan **22**; Sport Limousine **26**; Sport Roadster **25**
Model 60 Series F & Model F (Silhouette): Brougham 34; Four Passenger Touring **34**; Playboy **34**, **35**, 36; Seven Passenger Touring **34**; Town Sedan **33**, 34
Model 60 C: Aluminum Sedan **32**; Brougham 27, **28**, **32**; Sedan 27, **28**; Sport Limousine **27**; Sport Marine 28, **29**, **30**; Suburban Seven **31**; Town Car 27, **28**; Town Sedan **33**; Town Sedan (2nd version) 33
Model T (Standard Line Eighty): Coupe **101**; Sedan **101**
Model U (Line Seventy Sunshine Sedan): Convertible Sedan **103**, **104**
Model Z: Speedway Ace 107,**108**, **109**, **110**; Sportsman Sedan 105, **106**, **107**
Moore, A.B. 4
Murphy, L.F. 93
Murray Body Company 82, 85, 102

Nash, Charles 10
National Association of Manufacturers 119
National Automobile Chamber of Commerce (NACC) 23
National Cash Register Company 7, 8

National Organization for Public Health Nursing 119
New York Society for the Suppression of Vice 40, 77
Newcomb, Adrian G. 113
Nickel Plate Railroad 13
Noyes & Jackson 58

Ohio Body & Blower Company 37, 46
Ohio Press Bureau 7
Ohio Volunteer Infantry 3
Owen, Seena 74

Parish & Bingham **19**, 46
patents and trademarks **32**, **41**, **68**, **73**, 74, **86**, **112**
Patterson, John 7, 8
Peerless Motor Car Company 85, 116
Perfection Spring Company **13**
Perkins, Edna Brush 55
Pierce-Arrow 86
Pope, Albert "Colonel" 8
Popini 129

Quinn, Chester 87

Rambler (Automobile) 8
Reishel, R.C. 93
re-sale policy 52, **52**
Riley, W.B. 11, 15, 29, 39, 85, 93
Riley, W.B., Mrs. 39
Rolf, H.F. **24**
Roosevelt, Theodore (president, U.S.) 7
Rye, Gus **24**

St. Louis Automobile Dealers Association 94
Santa Fe Railroad 69, **70**, **71**
serial numbers (Jordan automobiles) 155, 156
Shaw, Welden W. Company 24
Sherman, Roger 88
Shields, E.M. 111
Shroeter, E. **26**
Sisters of Charity 68
Society of Automotive Engineers 68
Somewhere West of Laramie 53
Sparks, William 12
Sparks-Withington Company **12**, 15
Spaulding, Albert G. 8
Sperry, Elmer A. 111
Spitz, Walter 137
Stockwell, John W. 136
Studbaker Sales Corporation 117, 118
Stumbardt, John 72
Sumner, John S. 76,77
Sundblom, Haddon 131, 132
Surrell, Walt 51
Sweeney, John 115
Sweeney & James 115, 117

Tenney-Harding-Sherman 88
Thomas, Stanley R. 68
Thomas B. Jeffery Company 8, 9, 10
Tinker, Ben 117
Tobin, John (mayor, San Antonio, Texas) 72
trucks 6, **54**

Union Club 12
Union National bank 12
Union Pacific Railroad 3, 4
Union Trust Company 72
University of Arizona 111
University of Wisconsin 5, 6, 7

VerLinden, Edward 85
Vlchek Tool Company **46**
Vought, Lester **24**

Walker Body Company 46
Walker-Wells Company 17
Wallace, Caspian Oake 121
Wallace, David Andrew 121
Wallace, George A. (Cleveland fire chief) 86
Wallace, Kate Wilson Jordan 121, 122
Wallace, Maria Susan 121
Wallace, Richard William 121
Wanderwell, Nell 37, 63, **64**
Warren McArthur Corporation 118
Webb, J.W.S. & Son **113**
Webster, E. Ambrose 94
Wheeler, W.E. 24
Wildanger, Joseph **93**
Wilder, Amos P. 5
Wilson, Apolina Anderson, M.D. 118
Withington, Philip H. 12, 15
wiring diagrams (Jordan cars) 157–172

Zens, Paul 10, **11**, 15, **24**, 51, 82, 85,
Zens, Paul, Mrs. 28